FRESH
KING SALMON
$4⁹⁹
POUND

Created and Directed by Hans Höfer

INSIGHT GUIDES

SeaTTLe

Edited by John Wilcock
Principal photography by Jamie Wakefield
Managing Editor: Martha Ellen Zenfell

Editorial Director: Brian Bell

HOUGHTON MIFFLIN COMPANY

APA PUBLICATIONS

Seattle

First Edition
© **1993 APA PUBLICATIONS (HK) LTD**
All Rights Reserved
Printed in Singapore by Höfer Press Pte. Ltd

Distributed in the United States by:	Distributed in Canada by:	Distributed in the UK & Ireland by:	Worldwide distribution enquiries:
Houghton Mifflin Company	**Thomas Allen & Son**	**GeoCenter International UK Ltd**	**Höfer Communications Pte Ltd**
2 Park Street	390 Steelcase Road East	The Viables Center, Harrow Way	38 Joo Koon Road
Boston, Massachusetts 02108	Markham, Ontario L3R 1G2	Basingstoke, Hampshire RG22 4BJ	Singapore 2262
ISBN: 0-395-65989-2	ISBN: 0-395-65989-2	ISBN: 9-62421-176-0	ISBN: 9-62421-176-0

ABOUT THIS BOOK

Despite Seattle's frequent ranking at or near the top of "most livable city" lists, this quintessential Pacific Northwest city still gets stereotyped as a place where it rains all of the time. It wasn't the rain so much as the city's fascination with coffee, however, that most impressed this book's editor, **John Wilcock**. He says Seattle turned him into an addict – an espresso addict. "We caffeine fans are ubiquitous," he says, "but nowhere else did I ever see so many cup-holding, straw-wielding, rain-soaked believers standing on corners. I call it 'Sipping in the Rain'."

Seattle seemed the perfect destination to add to Apa Publications' expanding list of Insight Guides. With more than 180 titles spanning the globe, and a formula that combines frank writing with bold photojournalism, the timing was right.

Wilcock has written 16 books since the early 1960s, when he graduated from the *New York Times*'s travel section. Books on Greece, Japan and Venezuela, and *Insight CityGuide: Los Angeles* are his favorites, LA being where he lives. Wilcock's hobby is his cable TV travel show, which he hopes will bring him back to Seattle.

An Expert Team

The team that put together *Insight CityGuide: Seattle* is made up primarily of Northwest natives and transplants, with the expert guidance of travel veterans such as Wilcock and **Martha Ellen Zenfell**, editor-in-chief of Apa Publications' North American titles. A native of the American South now based in London, Zenfell chose the photographers and the pictures for the book, all the while keeping a watchful eye on the project from rainy Britain.

Assistant editor **Giselle Smith**, who wrote the chapter on South of the Kingdome and provided invaluable guidance in many other areas, is a lifetime resident of Seattle. A former editor of *Alaska Airlines Magazine*, she now edits *Greater Seattle* magazine.

Working with Wilcock to put together the CityGuide gave her a new perspective on her hometown, Smith says. "John helped me better appreciate Seattle by viewing it through the eyes of a visitor – a Los Angeles resident, no less, which some Northwesterners might label the classic anti-Seattleite."

Photography, an integral part of the CityGuide series, was assigned to Seattle native **Jamie Wakefield**. His freelance career has taken him from the cold of an Alaskan winter to the heat of the Indian monsoon. Capturing his own backyard on film was for him both a challenge and a rare delight. Other contributing photographers include locally-based **Joel Rogers** and Insight regular **Bodo Bondzio**.

Stanley Young, another resident of Los Angeles, came north to write the chapter on Seattle's history. As well as having worked with Wilcock on the LA book, Young has contributed to a number of publications, including *People* and *Los Angeles* magazines.

J. Kingston Pierce, the journalist who wrote "The Seattle Spirit" and "Twin Peaks and Other Mysteries," is a former editor at *Pacific Northwest*, *Washington* and *Oregon* magazines. "Seattle – if it doesn't burn itself out prematurely by trying to do too much too fast – may see its headiest days in the next 20 to 30 years," he says. "As East Coast cities suffer beneath the weight of crime and poverty and uncontrolled debt, the West can

Wilcock

Zenfell

Smith

Wakefield

position itself as the new power center of America."

The "Living with Water" essay was contributed by **Brenda Peterson**, an essayist and novelist who has lived for almost a decade on the waterfront in West Seattle.

Bruce Barcott ("Coffee and Culture") majored in philosophy at the University of Washington, and loathed the football team. Currently a staff writer covering ideas and culture for the *Seattle Weekly*, Barcott has written for obscure computer journals as well as for the *Seattle Post-Intelligencer*, the *Village Voice*, and *In These Times*. "Seattle thrills me in all respects but one," Barcott says. "Its politeness nauseates me. It's very easy to go soft-headed here."

Eric Lucas, who wrote the chapters on Boeing and the city's timbered past, moved to Seattle at the start of the longest period of drought the city had ever experienced: warm days, soft evenings and not a cloud in sight for 42 days. From a century-old home in Tacoma's north end, he has learned to love the area's attributes, such as butter clams and fireside coffee, and is a frequent correspondent on Northwest topics for magazines such as *Pacific Northwest* and the in-flight magazines for Alaska Airlines and Horizon Air.

A 20-year resident of Seattle, **Charles Smyth** is a former associate editor of the *Seattle Weekly* and the former managing editor of *KCTS Nine* magazine. He is a freelance writer and editor, specializing in assignments that pay well. Despite this, Smyth agreed to write the chapter on Central Seattle.

Molly Dee Anderson, who contributed "North Seattle" and "North of the City," is a freelance writer living near Lake Union. When she's not working on assignments for regional publications, Anderson explores the neighborhoods around Seattle on two wheels. She also contributed to this book's Travel Tips section.

Carlene Canton ("Eastside Places") is a freelance writer and editor who has lived on the Eastside since 1984. She resides with her husband and two daughters in Kirkland, a city she loves both for its distance from, and its proximity to, Seattle. She contributes to local and national publications.

Kristen Nelson, who produced the two out-of-town chapters (assisted by Connie Cooper, Jan Halliday and Helen Sutton) was born in Chicago's Old Town to a theatrical family; her ambition was to become a famous singer. After performing around the Midwest, she wound up in Seattle, where she taught music for several years, learned to play the Celtic minstrel harp, and gave birth to two sons. The hope is that they will one day fulfill their mother's dream of fame and glory and buy her a mansion. For now, she is special sections editor for the *Seattle Weekly* and *Eastsideweek*, a freelance writer and sometimes stage mother.

Anne Frichtl, responsible for the Travel Tips section, received her masters in journalism from Syracuse University. She moved to the Seattle area in 1987 with her family and is currently a freelance writer and editor.

The Final Touches

In Insight Guides' London editorial office, **Jill Anderson**, **Audrey Simon** and **Suriyani Ahmad** marshalled the text through a variety of Macintosh computers, using in the process some of the software that helped make Seattle's Bill Gates a billionaire. **Mary Morton** proofread and indexed the book.

Pierce

Peterson

Barcott

Smyth

History

Features

Places

Maps

TRAVEL TIPS

Compiled by Anne Frichtl

For detailed information see page 233

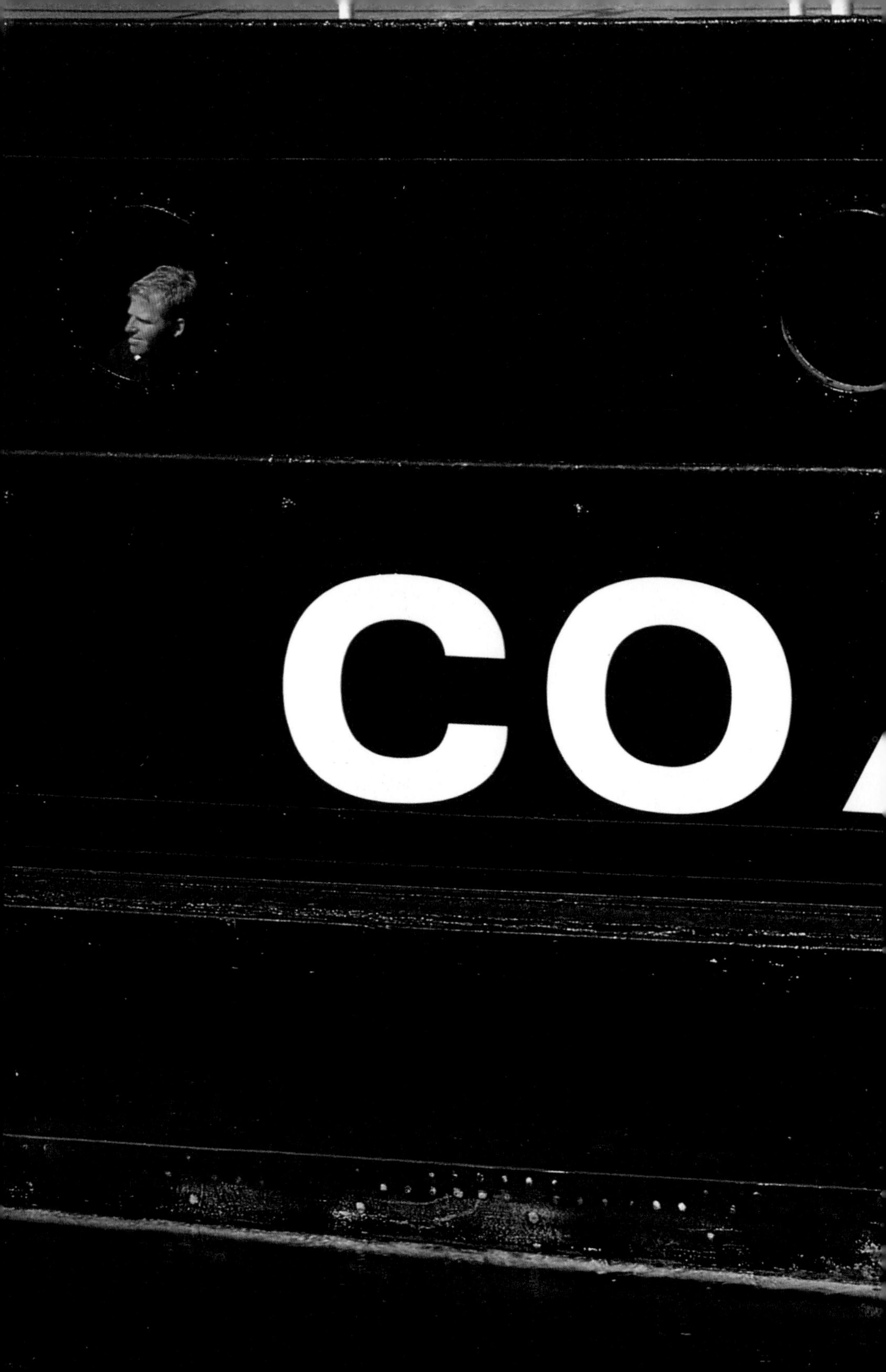
CO

AST

Seattle has become a media darling of late, touted as a most livable city by publications such as *Rand McNally's Places Rated Almanac* and written up kindly in American magazines from the *Atlantic* to *Esquire*. And while longtime residents smugly shrug and say they knew it all along, some newcomers criticize the city for being less idyllic than they had hoped when they shut down, packed up the U-Haul and headed northwest.

But it is those newcomers who will come to define the city, as did the travelers who settled here before them, and those before them, stretching back a mere century and a half to 1852. Seattle is a city of immigrants – mostly transplants from south and east, who longtime Seattleites now claim are spoiling their hometown.

Perhaps the residents of this mist-clad city on Puget Sound have taken the melting-pot approach to ethnicity too far. Members of some ethnic minorities, for example, have complained that despite the city's professed open-mindedness Seattle has no support group for its native cultures. The city has a recognizable Scandinavian community (in Ballard) and a strong contingent of several Asian nationalities in the International District, but few other identifiable neighborhoods by ethnic origin. Although there is a proliferation of Italian restaurants here, it speaks more of the current trendiness of Italian cuisine than it does of a sizable population that has Neapolitan ancestry.

Like many growing cities, Seattle has some problems. Arguments in favor of height restrictions on downtown skyscrapers culminated in a ballot initiative (the CAP initiative) that passed by a narrow margin. An increasing crime rate has arrived along with the surge in population as has an increase in the number – and therefore the visibility – of the homeless population.

It remains a much safer city than many others, however, and is consciously trying to prevent becoming just another big city. Actually, in one important respect it is exactly the right size, being – apart from an inconvenient hill or two – eminently walkable. A stroll along the bustling waterfront from 19th-century Pioneer Square to ever-contemporary Pike Place Market, for example, could certainly be accomplished within half an hour by somebody in a hurry. But, of course, who would *want* to make such a serendipitous journey in a hurry?

And even the aforementioned hills needn't be a problem in a city foresighted enough to invite non-paying passengers onto its downtown buses. A free bus service has been considered and rejected as impractical by many communities, but in Seattle it's an idea whose time arrived long ago. An addition to the city's excellent

Preceding pages: Public Market; welcome to Seattle; coasting into town; paddle boats at Green Lake; tangled transportation; sculpture and Space Needle. **Left**, the World's Fair put Seattle on the map.

bus system is an underground bus tunnel downtown. Shiny new and sparkling clean, the tunnel is closed at night to avoid its becoming a subway station nightmare. The tunnel was constructed, however, with a future light rail system in mind.

But what is it that sets Seattleites apart? According to *Seattle Times* columnist Jean Godden (who worked for years at the newspaper's crosstown rival, the *Seattle Post-Intelligencer*), they never carry umbrellas, never wash their cars, never shine their shoes and never turn on their windshield wipers unless it's absolutely pouring. Whatever the reasons for their distinctive identity, if such be the case, Seattle's coffee fanatics – and that seems to be most of the population – rationalize that they're synonymous with a preference for fine espresso. "Perhaps we're a bit independent and tend to taste things for ourselves," wrote an essayist in the city's *Cafe Ole* magazine.

In one memorable column, Godden also wrote that Seattleites seldom visit the Space Needle unless accompanied by visitors, seldom hail taxis, can describe 42 shades of gray and think a perfect day is 68°, partly sunny, with a light breeze from the north. Seattleites also buy more sunglasses than residents of any other city in the US, perhaps because we never expect to need them and thus invariably have left them at home.

The image of a Seattle resident is a modern mountain man, clad in GoreTex, plaid, sensible shoes and a beard. The reality is not far from that. It's true that local outfitters Recreational Equipment, Inc. (REI) registers future brides and grooms for outdoor gear ranging from crampons to campstoves, but this city also sports a growing local arts scene that is demanding attention from East Coast and Southern California critics and audiences. (Although an LA critic of the Robert Venturi-designed art museum did say the best thing about it was the giant interior staircase and you could save yourself five bucks by admiring that through the window.)

There's something about this city, though, a sense of style or good taste, that justifies most of the boasts concerning its quality of living. If you doubt that, check out the lobbies, basements and atriums to be found in the new architectural behemoths. Thick carpets, attractive decor, subtle lighting, giant photomurals, paintings or other imaginative artwork are some of the ways that the buildings' owners make the visitor feel pampered. And everywhere, of course, are spotless eating facilities and the ubiquitous espresso bars.

Seattle's sunny, polite disposition won't let most people dwell on any of the city's negative aspects for long. When the sun comes out in Seattle – after a day, a week or even a month of rain – most residents will tell you there is no better place to be.

Left, plane view of downtown.

The impression the visitor receives of Seattle today – stolid, self-confident, prosperous, and eminently livable – belies the eccentricity and gritty, ribald character that mark much of its brief history. Carved from the primeval forest beginning in 1851, Seattle has come into its own as a great American metropolis, but during its earliest days, it more closely resembled the Indian village of "seven ill-looking houses" that Merriwether Lewis and William Clark found "situated at the foot of the high hills" when they concluded their transcontinental expedition on the Pacific shore in 1805.

The "mellow" life for which the Pacific Northwest is famous existed long before the arrival of the first white settlers. The Salish Indians of Puget Sound inhabited a paradise mild in climate and abundant in resources. The Duwamish, one of the Sound tribes also known as the Renton Indians, occupied most of the present site of Seattle. They were a remarkably peaceable people. Fishing and hunting only on their own lands, they bought dressed deer and elk skins (using seashells as money) from more easterly tribes, whom the Sound Indians considered to be savages. These moutain dwellers, for their part, looked down upon the "fisheaters."

Fish, especially the ubiquitous salmon, played a major role in the lives of these coastal peoples. The man who caught the first salmon in the spring invited all his friends to a feast, each guest receiving a small piece of the catch, except the host who did not eat. The same ceremony greeted the first deer, berries, or fowl: the Duwamish were known to enjoy celebrating given any kind of excuse.

Tribal rights: During the summer, the eastern tribes came down from the mountains to trade for seafood they needed to help survive through the winter. Fishing, hunting, and berry-picking grounds were tribal property,

but requests to forage in another tribe's territory were not usually refused. Using a territory without the tribe's permission, however, was regarded as an invasion and frequently led to war.

When attacked by other tribes, as they often were by the more northerly Haida, Indians of the Sound preferred to retreat into the dense forests until the marauders left. Men unlucky enough to be caught unawares were killed, their women enslaved. Should a warrior kill an enemy in one of the more local conflicts, he was not allowed to touch food with his fingers for 10 days, and often scratched his cheeks with a sharp stone to make them bleed. Among some Puget Sound tribes, a warrior who had killed an enemy had to paint his face black to avoid blindness.

Fur traders: The first Europeans to see the Seattle area, under the command of Captain George Vancouver, landed near Everett in 1792. It was furs that drew the white man back to the Northwest. The Hudson's Bay Company, based in Fort Vancouver on the Columbia River, outfitted a rag-tag group of social outcasts to deal with the indigenous peoples and bring in the pelts of sea-otters and beavers. "The very scum of the earth, and the most unruly and troublesome gang to deal with in this, or perhaps any other part of the World," said Sir George Simpson, sent out in the 1820s to reorganize the company's holdings in the Northwest. For the next three decades the dour Hudson's Bay Company dominated the Northwest, but they saw themselves as stewards in a foreign land – a bureaucracy owned by distant landlords who were interested in profits, not settlements.

The discovery of gold in Northern California and the opening of new trails to the west pushed out the bureaucrats and fur-traders. Soon the pristine reaches of the Pacific Coast were being carved up by zealous citybuilders and determined capitalists. There were already a handful of settlers in Puget Sound when David Denny reached the sandy spit of Alki Point (in what is now West Seattle) on September 28, 1851. The settlers at the

Preceding pages: a Northwest scene by Alfred Jacob Miller, *circa* 1858-60. **Left,** 19th-century Goomokwey tribal mask, Seattle Art Museum.

newly named Alki-New York ("Alki" meaning "by-and-by" in Chinook jargon; and New York in honor of Denny's home town) had come by way of Illinois, and then through Portland, by that time already a bustling burg of 2,000 souls. But the Denny group preferred to establish their own city and with their arrival on the Sound, the formal history of Seattle begins.

Flattery and fraud: City-building was a commonplace enterprise of the 19th century. A determined land developer laid claim to a location he believed held promise, designed a town plan, then used every means at his disposal – from bribery and exaggeration to

flattery and fraud – to entice settlers and investors to fill out his vision of the future. Thus began Steilacoom, Olympia, Whatcom, Port Townshend and Tacoma, each born with hope and determination; yet of these neighboring settlements, only Seattle would become a world-class city.

Its first years were hardly auspicious. After a dismal winter, the Denny party discovered that Alki-New York was an entirely unsuitable site for a cabin, let alone a metropolis. Windswept and far too shallow for shipping, all it provided was a breathtaking view and pleasant breezes compared to the

dark swamps and dense forests that lined the rest of the Sound. But Denny knew that any successful city in the area would need at least a deep-water harbor, so he borrowed a neighbor's clothesline, tied several horseshoes to it and spent several days in a dugout canoe plumbing the depths of the adjacent coastline until he found his deep water in Elliott Bay, opposite several acres of mudflats (that reeked when the tide went out) guarded by impenetrable forest, steep cliffs and hills. Seattle had been discovered.

Denny, Charles Boren and William Bell staked out claims on the waterfront and were soon joined by Dr David Swinson Maynard, the first great man of Seattle history. Medical doctor, lumberman, blacksmith, entrepreneur and all-around visionary, Maynard, like many of those arriving in the Northwest, came by way of the Oregon Trail. This 2,000-mile-long trek from the Mississippi, through the Rocky Mountains by way of Fort Laramie and Great Salt, was the route that thousands of eager settlers would take to its terminus on the Columbia River and the new towns there, such as Portland.

The trip by ox-drawn covered wagon was fraught with death and disease, but it was an experience that bonded the pioneers. Maynard settled first in what is now Olympia, but was driven out by fellow merchants who, despite their common experiences on the Trail, were upset that the kind-hearted doctor's general store offered prices that were suicidally low and credit that was virtually unlimited.

When Maynard wandered down the Sound for a new location, both groups – those who stayed at Alki-New York, and the Denny trio on Elliott Bay – wanted Maynard to join them them "for the benefit," as one of them later wrote, "a good man brings." Maynard believed the new town on Elliott Bay was the more likely to succeed, and it didn't hurt that Boren, Bell and Denny offered to move their claims north by an eighth of a mile to make room for his.

The first store: Maynard measured out about 300 yards of the most southerly deep-water frontage and took the rest in marsh and hillside. He hired some Indians to construct a building down by the Sag, as they called the low land by the water, and within a few days he was in his new store selling, as one flyer put it, "a general assortment of dry goods, groceries, hardware, etc., suitable for the wants of immigrants just arriving."

In Olympia, Maynard had already befriended an Indian tyee (chief) named Sealth (pronounced See-alth and sometimes See-attle), leader of the tribe living at the mouth of the Duwamish River. Dressed in a breechclout and faded blue blanket, the 6-foot-tall chief with steel-gray hair hanging to his shoulders caused quite a stir among the settlers. Whites in the region considered him among the most important tyees in the territory; they were certainly more impressed with Sealth than his fellow Native Americans were. The multifarious tribes of the Sound had their differences, but they were all agreed on one thing: a chief had little authority, being merely a rich man with some eloquence, whose opinions carried a little more weight than those of his fellow tribesmen. Even so, when it was time to name the new city, Maynard's suggestion of Seattle, in honor of his noble friend, replaced the native name used by the local authorities, "Duwamps."

Ever since a ship captained by G. W. Kendall had nosed past the Strait of Juan de Fuca two years earlier in a misguided search for icebergs (to be used in drinks on the Barbary Coast) and had to settle for a load of piling, timber was the Sound's cash crop. Maynard set some of the Indians to transforming a stand of fir behind his store into shakes, square logs, and cordwood, while others caught salmon and constructed crude barrels, roughly hooped. When the ship *Franklin Adams* turned up at Maynard's tiny dock in October, the doctor-entrepreneur had ready for shipment 1,000 barrels of brined salmon, 30 cords of wood, 12,000 feet of squared timbers, 8,000 feet of piling and 10,000 shingles.

Even though the salmon spoiled and ruined most of his profits, nothing dimmed Doc Maynard's extravagant enthusiasm and exuberant friendliness for long. Anything

good for Seattle was good for Doc Maynard, and he did his best to make sure the town prospered. When Henry Yesler arrived at Seattle, scouting the Sound for the best location for a steam-driven sawmill, Maynard and Boren each gave up some of their land for the necessary waterfront frontage.

Skid Road: The determined city-founders knew that whichever settlement got Yesler's sawmill would have a headstart on the future and the town's rugged residents built a log cookhouse and started on the "Skid Road," a corduroy log slide that would allow the timber to slide down the hill to the sawmill. When Yesler returned from San Francisco

and set up his equipment, Seattle was put firmly on the map. "Huzza for Seattle!" wrote the editors of the paper in Olympia. "The mill will prove as good as a gold mine to Mr Yesler, besides tending greatly to improve the fine town site of Seattle and the fertile country around it, by attracting thither the farmer, the laborer, and the capitalist. On with improvement!" Within months, Seattle was named the seat of King County, with Doc Maynard's little store as the site of the post office and the Seattle Exchange.

Though the Native Americans had welcomed the whites at first for their wonderful

Left, Chief Seattle (*né* Sealth). **Right**, Dr David Swinson Maynard.

tools, blankets, liquor, guns and medicines, they soon came to see that other things were less desirable: new diseases, a religion that said that many things the Indians had always done were wicked (though the reasons why were less than clear), and most perniciously, perhaps, the concept of private property. By the time Doc Maynard helped broker an arrangement to buy their land, they were in little position to bargain. In 1854 the treaty was explained to the assembled Native Americans by a drunken Governor Stevens in Chinook jargon, a bastard tongue developed by fur traders more suited to commerce than to the subtleties of diplomacy.

comfortably," goes Smith's version of the speech. "His people are many. They are like the grass that covers vast prairies. My people are few. They resemble the scattering trees of a storm-swept plain... Every part of this soil is sacred in the estimation of my people. Every hillside, every valley, every plain and grove has been hallowed by some sad or happy event in days long vanished... and when the last Red Man shall have perished and the memory of my tribe shall have become a myth among the White Men, these shores will swarm with the invisible dead of my tribe."

The following year the treaty was signed

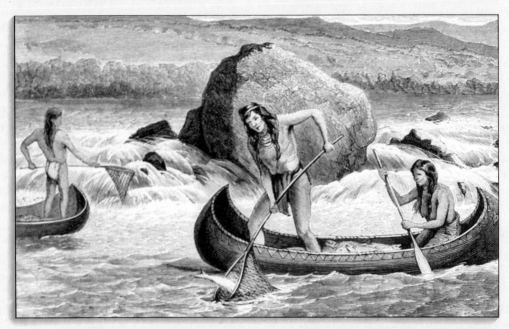

The American government offered the indigenous tribes $150,000 payable over 20 years in usable goods and a reservation in return for 2 million acres of property. Chief Seattle, towering a foot over Stevens, answered the ultimatum on behalf of all the Indians in his language, Duwamish. The speech was recalled 33 years later by Dr Henry Smith, an observer at the time much taken, as he put it, "with the magnificent bearing, kindness and paternal benignity" of Chief Seattle. "The Big Chief at Washington sends us word that he wishes to buy our lands but is willing to allow us enough to live

and most Indians moved to the reservations across the Sound. Some of the Indians fought the agreement and in 1856 rebelled. There was a lot of gunplay, but few casualties on either side and the US Army easily defeated the small rebel group. When one of the rebel leaders, Leschi, was later caught through the perfidy of a nephew, he was tried and convicted of murdering an officer ambushed during the war. (One of the two lawyers for the defense was H. R. Crosby, Bing's father). Leschi was hanged. Today he is considered a local hero with a park and statue dedicated to his memory.

The "Indian War" was over and the whites had won, but many issues were left unsettled and some, such as the continuing dispute over territorial fishing rights, remain disputed to this day.

Seattle was little more than an industrious village in its earliest years. Venison was caught and sold for 10¢ a pound in the "downtown" area, where 8-foot-thick trees still grew. Angeline, daughter of Chief Seattle, worked as a domestic, "a good worker," recalls Sophie Frye Bass, niece of David Denny, "but when she had a fit of temper she would leave, even though she left a tub full of clothes soaking." Yesler's saw-

unparalleled growth and prosperity.

Between the coming of the railroad and 1892, immigrants poured in, lumber output expanded, home and office building construction soared, electric streetcar lines opened up and new districts. Areas such as Queen Anne, Madison Park, Lake Washington, the Rainier Valley and West Seattle, unsettled in the mid-1880s, were substantial suburbs by the early 1890s – and sharply expanded the range of the city.

Racial problems: The mid-1880s, however, were hard times in Seattle. The city was hard hit by the national depression. Out-of-work fishermen, lumber workers and miners

mill sent off its lumber to San Francisco, and the sawdust was used to fill the swampy lowland south of the town.

The world became a smaller place for residents of Seattle in 1864 when the transcontinental telegraph tied the city to the rest of the country. But it was the coming of the Northern Pacific Railroad – a spur was extended to Seattle from the terminus in Tacoma, after a decade-long struggle, and two attempts by Seattleites to build their own railroad – that culminated in a brief period of

Left, netting salmon. **Above**, anti-Chinese riots.

found themselves competing for jobs not only with unemployed city clerks and carpenters, but also with substantial numbers of Chinese laborers discharged after the completion of the area's railroads. Not surprisingly, the Chinese workers became the scapegoat for the area's problems. Racial contempt was never far below the city's bustling surface as witnessed by a news item in the *Seattle Daily Chronicle* in 1882. "The cheerful intelligence has been received at Portland of the wreck on the coast of China of the steamer *Mary Tatham*, bound for this country with a cargo of 700 Chinamen. The officers and crew were saved, but, fortunately, not one of the 700 Chinamen survived. As yet no meeting of Pacific Coast citizens has been called to draft fitting resolutions of heartfelt grief."

The Chinese were considered to be both hard-working and uncomplaining, able to subsist on "a few handfuls of rice and a rat a day." Without their labor, the railroads would have taken far longer, but many unemployed Seattleites believed the Asian immigrants were also inherently inferior, unreliable, debased, immoral, given to gambling and smoking opium and riddled with diseases like syphilis and malaria. The Knights

the entire slate of the anti-Chinese People's Party in municipal elections. It would be a decade before the Chinese community slowly built itself up to its previous numbers.

By 1890 the population had more than quadrupled from 11,000 a decade before to 50,000. By 1893, the surge was over but Seattle was a very different place. The city was also developing a sense about itself. An 1882 visitor had found it a "self-reliant, determined, well-governed" community with "exceptional public spirit." Other observers stressed the "marvelous enterprise" of the city's inhabitants, calling it a virtual "paradise" for anyone willing to work hard.

of Labor wanted to eject the Chinese from the Northwest by force, and in 1885 rampaging whites destroyed the living quarters and drove about 30 Chinese from Newcastle, a nearby town. The contagion of hate spread to Tacoma and on February 7 and 8, 1886, Seattle exploded in anti-Chinese violence.

During the trouble, five men were shot, Chinese stores and homes were demolished, and 200 Chinese were forced to board a San Francisco-bound steamer. By March, when federal troops had restored order, the Seattle Chinese community of about 500 had been eliminated. In July, voters returned almost

One New Englander, after seeing all the major cities of the Sound, found that Seattle, though it had "few flowers, less laughter, and a scarcity of tennis courts," in its "dogged determination and energetic push… reminds me most strongly of Chicago."

The Great Fire: They called it "Seattle Spirit," and nothing, perhaps, demonstrates this can-do attitude more than the city's reaction to John Back's unfortunate blunder on Thursday June 6, 1889. Back, a handyman, threw a bucket of water on a flaming pot of glue in the middle of a paint store. The building exploded in flames, and 12½ hours later the entire commercial district – 60 city blocks – lay burned to the ground. "Oh, light-hearted, industrious Seattle," a reporter wailed in Friday's *Seattle Daily Press*, "to be reduced to ashes in a single afternoon." How ironic that 12 years previously, the *Daily Intelligencer*, after a fire struck Olympia, had warned "that Seattle's turn will come next, and our fancied security from the devouring element is only a delusion."

In fact, the Great Fire was the best thing to happen to the city. The commercial section of pre-fire Seattle had been a pestilential morass. Built on mudflats, the sewers would back up when the tide came in, spewing raw

Three years later a new Seattle – built of brick and up to eight storys high – stood ready to rule the Pacific Northwest.

When the new higher roadways were later built, they reached the second stories of the new buildings but had to leave the sidewalks and the ground levels accessible 12 feet below. Ladders were placed at intersections so the populace could cross the street and until the sidewalks were covered over (creating the now famous "underground Seattle") 17 people died, as a newspaper put it, "going from curb to sidewalk."

The streets were realigned after the fire. New wharves, railroad depots, freight sheds,

sewage out of the toilets. Huge chuckholes – pools of mud – would open up at major intersections sucking in horses, carriages and even one unfortunate schoolboy on his way home from school. Typhoid and tuberculosis were rampant. No wonder the populace called the fire a Godsend: it allowed them to overhaul the municipal systems and rebuild a city worthy of its industrious inhabitants. Civic improvement began three days after the fire, while the embers were still hot.

Left, Gold Rush miners. Above, mural of the Great Fire of 1889.

coal bunkers and warehouses in the mile-long waterfront strip were repaired or rebuilt. The sawmills moved out of town, leaving behind only the name "Skid Road," a remembrance of the days when the logs would come tumbling out of the hills down the corduroy pathway to Yesler's sawmills on the old waterfront. In later years, as this area of town became a drab repository of men and women with broken lives and shattered dreams, the name Skid Road would be corrupted to Skid Row and used as a description of urban decay in every city in the United States.

SPECIAL SEATTLE NUMBER

THE COAST

ALASKA AND GREATER NORTHWEST

VOL. 18 NO. 3

SEPT. 1909.

LOIS STO CO.

SEATTLE The METROPOLIS

The Coast Publishing Company
14th and Main St., SEATTLE, U.S.A.

AMERICAN ENGRAVING CO. SPOKANE

PRICE FIFTEEN CENTS

For much of the 1890s, Seattle was in a state of decline, its Skid Road crowded with the homeless and the poor. Business slumped to a fraction of its former numbers and Seattle might well have become a second-rate town were it not for the fortuitous arrival of the *SS Portland* on July 17, 1897. Fresh from Alaska, the *Portland* carried, as newspapers' headlines screamed across the country the following day, "A Ton of Gold Aboard."

When Seattle's mayor, W. D. Wood, heard news of the Yukon gold strike he wired his resignation from San Francisco where he was visiting, and headed for gold country. His reaction was typical. A kind of madness descended upon the Western World, as men from Sydney to Switzerland left their lives on a moment's notice and sailed and walked to the frozen fields and primitive camps at Dawson. And many of these treasure seekers passed through Seattle.

Fortune seekers: The Yukon Gold Rush wrenched Seattle out of its commercial doldrums and propelled it into the major center of the Northwest. Tens of thousands of prospectors and hopelessly naive and unprepared fortune hunters descended on the city to purchase supplies and tickets northward. Schwabacher's Outfitters rose to the top of a provisioning industry where supplies for the trek north lay stacked on the boardwalk in piles 10 feet high to keep up with demand. By springtime, following the *SS Portland's* arrival, Seattle merchants, who over the previous year had barely managed to make a gross total income of $300,000, now raked in some $25 million. Hotels and restaurants were overbooked and Seattle's banks filled up with Yukon gold. Schools opened to teach mining techniques; classes were given on how to drive a dog sled – in a city that rarely saw a snowflake.

And the transient population wanted entertainment. John Considine, patriarch of the

famous acting family, opened up the People's Theater and brought in famed exotic dancer Little Egypt who, clad in diaphanous harem clothes, gave a lesson in international culture, dancing the muscle dance, the Turkish dance and the Damascus dance to wildly appreciative crowds almost every night of the year. These "box-houses," so-called for the private plywood alcoves situated along the sides of the theater, had long been a part of Seattle's early nightlife.

The entry fee was only 10¢ but the profits were made on the drinks, cajoled out of the male patrons by "women with dresses nearly to the point above the knees, with stained and sweaty tights, with bare arms and necks uncovered over halfway to their waists," as a reporter for *Coast* magazine wrote. Sitting in their boxes equipped with electric bells to call for drinks, the women gold-diggers would entertain the male goldminers while Little Egypt danced for the newcomers in the main hall of the theater. Those newly met couples who wished to continue their conversations about goldmining or other subjects of mutual interest could walk to nearby rooming houses.

Prostitution had always been a facet of early Seattle life, a natural result of the vicissitudes of a nearly all-male lumber town. As early as 1861 an enterprising rake by the name of John Pennell established the Illahee (Salish for "homeland") over the mudflats, hard by the mill and in full view of arriving ships. Pennell's bordello soon became a landmark in the young town. Locals renamed it the "Madhouse," and some scholars hold that its presence helped establish Seattle in its formative years, serving "as the best mouse trap in the woods."

Once the gold from the Yukon poured in, the local bawdy houses went upscale. One house of pleasure spent $200,000 on tapestries and velvet. Honest Kate's "Parlor House" was more subdued: no rowdy behaviour or foul language was allowed in her salon, where customers and the working ladies met and conversed in tones of utter propriety. Lou Graham, a famous madam, paraded her newest arrivals in fine carriages on Sunday afternoon, and also served as an unofficial banker, helping to start many a business in boomtown Seattle.

The Klondike Gold Rush also solidified Seattle's position as the center of trade in the

The demographic discrepancy between males and maidens prompted Asa Mercer, a carpenter on the newly built Territorial University (and its first president), to secure a $300 fee from lonely northwest bachelors with the assurance he would bring them marriageable young maidens from the East Coast. Promising delivery of some 500 women, he arrived in Seattle a year later with 100, but managed somehow to placate his male clients. Mercer married one of his imports and promptly moved inland.

Bordellos persisted in the Skid Road area, helping solidify its already gamy reputation.

Northwest, allowing it to surpass the older and up to then bigger city of Portland. The boom raised Seattle's population to 80,000 by 1900 and, with the arrival of three new railroad lines and a road over the Cascades, those numbers rose to a quarter of a million by 1910. Most of the immigrants were from the Midwest of America and Europe, particularly Scandinavia. (Swedes, in fact, populated the separate sawmill city of Ballard.) Japanese laborers began arriving in large numbers in the late 1890s, an indication of Seattle's position as a major shipping outlet to Asia and the Pacific.

Seattle was also growing increasingly legitimate. The entire downtown area was regraded to reduce the steep inclines of the original hills. Areas such as Capitol Hill became neighborhoods of the utmost propriety. The high-class bordellos and cheaper "crib-houses" were closed down and John Considine moved out of his first box-house on Skid Road, and into a countrywide vaudeville theater chain that extended from coast to coast and guaranteed performers 70 weeks of work. Alexander Pantages, who had also started with a single box-house theater during the uproarious Gold Rush days, rivalled Considine's chain, earning a reputation for

War I brought an increased demand for navy vessels, Seattle was convinced that its future lay in shipbuilding and the sea. But there was one wealthy resident who disagreed. In January 1910, at a makeshift airport south of Los Angeles, William Boeing attended the first international flying meet held in the US. The scion of a wealthy Minnesota iron ore and timber family, he had made his own fortune in the timber of the Pacific Northwest.

Although Boeing's initial interest in flying may have been on a par with his decision to buy the Heath shipyards in order to finish a yacht, during tests over Lake Washington

booking superior acts. By 1926, Pantages, who had once worked as a bartender in a saloon in Dawson during the Gold Rush, owned the largest chain of theaters in the country, which he later sold, although the name lives on as a little known memento to the days of the Seattle box-houses.

Birth of Boeing: Seattle already dominated the Alaskan shipping routes. When the Panama Canal opened in 1914 and World

of a Curtiss-type hydroplane he had built with his friend and fellow Yale graduate Conrad Westervelt, he discovered a profession and a mission. On July 15, 1916, after a couple of years of experimentation, Boeing was incorporated in Seattle. Eleven years later Boeing Air Transport flew the country's first commercial air flight from Chicago to San Francisco. Eventually, Boeing Air Transport would become known as United Air Lines.

With the signing of the Armistice, government contracts for ships evaporated, and Seattle was saddled with 35,000 skilled but

Left, *SS Victoria* sails to Alaska from Seattle, 1900. **Above**, Lou Graham, the city's most famous madam, at home.

unemployed laborers who had been enticed to the city by the promise of high wages and permanent employment and who now found themselves out of work. Rapid industrial expansion had provided a fertile soil for the growth of strong labor unions and radical politics in the early decades of the century. The Northwest became a stronghold of organized labor, but some unions fared better than others. The International Workers of the World, better known as the "Wobblies," were often the target for violent suppression by the police, the American Legion and the companies attempting to break the unions.

In Seattle, all the conditions were ripe for

alive in Seattle and Washington State to this day: even the state's Republicans are decidedly progressive.

Yet, even trade unions could not guard against the economic body blow that would follow in the wake of the Great Depression, which hit Seattle harder than most cities. Skid Road, south of Yesler's Way, saw an ever-growing population of the haggard and the hungry. A meal cost 20¢ but few down on Skid Road could afford one. Still, there was a surprising degree of order among the destitute. The city's Hooverville, built on the tideflats in an abandoned shipyard, was among the largest temporary communities in

a confrontation and, in February 1919, the Central Labor Council organized the country's first and – at five days – longest general strike, driving a spike of fear into the hearts of the propertied classes. The fear exceeded any reality of danger, and the general strike proved to be a tactical error. Anarchists, socialists and communists were targeted as agents of the "Red Scare," and, though Seattle and Washington State continued to be highly unionized, labor leaders prudently adopted a strategy of cooperation with management instead of confrontation. This union orientation and liberal heritage is still

the country, but also had its own self-appointed vigilante committee to enforce the sanitation code. The Unemployed Citizens' League, which reached a peak membership of 50,000 in 1931, formed a separate community (the so-called "Republic of the Penniless") which used an elaborate system of work and barter to keep its members fed and housed. Those lucky enough to hold jobs were members of a well-organized network held in lockstep with "Brother" Dave Beck's powerful teamsters. When Eastern non-union beer began appearing in the Seattle area, Beck's teamsters refused to move it out of the warehouses. Local breweries benefited, helping to establish a tradition of strong regional breweries in the Seattle area.

Big bombers: With World War II came Seattle's second great boom. Although based partly on shipbuilding, this time the recovery was centered predominantly on one industry and one company, aircraft and Boeing. Borne on the wings of Boeing's mass-produced B-17 Flying Fortress and B-29 Super Fortress bombers, the metropolitan population of about 450,000 in 1940 climbed to just shy of three-quarters of a million by 1950.

But the burgeoning Seattle economy was

Chinese before them, the Japanese returned to Seattle after their expulsion, despite the often overt racism they encountered.

Race relations were always a matter of tension in Seattle. Long before the Asians, the Swedes were the first object of derision; and after the Japanese were evacuated, the city faced its first real influx of African-Americans as wartime jobs opened up in factories. Most moved to the Central District, and in 1944 Mayor Devin formed the Seattle Civic Unity Committee to promote racial accord. In 1968, after the arrest of two Black Panther leaders, seven police officers were injured in a riot in the Central District

placed out of reach for the local Japanese population. When President Roosevelt signed Executive Order 9066 on February 19, 1942, 110,000 Japanese were summarily removed from their jobs and homes and placed in camps up and down the West Coast. In Seattle, 6,000 Japanese, many who had been in the city for half a century, lost everything they owned, moved out of "Japtown" to spend the next three years in a camp in the state of Idaho. Yet like the

Left, Seattle's Hooverville during the Great Depression. **Above**, strikers pose with food, 1919.

with disturbances that included gunfire, fire bombs and rock throwing. By 1980, despite a steady rise in the black population, Seattle was not even among the top 50 cities in terms of percentage of the population which were African-American. Nevertheless, Ray Charles, born in Florida, put together a trio in Seattle in the early 1950s in his late teens that had the distinction of being the first all-black unit to have sponsored TV shows in the Pacific Northwest. Quincy Jones and Jimi Hendrix also hail from Seattle.

Post-war elation led to a brief depression in 1950 which, in Seattle, was squelched by the Korean War and its demand for high-ticket B-47 and B-52 bombers. It was only with the advent of the civilian 707 airliner – a 1954 spinoff of a military jet tanker design – and the subsequent boom in commercial jet aviation that Boeing was at last released from its dependence on military contracts.

By 1960, the metropolitan population crested 1 million inhabitants – and Boeing employed one out of every 10. The Seattle Spirit had confidently entered into the Jet Age, and nothing symbolized this attitude of onwards and upwards more than the Space Needle, built in 1962 as part of the World's Fair. Unfortunately, Boeing had over-

estimated its market. The city's fortunes plummeted almost overnight, and in the single business year 1969–70, the company was forced to lay off nearly two-thirds of its employees as the demand for commercial jets crumbled. Seattle seemed bereft. Aircraft engineers, unable to secure work anywhere else, opened up hamburger stands and when the unemployment rate hit one of every six workers in the city, tens of thousands left the town where they had been promised lifelong security.

Despite the bust at Boeing, Seattle continued to draw newcomers. By 1970, the population topped 1.2 million. Several attempts were made to raze the older sections of the city, only to be countered by a growing population of individuals intent on preserving what little remained of the Seattle of old. For the most part, it is visitors and tourists to areas such as Pioneer Square who appreciate the city's colorful beginnings.

On May 18, 1980, nature took a last stab at containing the growth of the Pacific Northwest when Mount St Helens, located about two hours south of Seattle, finally lived up to its Native American name of Fire Mountain. After 200 years of near-dormancy, 9,665-ft Mount St Helens erupted, sending more than 150 square miles of mountain 60,000 feet into the air. The eruption came after warnings from scientists and attempts to evacuate the area, but the flow of molten rock and clouds of ash still resulted in almost 60 deaths. Damage was estimated at $1 billion.

Within three days the ash cloud had crossed North America, and within two weeks of that it had traveled right around the globe. Mount St Helens itself was now 1,300 feet shorter than before the blast. Fortunately, the ash has brought essential nutrients to the soil and the devastation has made space for new growth. A million people a year now visit the crater, which is preserved as a national monument.

Industrially, Seattle and the surrounding area has now become less dependent upon Boeing for its business, developing an extensive high-tech industry in the suburbs that includes Microsoft, the company built up by Bill Gates, "America's richest man."

The city continues to draw new "settlers" to its wooded hills. They arrive by the Interstate 90 rather than the Oregon Trail and are drawn by Seattle's standing as the nation's most livable city, the No. 1 recreational city in the country with a good transit system. And some claim that on mist-soaked evenings, they can hear the Gold Rush crowds south of Yesler Way, and feel the ghosts of Chief Seattle's people lurking in the streets of the city that bears his name.

Left, Elvis on location in *It Happened at the World's Fair*, 1963. **Right**, NASA photo of Mount St Helens two months after it erupted, 1980.

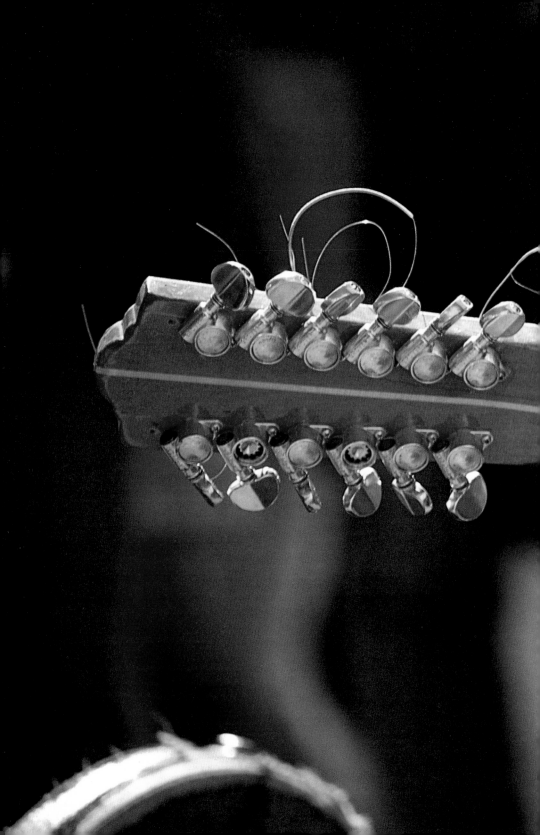

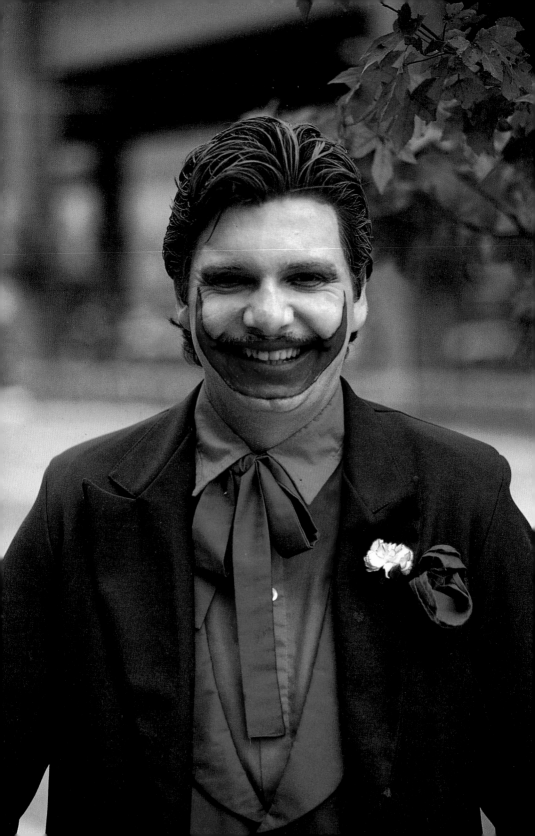

Native Northwesterner J. Kingston Pierce reveals what makes Seattleites different.

Californians and Seattleites have a symbiotic love-hate relationship. They love us. We hate them. Both sides consider themselves to be virtuous.

Actually, *hate* may be too strong a word to describe how Seattleites feel about visitors. We usually deny hating anything. We're too polite for that, thank you, a fact that might be traced to decades of Scandinavian influence. (Many local families can follow their bloodlines back to Europe's emotionally reserved northern quadrant.) Or perhaps we are just reticent to voice any definite opinion, for fear that it will turn out to be politically incorrect. Locals worry about being labeled incorrigible hicks, because we're either too trusting or we're out of step with East Coast towns from which so many of our members recently moved. We were humbled greatly in the late 1980s when it was discovered that the organization, chartered by the city to operate the popular Pike Place Market, had apparently been selling off financial control of this historic civic cynosure to a New York investment company. Even the local press couldn't find enough words of rebuke for city officials. Seattle, it appeared, didn't have the fins to be swimming with sharks.

Happy face: Every once in a while, there will be a splenetic public offensive here against something that wouldn't provoke so much as a yawn elsewhere – like nude dancing clubs or the issue of whether guys who dress up as pirates during the summer's Seafair Festival and leer at beauty queens are actually encouraging sexual violence. But for the most part, Seattle wants to portray itself as upbeat and friendly. It was no mere coincidence that the Happy Face, that loony, lemony, noseless symbol that now decorates everything from headlamp covers to boxer

Preceding pages: stringing along; outdoor lovers; 1st Avenue; stars in her ears. **Left** and **right**, the "Happy Face" smile badge was created here.

shorts to sanitation straps on motel toilets, was created in Seattle in the 1960s. This is a town that doesn't want to raise a ruckus, that likes to get along with everybody.

Everybody, that is, except all those carpetbaggers who've descended upon Puget Sound since the mid-1980s, fanning fistfuls of greenbacks they gleaned from selling homes in pricier areas and snapping up property here that would cost many times more elsewhere. Californians are a special focus

of disgust, usually because we stereotype them as money-oriented, tasteless and self-obsessed. Oregonians struck back at them first, with their "Don't Californicate Oregon" bumper stickers, but Seattleites have followed at a heady clip. We live in a spot shoved far up into the northwest corner of the United States, at least 3,000 miles away from the New York/Boston/Washington, DC corridor and 1,133 miles from the glitzed-out floor show that is Los Angeles. We thought we were safe here from the attentions of the world. We were, unfortunately, dead wrong.

Exclusionists have done their utmost to

discourage outsiders from seeing and then staying in Seattle. Their secret, if subtle, weapon used to be rain jokes, playing on the frequent local drizzle as a deterrent. "Last year 299 people in Washington fell out of bed… and drowned," went one jibe. "What comes after two days of rain?" *Monday*, of course. "The most popular movie in Seattle?" *The Sound of Mucous*.

But while it's true that in an average year, Seattle records only 55 clear days, with another 90 registering as partly cloudy and the remaining 220 recorded beneath the rubric "cloudy," climate is not a part of the ratings systems used to rank "livable" cities. Even if

Media across the nation picked up on the story of a young woman from Los Angeles who, shortly after relocating to the Puget Sound area, advertised in the *Seattle Weekly* personal columns "hoping to meet fellow Californians." Instead of dates, she received calls "from angry Seattle natives telling her in no uncertain terms to go back where she came from."

Emmett Watson, the *Seattle Times*'s curmudgeonly columnist and enthusiastic proponent of wrapping the city in an amber that's impenetrable to all but the longest-term Seattleites, constantly blames this town's ills on immigrants – and that means

it were, that still wouldn't make Seattle look too bad: New York, Atlanta and Boston are all pummelled with more precipitation annually than is this city. While New Englanders and Midwesterners battle through their winters looking like leftovers wrapped securely for freezer storage, Seattleites enjoy moderate, if again rainy, conditions. Polls show that weather doesn't figure prominently in how Puget Sounders – native or new – measure quality of life. Besides, without the rain we wouldn't have all those fir trees.

Go back home: Recently, though, the calumny over new residents has intensified.

not only the traffic jams… and the gang violence… and the pollution… and the runaway housing prices, but even what Seattleites have labeled The New Rudeness. Time was when locals would sit patiently at stoplights for hours, watching one yutz after another try unsuccessfully to make a turn into heavy traffic, and nobody would utter one word. Now, car horns can actually be heard bellowing through downtown streets. Heaven forfend! Whatever happened to Seattle's storied mellowness?

Even big business has played a hand or two in the "We Hate Outsiders" game. Rainier

Brewery, ranked only behind Boeing Corporation and computer colossus Microsoft as the most-recognizable Seattle company (even if it is owned by an Australian firm), erected billboards all over the city one recent summer that featured a bottle of Rainier Beer along with the slogan "Californians Don't Get It." Indeed, Rainier isn't marketed below the Oregon border. But for thousands of Seattleites, Rainier's message took on a distinct – and peculiarly appealing – xenophobic air. Curiously enough, the advertising company that put together the ads was, itself, California-based.

If outsiders are feeling unfairly maligned,

beneath Pioneer Square and listen while tour guides explain that sidewalks in this historic district were at one time a full story lower than the roads, so people had to climb ladders just to cross the streets. Most important of all, they come to spend money, millions of dollars annually, and that's something that should put a shine on the image of even the snobbiest, most acquisitive, most tasteless tourist riding around on four chrome wheels.

Self esteem: Not that everybody is concerned with how Seattleites think of them. Indeed, it was only a few years ago that a columnist with the *San Francisco Examiner* called Seattle "a prim and proper, almost

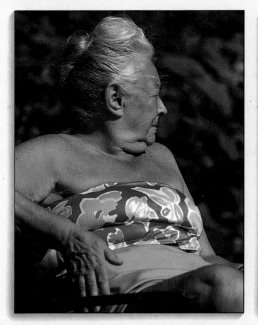

it's because they figure Seattle should be more grateful for their interest. California, for instance, ranks number one among states sending tourists to this city every year. Visitors come north to scope out the view from the Space Needle; to chug across Puget Sound in one of the many ferries that connect Seattle with its nearby island communities; to stare in curiosity as fishmongers shout forth the freshness of their catch at Pike Place Market; and to venture into tunnels

<u>Left</u> and <u>right</u>: Seattleites young, old, friendly and feathered.

prissy, little city" and wondered why stay-put locals tend to stay put. He concluded finally that "There must be drugs in the water." There's nothing wrong with a little enmity from both sides in this case. After all, as essayist Roger Rosenblatt once pointed out in a *Time* magazine article, both people and places can be more clearly defined by the quality of their enemies. "[Enemies] offer a criticism of one's conduct (albeit unsought) that is not always provided by friends," Rosenblatt explained in his piece. "They also encourage self-esteem. How would we know the magnitude of our own worth without someone so worthless attacking it?"

In a weird way, then, Seattle's exclusionists are actually demonstrating their respect for Californians and others by casting them as spiritual and philosophical opposites. If the people of Puget Sound honestly did hate newcomers, we would do better to ignore them completely, as architect Howard Roark dismisses his arch-enemy, Ellsworth Toohey, in Ayn Rand's hypnotic novel *The Fountainhead.* "Why don't you tell me what you think of me?" Toohey asks in the book. To which Roark replies, "But I don't think of you."

Reading the Seattle papers, it seems that architectural scale, the preservationist attitude and even the "eccentric personality" of this place called the Emerald City. (Efforts to change Seattle's silly nickname have so far failed, although two substitutes – "Jet City," in recognition of our associations with Boeing, and "Lady Gray," playing on this area's drizzly climate – can be spotted occasionally in local writings.) Several local publications, too, have bought into the most-livable-city notion of Seattle, although they know deep down that most of it is just tourist-oriented bunk.

These reports often seem loaded unnecessarily with jealousy. They make much of the

locals are constantly speaking and writing with anger about those souls who deign to encroach, like H.G. Wells' Martians, past our city limits. Call it the War of the Words. We're starting to act frightfully defensive about our place in the world.

World-class city?: The word has gone out, right or wrong: Seattle is the coming place. Rare is the month when at least one national magazine doesn't now trumpet its virtues. "The Last Best City in America," *Lear's* magazine called Seattle. "A City That Likes Itself," read the headline on a lengthy piece in *The Atlantic* that applauded the muted high per-capita rates at which Seattleites buy books and attend the theater. They portray us accurately as dedicated in our regard for serious films and supportive of both fringe and established arts. We're fervent gardeners and astute in our understanding of cutting-edge architecture (hey, wasn't distinguished designer Robert Venturi brought all the way from Philadelphia to create the Seattle Art Museum downtown?). And we're trend-setting in our relentless fondness for *caffé lattes.* So popular have these Italian espresso drinks become here, in fact, that one columnist now regularly refers to much of the Seattle area as "Latteland."

Seattle's character might best have been embodied in Ivar Haglund, the late and lovably cornballish entrepreneur who left behind a chain of seafood restaurants that bears his name. But we are more than that. We're Boeing line workers who rise before the sun each morning. We're ex-hippies or hippie wannabes who settle out on Bainbridge Island, just west of the city, where we're told all of our kind eventually migrate. We're aspiring intellectuals who can quote Tolstoy and Shakespeare, but know just enough about local writer Tom Robbins (*Even Cowgirls Get the Blues*) that

made a difference in the world would include Kung Fu cult hero Bruce Lee; Hank Ketcham, creator of cartoon character Dennis the Menace; Microsoft computer mogul Bill Gates; expatriate author Alice B. Toklas; art photographer Imogen Cunningham; packaging whiz Jim Casey, the man who created United Parcel Service; musician Jimi Hendrix; cartoonists Gary (*The Far Side*) Larson and Lynda (*Ernie Pook's Comeek*) Barry; and modern dance choreographer Mark Morris. Even locals are often surprised to discover that so many big names came from such a small place.

What visiting writers don't see is that

we don't look completely like square pegs. We're weekday computer programmers who spend every minute of our weekends in sailboats on Lake Washington. We're architects and journalists and ferry workers and just teenagers with high hormone counts who want to make something of ourselves in a town that's still trying to make something of itself.

An all-star lineup of Seattleites who've

Left, Seattleites buy more sunglasses than residents of any other US city. **Above**, but they never shine their shoes.

Seattleites, while we may survey out as enviable, can also be strident and humorless in our desire to be taken seriously. Rush-hour drivers in the Fremont neighborhood weren't at all surprised to discover a cab company billboard, which suggested that women whose dates become intoxicated "go home with another man" (a cabbie, that is), sprayed over in black paint with the legend "SEXIST." But this stridency is not something that generally makes the public press and, even if it did, the modern correctness would, to some people, make Seattle look even more attractive than it already does.

If Ronald Reagan was the (unscratchable) Teflon President, Seattle is the Teflon City: during its present honeymoon period, nothing can harm its image. Yet we show a streak of fear when it comes to maintaining our image. You can see it in newspaper stories that compare other, now-burgeoning cities – notably neighbors Portland, Oregon, and Vancouver, British Columbia – with the Emerald City. Check to see how often those out-of-state places are described as "what Seattle used to be like." Seattle worries that it's losing its freshness.

So it is actually worrisome when national and international media speak so cheerily of

with its seat covers and stereo gone and its wheel-less chassis mounted on blocks. Any such comparison would be a blow to hard-core Seattleites, for we unfortunately regard our own 'burbs with mild (and sometimes not so mild) disdain or at least humor.

While they aspire to be cities – and, indeed, the metroplex of Bellevue and Kirkland on Lake Washington's east side is the fourth largest population center in the state of Washington – Seattle suburbs are only now beginning to receive some guarded respect from inner-city habituees. Those suburbs have the reputation of harboring money-oriented residents with minimal ar-

Seattle as an aspiring "world-class city" (whatever that really means). Places that are already fit to carry such a mantle (New York, Tokyo, London, etc.) are also those that people so often try to run *from*, not *to*.

Suburbs disdained: And it's funny that many stories spun out from Seattle make it sound, not inaccurately, like some large-scale possessor of the qualities that Americans used to prize in suburbs: cars parked neatly in rows, smiling automatons to greet you at clean movie theaters, neighborhoods where a BMW can be left unlocked overnight and not be discovered in the morning

chitectural tastes, who live in sprawling, characterless homes and carry on all their social rites in shopping malls. Perhaps that will change only as more and more urbanites move outward from Seattle proper to find affordable property, more responsive school districts and greater elbow room, and in the course of it help to reshape the 'burbs using a more urban vernacular of "city."

Jonathan Raban, a well-known British travel writer who relocated not long ago to Puget Sound, is less quick with his hosannas than are other students of Seattle. In his de Tocquevillesque non-fiction book, *Hunting*

Mister Heartbreak: A Discovery of America, he makes clear that newcomers see only a polished-glass, water-fronted, confidence-driven facade of what this city is really like. "If you had the bad taste to look at Seattle from the back," he comments, "all you'd see would be plain brick cladding and a zig-zag tangle of fire escapes." Yet even Raban makes Seattle sound honestly like the Emerald City it wants to be, a place where anything is possible.

"One could tell that Seattle was on a winning streak," Raban writes, "by the number of men in cranes who were trying to smash the place to bits with wrecking balls. The

recast it in the image of home, arranging the city around themselves like so many pillows on a bed." Despite more than a century of history, Seattle still seems very new, protean, waiting to be fully defined.

Which isn't to say that Seattle is a blank slate. Nor is it the proper capital of Ernest Callenbach's *Ecotopia* – a place bereft of trouble and cleaving to a relationship with nature. It's just another city, with all the strengths and weaknesses that label implies. Seattle's history is pocked by racial prejudice and the Ku Klux Klan, by terrifying conflagrations and threatened violence on the highways, by ups and downs at Boeing

pink dust rose in explosive flurries over the rooftops and colored the low sky.

"Pitched on a line of bluffs along Puget Sound, with Lake Washington at its back, Seattle had ships at the ends of its streets and gulls in its traffic. Its light was restless and watery, making the buildings shiver like reflections. It felt like an island and smelled of the sea."

As Raban puts it, the people who've decided to settle in Seattle "could somehow

Left and **right**, Seattle likes to portray itself as upbeat and relaxed.

and the loss of civic attributes both built (like much of the old terracotta architecture downtown) and unbuilt (such as a downtown park on the present site of Westlake Center, which would have given Seattle the spiritual, if not geographical, center that it so needs). It is a place where homeless people – whose numbers grow alarmingly every year – share bottles of screwtop wine in gutters, while stockbrokers stride blindly by, comparing the expense of their automobiles. Where floating bridges have been known to sink into Lake Washington just after planners insist that traffic problems are on the downswing. Where the Green River Killer, Seattle's answer to Jack the Ripper, began a string of murders that now numbers more than 49... and is still growing.

"We're not all that serene and peaceful; we're cold and sullen," said *Misc.* editor Clark Humphrey in a recent edition of *Greater Seattle* magazine. "Imagine old Swedish-Americans whose silence doesn't come from being an alternative to New York noise but out of just not caring to be all that sociable and affable."

Yet locals love this place, and they don't even have to be influenced by drugs in the water. Notice the use of "locals" rather than

"natives" to describe the majority of Seattleites. That's because so many residents here have logged fewer than 10 years within the city limits. Between 1980 and 1990, Washington State's population grew nearly 20 percent, or twice as fast as the rest of the country. The Seattle metropolitan area itself grew by 18 percent, to reach a population of almost 2 million.

Remembering when: Although natives like to depict themselves as the only true Seattleites, anybody who's lived here for more than a month can sometimes be heard saying things like, "You know, so much is

different here than it was. Why, I remember when..." Such is the fate of a city that's just seriously establishing itself: everybody wants to be thought of as present when the boom began.

So the first thing newcomers do after signing a mortgage here is gather the trappings of established residency about themselves. They register for membership with REI (Recreational Equipment, Inc.), the consummate local wilderness outfitter. They procure a credit card from the clothing giant, Nordstrom, and subscribe to *Seattle Weekly* so they can share in gossip about politics, this city's burgeoning art scene and prominent restaurant closings. If they're unmarried, they start dating someone with family connections to Boeing or Microsoft. They start drinking local craft beers and, once they find a brand they like, they zealously contend that it is *the best in the world* – bar none. They buy a dog (there are now 2.8 for every fire hydrant in this city). Even if they despise the game of baseball, newcomers are obliged to insult the closed-roof Kingdome at every opportunity as an inappropriate venue for America's Great Game.

If they live within the Seattle city limits, they go out and kick the tires on a Volvo station wagon, which the *Seattle Post-Intelligencer* proclaimed as "a perfect match" for the semi-individualist, seemingly liberal and sensible nature of locals. If they've chosen instead to locate in one of the (gasp!) suburbs on the other side of Lake Washington, they opt for a Jeep Cherokee, which in turn was acclaimed by the newspaper *Eastsideweek* as "the national car of the Eastside." It's all a part of fitting in, of getting along with everybody.

Finally, these new Seattleites try to close the gates behind them. As is true of anybody who discovers a fresh, barely trammeled place, newcomers want to keep it to themselves. "No more immigrants," they bellow, even louder than the people who've lived here for decades and are now beginning to feel crowded. And you just know the next words out of their mouths will be, "especially no more Californians."

Left, a piece of cake.

SEATTLESPEAK

Mukilteo. Sequim. Humptulips. Enumclaw. Influenced especially by local Native Americans, cartographers have made the state of Washington a minefield of barely pronounceable monikers. Pysht? Skookumchuck? Puyallup? The dangerous days when men spoke "with forked tongues" may be long gone, but they've been survived in Seattle by the era of the twisted tongue.

It's disappointing sometimes to learn that the most colorful place names have been taken from Chinook jargon, a regrettable mishmash of Indian dialects that white explorers and settlers used to communicate haltingly with the previous stewards of this land. Alki, for instance, which today graces a beach and an area of Seattle, means "by and by" in this jargon. La Push, referring to a town at the mouth of the Quillayute River ("river with no head"), is at least geographically correct: it means, simply, "mouth."

Other names are really garbled versions of Indian words. Snohomish, which refers to a city, a river and a county north of Seattle, does not exist in any known Native American language, according to linguists. Its suffix, however – "ish," which translates as "people" – stands out on road maps like pimples on a high school kid. Sammamish means "the hunting people." Skykomish translates as "the inland people." Stillaguamish, Duwamish. The words may come from different native dialects, but they both mean "people living on the river."

So prominently did rivers and other bodies of water figure in the language of Northwest Indians that if someone were to ask you what a peculiar-sounding Washington name means, you could say "water" and stand at least a 50 percent chance of being correct. Lucile McDonald, a prolific historian living in the Seattle-area town of Enatai (meaning "crossing" or "across" in Chinook jargon), writes that "Skookumchuck, Entiat, Cle Elum and Skamania all have to do with strong, swift or rapid water.

Walla Walla and Wallula mean small, rapid river; Washougal is rushing water; Tumwater, a waterfall; Wenatchee, a river issuing from a canyon; Selah, still water; Pilchuck, red water; Newaukum, gently flowing water; Paha, big water; Palux, a slough covered with vines; Yakima is lake water. Sol Duc is magic water. Chelan is deep water." Which is exactly what

outsiders find themselves in when trying to pronounce the majority of these monikers. When in doubt, refer to the book *Washington State Place Names*, by James W. Phillips, which offers not only the source of local appellations, but – thank God! – pronunciations as well.

Locals sometimes look at all these mispronounceable monikers as their special revenge against the incomprehensible accents present in other regions of the country. After all, as linguists are wont to remind Seattleites, Northwesterners have no discernible accent.

The Northwest's language differences are more subtle than swallowed or drawled vowels. In New England, men who used to risk their lives cutting down the forests of Maine were called "lumber-

jacks." In the Northwest, they're known as "loggers." Call somebody riding a horse in eastern Washington State a "cowpoke," and you're liable to earn a mean stare at best, a poke in the nose, at worst. They prefer the name "buckaroo," pardner.

Despite its tenuous connections with the old West of legend, Washington has appropriated some discernible Westernisms. It's not uncommon in farming country to hear someone say "That's as useless as tits on a boar hog" and, despite the fact that weather here is generally mild, somebody may describe a particularly thick-headed outsider as being so dumb that he "couldn't drive nails in a snowbank." ∎

Seattle boasts an artistic culture that would be the envy of a city twice its size. News of its creative climate has seeped into the national press and acted like an artistic pheromone, drawing a young generation of talented writers, actors, artists and musicians. Both high and low flourish here: the Seattle Symphony Orchestra and Seattle Opera consistently pack the Opera House, while fringe theaters and avant-garde galleries are born and die on 6-month cycles.

Seattle's creative forces are inspired by climate and driven by caffeine. The thermometer outside registers 62° and the sky is the color of raw oysters, dripping a steady curtain of rain in sheer vertical paths. It is mid-July. A few friends – two writers, a visual artist, an actor – are ecstatic. The work is going well, unlike yesterday which for most of them was a complete wash: the temperature hit 99°, an all-time record high. It was a dreadful day for the muse.

The city's sodden reputation notwithstanding, it rains no more here than in other American cities. Seattle is distinguished by *how* it rains. Water falls in a fine mist, creating a peculiarly rich quality of light. Colors are dark and true, the mood is introspective, ambiguous, mysterious. "Contemplative weather" is how artist Ginny Ruffner, whose studio overlooks Elliott Bay, once described it. She called it "a beautiful gray day:" interior weather. You want to stay inside and imagine, play make-believe. Which is often the first step towards art.

If the weather turns Seattle's artistic community to brooding, the city's drug of choice prevents them – and a sizeable percentage of the remaining citizenry – from melting into a melancholic droop. This is a city hooked on caffeine. The typical worker checks into the office in the morning and then sprints for an espresso at the cart on the corner, banters with the clerk, then saunters back clutching

Preceding pages: the J & M Café. **Left,** *Nutcracker Suite* performed by the Pacific Northwest Ballet. **Right,** Seattle has theaters big and small.

a foamy latté in a white paper cup. People drink coffee here like nowhere else in America; espresso stands crop up on sidewalks, in department stores, in dental offices, car dealerships and floral shops. It's as if we're all convinced that Thanatos will spirit us away should we lower our guard and drop asleep.

Café life: In the arts community, the day is more likely to start and end at a coffee house, one of a dozen smoky cafés located mainly in

neighborhoods outside of downtown. Pulling espresso is a common day job for aspiring writers and artists. It offers odd hours, cool atmosphere and no dress code. One espresso cart near the Pike Place Market is staffed by a classical musician who pulls coffee in the morning and plays in a string quartet at night. Another cart nearby is owned by an actor who spends his evenings at rehearsals.

For actors especially, coffee is a personal body fuel, although no coffee house is especially known for its dramatic clientele. The Still Life in Fremont may come closest, as it once hosted improvisational theater groups on a makeshift stage. Big and open, with huge windows conducting streams of sunlight into the room, the Still Life is funky and friendly, like the living room of an eccentric aunt, with a very much low-key artistic crowd. You're more likely to find environmentally-conscious baby boomers here than angst-ridden teens.

If there is no common watering hole for theatrical Seattle, there is at least a common institution: The Seattle Repertory Theater. The Rep is largely responsible for establishing the city's reputation as a terrific theater town, although in the past few years some of

groups, visual art exhibits, an avenue of restaurant booths, an army of street performers and very little breathing space. Bumbershoot's smaller twin, the Northwest Folklife Festival, hosts folk musicians and craftspeople during late spring.

The Rep has become a major player in the country's regional theater movement, in which significant new dramatic works (Broadway having found it all but financially insupportable to put on anything but lavish musicals) are nurtured in such provincial incubators. The Rep itself was recently awarded a Tony award as the country's outstanding regional theater company.

the most innovative work has taken place in the city's lesser-known spaces. The Rep was founded in 1963, when the Seattle World's Fair was winding down. Modern-day Seattle arts all essentially date from the World's Fair when the Seattle Center complex – home of the Rep, the Seattle Opera, the Seattle Symphony, Pacific Northwest Ballet, Intiman Theater and a number of annual festivals – was created. The Center's major cultural event takes place on Labor Day weekend; at the Bumbershoot Festival, an inexpensive ticket pays for a day of performances by national musical acts, local theatrical

It has such vast comparative resources (annual budget of $5 million, staff of 200), however, that production values tend to overwhelm the plays. Many playgoers have found themselves so absorbed in admiring the elaborate sets that they missed some crucial opening lines.

Younger work: In the past few years, Seattle's other major theaters have also begun to stage new and provocative productions. A Contemporary Theater (ACT) has been developing strong relationships with young playwrights.

Outside the well-heeled circles of the major theaters exists a whole generation of daring smaller and fringe theaters. Top among these are New City Theatre and Alice B. Theatre, which bills itself as "a gay and lesbian theater for everybody." Productions here can be both risky and risqué. The theaters take chances on radical scripts that in their best moments pay off wonderfully; even when they don't the audience is usually tolerant, if a bit weary. New City hosts festivals featuring both directors and playwrights, staging marathon sessions that afford the city's fledgling dramaturges the opportunity to air their material in front of an audience, even if that audience is infinitesi-

August performances). Tickets are extremely cheap, production values bargain-basement, but occasionally you'll share a flash of brilliance. Three struggling actors once staged an excellent production of David Mamet's *American Buffalo* in what was essentially a converted attic with an audience of 20.

The coffee culture is most apparent in the city's visual arts community. Espresso Roma, with outlets on Broadway on Capitol Hill, and on University Way ("The Ave") in the University District, is notorious for hiring hardcore young artists, beatniks and itinerant bass players to work the counter; the

mal. New City closes each festival with "Best of Fest" nights which repeat the most provocative and polished works.

Seattle's reputation as a theater town has lured scores of aspiring actors and playwrights but, as in any city, there's not enough work to go around. Many stage fringe-theater productions in whatever odd spot they can find: church basements or the sweaty fourth-floor room in the Oddfellow's Hall on Capitol Hill (beware of July and

Left, the art of recycling. **Above**, Tacoma's most famous coffee cup.

artwork of the clerk or the clerk's friend, often hangs on the walls, priced to sell. Café Septième is set in Belltown, an area that runs along First, Second and Third avenues from the Pike Place Market north to Seattle Center. Rents are still cheap enough here to attract a sizeable number of artists. Bleary eyes, black clothes, cigarettes and attitude are *de rigueur*.

First Thursday: On the first Thursday of every month Seattle's art galleries collectively stage an open house of their newly-installed exhibits and between 4pm and 8pm a crush of viewers flows in and out of the artspaces, simultaneously creating and making a scene. Not all come for the art, especially on summer evenings when the mobs prevent even the most ardent connoisseur from seeing anything. Some come only to be on the scene: young couples out on cheap dates, downtown lawyers looking for a classy boardroom canvas and the artists themselves, usually dressed down for the occasion and checking out what's in demand this month.

First Thursday began as a gimmick to attract a broader audience to Seattle's art galleries, most of which are located within a six-block area of Pioneer Square. In the early

days, wine and cheese flowed freely but as the crowds have grown, the taps have stopped; free grub nowadays is reserved for those invited to the Wednesday soirees which precede the First Thursday openings. (Dogged party crashers can usually slip in unnoticed.) The Occidental Park gallery openings often turn into mini-festivals with steel drum bands, entrepreneurs hawking their wares and occasional guerrilla performance art. When a heavy metal concert is scheduled at the Kingdome and thousands of teenyboppers cross the brick park, it can get very messy indeed.

Of all Seattle's cultural milieus, the visual arts is the most accessible. *Reflex*, an independent monthly newspaper available at galleries and some of the hipper bars and clubs, is the fastest way to enter local artspeak. It's worth the effort to weave through jargon ("the Lacanian implications of the mixed-media symbols bode ill for those neo-deconstructivists who…") to read some creative thought and biting criticism. In Seattle, alas, the latter is mostly absent. But *Reflex* gives a voice to off-the-wall praise as well as scathing criticism. No other publication in town would print a review that ends (as one recently did): "[The artists] and their mentors all deserve to be thrown to an angry mob of homeless Cuban winos wielding post-modern shit-shovels by Buster Simpson." (Simpson is a Seattle-based environmental artist whose public artwork includes the planting of latrine shovels on homeless campsites around the city.) *Reflex* also sponsors Second Thursday, an 8pm discussion series in the bar of Italia restaurant, where the most intense of Seattle's artists gather to address contemporary issues.

The staid ones: The city's larger art institutions are, in decreasing order of staidness: the Frye Art Museum, the Seattle Art Museum and the Henry Art Gallery. The Frye contains a private, traditional art gallery, very quiet, upright, uptight, with fine 19th-century European impressionists on the walls. The Seattle Art Museum, a 20-foot giant on the local art scene, has often been the talk of the town. The Henry, on the University of Washington campus, launches more daring shows than the others.

The old and not-so-old masters are hanging on the walls of the museums, but where is the *new* stuff, the work in progress? The best two venues to catch cutting-edge talent are COCA and On The Boards.

COCA is the Center for Contemporary Art, a storefront across the street from the Seattle Art Museum and neighbor to a burlesque joint. COCA seems to take as its mandate the obligation of shocking the city at least twice each year. Its Modern Primitives show some years ago featured the work of tattoo artists and body piercers, many of them piercing live on opening night. COCA keeps its gallery stocked with everything from comix-as-art to environmental sculpture and until recently its artistic director was a fellow named Larry Reid, notorious for showing up on opening nights in torn jeans, old T-shirt, scraggly hair and baseball cap, a can of Black Label beer in hand.

On The Boards promotes a New Performance Series every year featuring new work by established choreographers and performance artists, but the real excitement at OTB happens at its experimental venue known as Twelve Minutes Max. Every six weeks, half a dozen performers are each given 12 minutes to air new performance works. Some

salons. Writers escape to the Northwest to find quiet and solitude; they come to work. Mark Helprin (*A Soldier of the Great War*), Jonathan Raban (*Hunting Mister Heartbreak*), Charles Johnson (National Book Award-winning *Middle Passage*) all live and work around Seattle but few are identified in the national book-buying conscience as "Seattle writers." There is no body of work yet that can be identified as Northwest, as there is for Southern or New England literature.

But certain literary circuits can be tapped. The Elliott Bay Book Company is the nerve center of literary Seattle; tickets for its read-

works are brilliant, others mediocre, but rarely is a performance downright lousy. The program is usually half performance, half dance. There was once a mini-opera devoted to office products in which a woman sang the virtues of Liquid Paper to a rapt audience. The upstairs bar serves shots of Jack Daniels during the intermission.

The literary set: The literary life in the New York sense doesn't exist here; there are no lavish publishing parties, few intellectual

Left and **above**, two versions of the Seattle sound: Jimi Hendrix and Nirvana.

ings, available at the front desk, are usually free but get snapped up early. The Elliott Bay Café downstairs from the bookstore doesn't serve hard alcohol, but does of course provide strong coffee. The Café's annex, an underground bookreading grotto, serves as Seattle's unofficial literary bunker where authors famous and obscure stage nightly readings. Overflow crowds often jam the Pioneer Square store when writers such as Amy Tan or Alice Walker come to town, and these readings are memorable.

On the grittier side, the Red Sky Poetry Theater holds weekly outbursts of spoken-word performance in a local bistro or bar. The work is more outrageous than insightful; a poem from two years ago at a Red Sky reading at Squid Row Tavern (since converted to Tugs, a dance club) still resonates. Marion Kimes, a local poet and denizen of the literary scene, flew from her barstool yelling "No no no Pete Rose" and jammed on from there, throwing fastball poetry at baseball's foremost gambling man.

At the movies: During the annual Seattle International Film Festival, the espresso counter at the Egyptian Theater keeps ticket holders caffeinated nearly round-the-clock. The Egyptian snack bar serves the outside

The Seattle Art Museum exhibits films in series – Bette Davis, film noir, westerns, British comedies – but cineasts seeking the truly bizarre must visit the Pike Street Cinema, which programs esoterica along the lines of *Reefer Madness* and Roger Corman's low-budget schlockfests. The occasional film is also screened at the Jewel Box Theater, tucked away in a back room of the Rendezvous Tavern. The Jewel Box is so covert that longtime patrons of the Rendezvous may be unaware of its existence. A local film-maker once premiered his low-budget horror film here; called *The Attack of the Fertilichrome Cheerleaders*, it attracted

 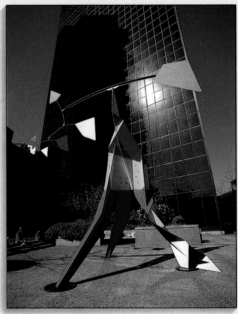

sidewalk as well, so those queuing up for the next show can purchase a pre-screening java stoke. The festival inspires mad loyalty among local cinema buffs.

Beyond the festival, Seattle's independent film culture is more hidden than any other artistic scene. A few intrepid souls sponsor underground screenings in shoebox theaters. Film-maker Janice Findley produces "New Film New City," a program of short films at New City Theater on Capitol Hill the first Friday night of the month. Findley unearths bizarre unheard-of film reels along with early work by now-successful directors.

the kind of audience one might have expected at a Sex Pistols performance.

The soundtrack for that film was provided by a then-struggling band called Screaming Trees. The band has since gone on to sign a major record deal as part of the "Seattle Sound," a brand of grunge-rock spearheaded by bands such as Soundgarden, Nirvana, Pearl Jam and Mudhoney. In the early 1990s, the movement broke nationwide (*Spin* magazine called '92 "The Year of Grunge"), Nirvana and Pearl Jam became MTV stars and the town was flooded with record company A&R scouts seeking bands, and bands seeking the A&R folks with their lucrative contracts. The Seattle Sound grew out of clubs such as the Central, Squid Row, Rockcandy and the Off Ramp. A number of the bands still gig around town between national tours, but only Rockcandy and the Off Ramp remain alive as grunge venues.

Aspiring local musicians frequent bistros and coffeehouses that often host open-microphone nights; the premiere spot for anyone-sings musicianship is the Last Exit On Brooklyn, the grand-daddy of all Seattle coffeehouses. A favorite hangout for anti-war activists and draft dodgers in the 1960s, this place is still Discontented Youth Cen-

hero Jim Page might be followed by a starry-eyed University of Washington sophomore.

Gutsy audiences: Finding culture in New York or Los Angeles is fairly simple. You hit a Broadway show, go to the Met, buy a map of the stars' homes, crash a movie opening. You must do a fair amount of digging to find indigenous Seattle culture. You can get it the easy way, by hitting the Seattle Art Museum and seeing a play at the Rep, but that is showy Seattle. That, and the Space Needle, is what the chamber of commerce wants you to see. See that in a day. Then pick up the culture listings and turn to the fine print in the back; see "fringe theaters" or "films in series" or

tral. Speed-chess players will ignore your presence at their table, so don't bother asking to sit down. Just do it. Circular, open-to-all tables encourage you to get friendly with the person reading Sufi poetry next to you. The open-mike performance series has been running here for more than 20 years (every Monday at 9pm) and never fails to bring out the good, the bad and the downright tone-deaf. On a typical night, local folk-guitar

Far left, land shark. **Left**, Calder sculpture. **Above**, origami designs for the International District Metro Bus Tunnel.

"performance, etc." Dress casual and look like you know what you're doing. Immerse yourself in the cultural trenches; you will see *Attack of the Fertilichrome Cheerleaders*, you will see brilliant David Mamet. You will see what makes Seattle culture electric: people willing to fail.

Artists are given much more room to risk here than in New York or LA. This is the place to air experimental works; critics won't puncture your balloon before it's fully inflated. But this requires something besides gutsy artists. It requires a gutsy audience. Welcome to it.

"She's *de-e-e-ead!* Wrapped in *plassss*-tic!" That line, silly and melodramatic and uttered by a fisherman who discovered the cellophaned corpse of homecoming queen Laura Palmer in the opening episode of a cult television series called *Twin Peaks*, kicked off one of the most bizarre viewing experiences of the 1990s. Along with true stories about serial killers still at large in this area and sociological reports that Northwesterners are given to violence, it also helped change – at least temporarily – the way the world looked at Seattle and northwestern Washington. After years of being characterized as a casual, carefree place, Seattle was suddenly showing its darker side.

Before *Twin Peaks*, Seattle may have been best remembered as the setting for *Here Come the Brides*, a 1960s "family drama" based loosely on an authentic 1860s scheme to match eligible Puget Sound gents with virgin women imported from Massachussetts ("Mercer's Maidens," they were called, after the originator of the scheme, future legislator Asa Mercer). Of course, *Brides*, featuring the apple-cheeked teen heart-throb Bobby Sherman among its eminently forgettable cast, confirmed for the world what it already thought it knew: that Seattle was far too backwards ever to be taken seriously.

Later television efforts to portray Seattle only worsened the image. Who could forget that 1973 movie-of-the-week, *The Night Strangler*, which sent a wide-eyed Darren McGavin creeping around the underground tunnels of Pioneer Square in search of a ghastly murdering creature said to be the undead remains of a Civil War physician? No doubt, the local tourist bureau had a fit over that little bit of cinematography. ("Sorry, Helen, we're not going to Seattle this year. I hear there are crazy, undead

Preceding pages: "Fremont Troll" under the Aurora Bridge. **Left,** Snoqualmie Falls and Salish Lodge provided exteriors for *Twin Peaks*. **Right,** who killed Laura Palmer?

people running around beneath its streets.") Then there was the syndicated sitcom, *Harry and the Hendersons*, based on the 1987 movie of the same name, which asked America's gullible viewers to believe that the nearby Cascade Mountains were inhabited by the Sasquatch, or Bigfoot, a dubiously photographed but never scientifically confirmed creature that is related to the Abominable Snowman or *yeti* of the Himalayan Mountains.

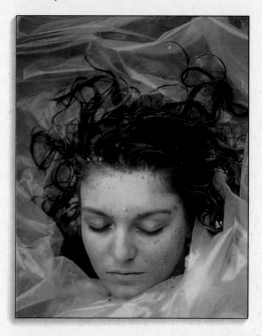

A weird place? No question about that.

The *Peaks* experience: *Twin Peaks* didn't enhance the image of Seattle and its outlying rural towns so much as it just twisted their rube-ish renown into something that was… well, *cool*. Bizarre, yes. Often demented, without a doubt. Outlandish, always. But *cool*, nonetheless. Director David Lynch, still fresh from another cultish noir success, *Blue Velvet* (1986), set out with *Hill Street Blues* veteran Mark Frost to offer tube-aholics a meta-soap opera with surrealistic undertones that might be reviled by critics and despised by those people who always think they have to control the viewing habits of their children, but which was so unlike anything that had come before it, it couldn't help but be talked about.

Rather than being repudiated, the show was embraced. Exalted. It was Topic A at water coolers during its first season. Elements from the script infiltrated daily life – suddenly everyone wanted "a damn fine cup of coffee" and a rich hunk of cherry pie. Reviewers started calling *Twin Peaks* a "phenomenon," something that existed beyond the petty parameters of a Magnavox or Motorola, a program that transcended the traditional shallowness of its medium. Fac-

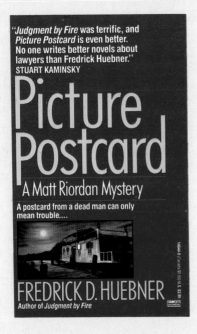

tory workers, fishermen, architects, bankers – Americans everywhere assembled the morning after an episode to discuss what had happened and, more importantly, *what it had meant.* As one magazine so eloquently phrased it, *Twin Peaks* "has twisted the concept of night-time soap opera and sent it reeling down Alice's rabbit hole."

Marketing opportunities: The vision of Lynch and Frost may have been original, but at times, it was also downright confusing. By the end of its first season, even staunch admirers said the show was just too obtuse to follow. But by then, *Twin Peaks* had become

the phenomenon it was supposed to be all along. A national publisher issued a paperback book (written by David Lynch's daughter) titled *The Secret Diary of Laura Palmer.* Another company started marketing audio cassettes of Dale Cooper's taped memos to his never-seen assistant Diane.

Newspapers and travel magazines ran stories about the area where the show was set, making clear the sources of Lynch's fictional settings. Elegant Salish Lodge, a historic hotel perched right above Snoqualmie Falls east of Seattle, provided the exteriors for Twin Peaks' Great Northern Hotel. The Colonial Inn, a short way off in Fall City, became the fictional town's notorious Roadhouse Bar.

And crowds were pouring into the hamlet of North Bend to see the dowdy Mar-T Cafe, which doubled as the Double R Diner (and was also where David Lynch ordered pie and coffee every day that his people worked in the area). A BBC film crew even flew over to interview Mar-T owner Pat Cokewell and pie-maker Garnet Cross, and basically plumb the popularity of *Twin Peaks* in England for every viewer ratings point it could grab. One tenant of a British prison wrote to Cokewell, telling him that he'd like to visit the Mar-T Cafe as soon as he was released.

"*Twin Peaks*," wrote a columnist in the *Seattle Times* about the show, "flawed or not, probably did more to put Washington on the map than the millions the state has spent promoting tourism."

Tours of the area continued even after *Twin Peaks* ended and David Lynch's movie – a prequel to the *Twin Peaks* story – brought scores of Japanese fans to the area on conducted tours.

Real-life mystery: It was just about that time that a new book, based on a survey conducted by two New Yorkers, made the worrisome case that Lynch's dark-side portrayal of Pacific Northwest life may be closer to the truth than anyone here would like to think. In *The Day America Told the Truth*, authors James Patterson and Peter Kim, both senior execs at the J. Walter Thompson advertising agency, reported that Seattleites and others living in what they called the "Pac [or Pacific] Rim Region" (representing western

Washington and Oregon, as well as northwestern California) tend to be sex-crazed, prone to violence, fixated on suicide, unpatriotic and given to laziness at work.

You could find thousands of people in this area to discount such conclusions, but by the authors' reckoning, about one in four residents of the Northwest could be classified as a "sociopath" – a person lacking in the restraints of conscience. The book explained that nationwide, the average was one in every 10 people. "Coupled with the observation that Pac Rimmers are the regional respondents least likely to present themselves to others as they really are, it seems that David Lynch may be on to something," the book concluded.

Patterson and Kim based their report on what they claimed was the "largest survey of private morals" ever carried out. Personal interviews were conducted with more than 2,000 Americans from every region, and 3,600 more responded to a questionnaire.

The survey determined that more than 40 percent of Northwesterners regularly experience violent fantasies (about the national average); that 40 percent have considered committing suicide (the nationwide average was 32 percent); and that 58 percent admitted using drugs, compared against a national average of 41 percent.

Killers in our midst: This wasn't the first evidence of the Northwest's dark side. The area hosted anti-Chinese raids in the 19th century and slaughters of Native Americans before that. One of the biggest public events mounted by the Knights of the Ku Klux Klan occurred in the Seattle area in 1924, when as many as 55,000 people gathered in the town of Issaquah for a membership rally. That was a lot of folks to show up in this then-tiny burg on the east side of Lake Washington for *any* reason, much less the "naturalization" of 250 candidates as members of the KKK. But the so-called Invisible Empire had promised to "put Issaquah on the map" with its rally and, at least to historians and secret-society

watchers, the empire did just that. Even today, Seattle newspapers occasionally report cross burnings and threats against the area's minority residents.

For years, novelists have plumbed the often dim, misty environs of Puget Sound for dramatic effect. J. A. Jance (*Until Proven Guilty, Injustice for All*) has a homicide cop discover a blonde dragging a dead man from the water at Rosario Resort, a historic lodge in the San Juan Islands, north of Seattle. Portland scribe Richard Hoyt (*Siskiyou, Fish Story*) pitched his detective, screwtop wine-lover John Denson, against a person who's been leaving chunks of human flesh around

Seattle's Pioneer Square. North Bend resident Earl Emerson, author of a series featuring Seattle private eye Thomas Black (*The Rainy City*, *Yellow Dog Party*), once sent his protagonist after a woman who used to work on fundraising drives for Seattle public television station KCTS. He's also had Thomas Black discover a body in a closet at the downtown Four Seasons Olympic Hotel – barely clothed, riddled with four bullet holes and a statuesque trans-sexual lying dead as can be nearby.

The roster of local authors who commit dastardly deeds on paper, and often decrease

Left and right: books by local thriller writers Fredrick D. Huebner and Aaron Elkins are read avidly. Even Dashiell Hammett's fictional detective Sam Spade once practiced in Seattle.

Seattle's population by one or two in the process, must also include Aaron Elkins (*The Dark Place*), Robert Ferrigno (*The Horse Latitudes*) and Fredrick D. Huebner (*Picture Postcard*).

Even Dashiell Hammett once lived for a spell in Washington before he became famous (although his time was spent mostly in Spokane, on the state's eastern end). In Hammett's *The Maltese Falcon*, Hammett has San Francisco gun-for-hire Sam Spade saying that way back in 1927 "I was with one of the big detective agencies in Seattle." Black and Denson and the rest of the crew are in good literary company.

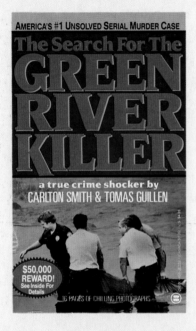

The Day America Told the Truth wasn't even the first published study in which authors and researchers made the case that Seattle and the surrounding Northwest might be spawning or at least attracting seriously violent individuals.

Since 1982, the media have deluged Americans with stories about the Green River Killer, so named because his first female victims were discovered in the fertile Green River valley, south of Seattle. At last count, the death toll was 49, making the Green River Killer the most prolific murderer in the crime annals of America – and

law enforcement agencies still don't know if he's out there somewhere, waiting to commit more of his heinous acts.

In a sensationalistic, but reportedly accurate book on the subject, *The Search for the Green River Killer*, two *Seattle Times* reporters, Carlton Smith and Tomas Guillen, gave only the most general sketch of the person who took 49 lives. "He was a man," they wrote, drawing from years of police investigations, "probably white, experts thought, and possibly between the ages of 30 and 50. He was a man familiar with hidden areas often found near golf courses, cemeteries, plant nurseries, parks and places where household garbage and yard waste were illegally dumped.

He may have had experience in the military or as a security guard. He was familiar with police procedures. He probably was in the Seattle-Tacoma International Airport in late May of 1983, either flying somewhere or meeting someone on a flight. He read the newspapers and followed the coverage of the murders on television. He kept things that belonged to his victims."

And he may still be alive. Maybe not. He may already be in custody. The most disturbing suggestion thus far is that he may also be a cop.

Other serial killers: So far, the case of the Green River Killer is still open. Other Northwest serial killers have not so successfully escaped justice – former Green Bay Packer and Oregon's "I-5 Killer," Randall Woodfield; "Lust Killer" Jerome Brudos, also of Oregon; Harvey Louis Carnignan, who procured his victims in the region through newspaper want-ads; and Theodore "Ted" Bundy, a handsome aspiring attorney who was posted to former Washington Governor Dan Evans' 1972 re-election campaign, but later wound up on the FBI's 10 Most Wanted list.

How many women Bundy may have killed in Washington (his first victim perished in Seattle in 1974), Oregon, Colorado, Florida and elsewhere in America is anybody's guess. Some police detectives estimated that the figure was 36; others have pegged the number as high as 100. Bundy hadn't provided a firm figure before he was executed in Florida on January 24, 1989.

Author Ann Rule (perhaps the second-best-known true-crime writer from Seattle, behind Jack Olsen, author of *Son: A Psychopath and His Victims*, about the man convicted of Spokane's notorious South Hill rapes) knew Ted Bundy, and her largely first-person book, *The Stranger Beside Me*, remains the most readable account of that slayer's exploits.

She offers several theories as to why serial killers may be attracted to Seattle and the rest of the West Coast. One may be that the killers are drawn to water. "Rain, fog and clouds create shadows to hide crimes not meant to be seen," Rule has explained. "Eight months

with fewer convenient routes of escape from state and US national jurisdictions than Interstate 5 provides." And finally, Rule speculates that these hardened killers might possibly come here because they see it as a challenge. "Serial killers... relish playing games with the police," Rule has written, "but a chess game without a worthy adversary holds no fascination."

Through baptisms by fire with the Ted (Bundy) Task Force and now the Green River Task Force, Northwest law-enforcement personnel have played "the game." Detectives here are familiar with the psychopathology of serial murderers. They may be

out of the year, the Northwest's climate provides more stormy nights than does any movie thriller."

Then there's Ann Rule's "Last Frontier Theory": "Serial killers may gravitate here in search of the same sort of grudging acceptance that Billy the Kid, Butch Cassidy, even Idaho mountain man/murderer Claude Dallas have been afforded. There are other Old West states but, unlike Washington and Oregon, they are landlocked and endowed

Left, real-life mystery. Above, the Mar-T Cafe, home of real fine cherry pie.

more able to see patterns in these crimes. At the same time, smart serial killers may be able to find patterns in the way that detectives go about tracking them down. Do assassins still at large consciously or unconsciously salivate at the chance to joust with task-force veterans?"

Faithful watchers of *Twin Peaks* will remember that the killer of Laura Palmer engaged in just such a dangerous joust with FBI agent Dale Cooper. David Lynch may, indeed, have been playing closer to the boundaries of reality than we, and even he, might have thought.

On a hazy summer day in July, the Boeing Co. threw a party. It jammed 3,000 employees on buses, invited about 30 media people, hired the University of Washington marching band and a local sports broadcaster whose claim to fame was several years' playing for the Seattle Seahawks football team. All were ushered inside a dim, cavernous, ancient hangar – a place where World War II bombers were built – to hear big news: the company had decided to introduce a new plane, the 777.

Boeing Chairman Frank Shrontz made a short, dry speech. The band played, a pep squad led a few cheers and everyone ate the fried chicken box lunch they found under their chairs. A videotape reeled off a quick history of Boeing successes, from the B-17 and the China Clipper to the 747. The public was not invited, and what razzmatazz there was resembled a college football halftime in a small town in the midwestern part of the US. A little more than an hour later it was all done, and everybody filed back onto the buses and returned to work.

Multi-billion: Shrontz and three of his executives, dressed in their customary plain gray suits with diagonally striped ties, traipsed over to a dull brown Ford Taurus and carpooled their way back to headquarters. No uninitiated onlooker would have known their provenance: the leadership of one of the world's pre-eminent, multi-billion dollar manufacturing companies.

That's Boeing for you. Not only is the company studiously low-key, it is mysteriously inconspicuous in its home city. The question is which has caused the other. It's not surprising that few Seattleites would recognize the company chairman if they bumped into him on the street; Boeing executives detest the high-profile approach to corporate management and generally stay out of sight. It's the company's own invisibility that is so puzzling to outsiders; because in all respects, Boeing is a behemoth.

Its annual sales are in the $30 billion neighborhood, profits around $2 billion. It exports more goods than any other US company, $16 billion a year. Its business backlog is about $90 billion, the largest in industrial history. It employs 100,000 workers in the Puget Sound area, 150,000 worldwide. It owns thousands of acres of property and owns or leases more than 20 million square feet of office space. Its annual Seattle-area payroll is $5 billion. Its outside purchasing, taken by itself, would rank as a Fortune 500 company at $12 billion.

Recognition: Economic studies show that, when you add in the effect of Boeing work done by subcontractors and the multiplier effect of its payroll, one in four jobs in the Seattle area depends on Boeing. In the heart of Boeing country, such as King County, demographers figure half the households depend on Boeing either directly or indirectly. Overseas, Seattleites find people do not know their city until they say "Boeing," which causes a foreigner to crack a grin, point to the sky and reply, "Ah, Boeing!"

Boeing is Seattle's Hollywood. It's Chrysler, General Motors and Ford all rolled into one. No other metropolitan area in the world is so dependent on a single corporation, a fact of which most area residents are oblivious. If Boeing is evident in any single aspect of Seattle life, it is during rush hour – which begins at 5.30am and 2.30pm – for one simple reason: that's when shifts change at Boeing plants. But residents and visitors alike search in vain for other overt signs of the company's ponderous magnitude.

Where, for example, is the gleaming downtown tower which serves as Boeing's headquarters? It's nonexistent; the company's executive offices are housed in a drab three-story building on an industrial street south of the city – a description that fits most of Boeing's hundreds of buildings. You can't go in; as at most Boeing sites, headquarters' access is limited to employees and scheduled visitors. To see its neighborhood,

Preceding pages: Museum of Flight. Left, a tail of two cities: Everett and Seattle.

drive south on Interstate 5 from downtown Seattle. You'll see an airfield with dozens of new jets lined up alongside; that's Boeing Field, where 737s and 757s are prepared for delivery to buyers. The headquarters is on the other side, hidden from view, and the air strip's actual name is King County Airport.

If there's no skyscraper to represent Boeing, where is the company's annual meeting held? In the main cafeteria out at the headquarters where stockholders and directors alike sit in folding chairs and discuss their $30 billion global enterprise. That's an apt allegory for Boeing's political power. It contributes faithfully but moderately to can-

complexes that reflect the hopscotch way the company grew from its beginnings on the shores of Lake Union in 1916. Most Boeing buildings are marked only by numbers – the headquarters is 10-06, for example – and your surest clue there's a plant nearby is a gate with a guard. Only in one place would you know at first glance that one of the world's biggest industrial enterprises is housed therein.

World's biggest: That's in Everett, 45 minutes north of downtown Seattle, at the plant where 747s and 767s are assembled. The 747 hangar is 200 million cubic feet, the world's largest building, one of the few grandiose

didates, largely eschewing issues. It rarely takes public stands, although in the Washington State Legislature Boeing is described as a 1,000-pound gorilla. If your bill's in trouble, the axiom goes, the timber industry doesn't like it. If your bill vanishes without a trace, Boeing didn't like it. That's what the city of Seattle discovered in the late '70s when it aspired to annex the company's headquarters; just a few weeks later the legislature had abruptly changed the annexation rules to make the city's scheme impossible.

Boeing's planes, and the parts which comprise them, are made in large helter-skelter

claims Boeing allows itself. Tours are offered daily – the only Boeing site open to the public – and visitors find themselves flabbergasted by the sheer size of the planes and the plant, and by the apparent lack of activity. Assembling the world's largest commercial jet appears to be a leisurely process; on each fuselage a few workers are driving rivets or bolting flanges. In the whole place there's no more than 700 workers on any shift. How on earth do a 747's 4 million separate parts coalesce into one massive whole that can take 450 people a third of the way around the globe in half a day?

Actually, most of the parts are pre-assembled. The planes are pieced together methodically during a 21-day journey through the assembly hangar; every few nights the graveyard shift's task is to move the line, which means picking up and shifting every single 747. They emerge at the other end ready to be painted for delivery to the international airlines which have made it, according to one popular legend, the most universally recognized manufactured product in the world. This is also the world's most expensive commercial plane; at $125–140 million per airplane, the 747 is the foundation of Boeing's finances.

60,000 Puget Sound workers, shrinking its workforce from 105,000 to 39,000.

Boeing was at the brink, and so was Seattle. Thousands of families packed up and left; Houston, where unemployed engineers sought jobs in the space program, was known as Seattle South. The Boeing Crash remains an intrinsic part of Seattle folklore.

Boeing embarrassments sometimes generate as much unwanted visibility as the company's success, even though it is the latter which has spurred Seattle's spectacular growth. A Boeing military procurement executive proved an exemplary culprit in the Pentagon defense-spending scandals of the

Most Seattleites nevertheless think of the 747 as the force that almost drove the company down, and the city with it. In 1970 Boeing had over-committed itself to develop the jumbo jet, investing more in the project than the corporate net worth. Banks refused to loan Boeing money; when the government cancelled the supersonic transport (SST) project in 1971, it was a double blow that provoked catastrophic action. In less than two years Boeing pared down more than

Left and **above**, one in four jobs in the Seattle area depends on Boeing.

mid-1980s; he went to prison for trafficking in procurement secrets, and Boeing scrambled to institute ethics policies. Toxic waste surveys of King County have uncovered a string of sites at which Boeing wastes were dumped; the company sued its insurance carrier over responsibility for cleanups. When a Boeing 747 went down in Japan, the company wound up apologizing to the families of the victims for its role in the plane's crash.

That sort of exposure helps prompt the odd adherence to obscurity. The company's character was forged in the Boeing bust of

1970 every bit as much as Seattle folklore depends on it. Any longtime resident discussing prosperity will recall how recently catastrophe came to call; Boeing executives recall it, too. The company hoards cash, liking to keep more than $3 billion on hand. It owns no executive jets, and its few limousines are reserved only for customers. Advertising is sparse.

In many respects, this is much like Seattle, the city which has gaped at its recent discovery as a major metropolis. Thinking of this as merely a timber town is a half century too late. But despite its pivotal role in the Seattle community, past and present, Boeing strikes

even local experts as a surprise.

"Well, I can't say I've thought about it much," acknowledges Murray Morgan, the dean of Puget Sound historians and author of several crucial books about the area. "I guess we wouldn't be anything like we are without Boeing." Indeed, Boeing is partly responsible for the region's evolution into a middle-class domain, the home of the neighborhood espresso cart.

Designers predominate: How did a manufacturing company transform a working-class city? It began in 1947, when new Boeing President William Allen broke a long and bitter strike by out-bluffing the International Association of Machinists with a threat to replace workers. The company's simultaneous shift toward high-tech aerospace started its evolution from a blue-collar to a white-collar corporation, a key change. In 1942, at the height of the World War II bomber production effort, there were three hourly employees for every salaried worker. Now the proportions are reversed; it takes far more designers and technicians to build a modern airplane than it does production workers.

"The company created the middle class around here," marvels University of Washington historian Richard Kirkendall, who has fashioned a course he calls "Boeing and the Taming of the West." "Nobody realizes it, I guess. People seem to be peripherally aware of Boeing's significance, but why it hasn't attracted more attention is a mystery to me. We belong to Boeing. It's the great economic and cultural shaping force of the region." Kirkendall credits Boeing for the political transformation of the area, too. Puget Sound was once home ground for the Wobblies – the International Workers of the World – and left-leaning political parties got more than twice the vote in Seattle than they did nationwide.

That was in the early 1930s. Then came Boeing's first big boom, the post-war union struggles, the growth of high-tech and defense work. By the '70s, Seattle was home ground for US Senator Henry "Scoop" Jackson, the prototypical conservative Democrat who never met a defense project he didn't like. Scoop and colleague Warren Magnuson together wielded immense power in the US Senate, and funneled all the defense work to Boeing that they could manage, including the Minuteman nuclear missiles and the immense fleet of B-52s which is still the heart of the US intercontinental strike force. But even Scoop and Maggie couldn't keep the orders coming. When Congress killed its multi-billion-dollar funding of the project, Boeing found itself with no other direction to take but the one that led it to its current status as the world's leading maker of commercial jets.

Now Boeing owns almost two-thirds of

the global market in its field. Its planes are sold to China and to South Africa, to Israel and Hungary and Britain, Germany and Japan. Its jets are by far the leading Washington state export. Not apples, not wheat, not wood. And it's all an accident of history.

Bill Boeing, the company's founder, was a prosperous Seattle lumberman who developed a fascination with planes. In 1916, he set out to build one, a pontooned biplane called the B&W made of spruce and linen. Only one B&W was built, but it impressed government authorities sufficiently to earn the fledgling Boeing Co. contracts to build military trainers during World War II. The

The museum is in Seattle because Boeing is – the company donated the land – but at no point in the seven-decade history of the company has Seattle proved crucial to Boeing. In fact, a 1948 study found no economic reason why the company should operate in Seattle at all. But operate it does.

Boeing is as pervasive as rain, and the company and the region regard each other like an old married couple, hardly ever stopping to take a close look. North, south and east of Seattle, the largest employer is Boeing. Even in the Tacoma area, where it has just one small plant, it's the biggest employer. Boeing is the one business ac-

company earned world prominence with the legendary B-17 and B-29 bombers of World War II. Initial commercial dominance came with the 707, the first successful passenger jet, in 1958. Some of this history can be seen at the Museum of Flight, a facility just down the street from Boeing headquarters which compresses one of the world's major modern industrial endeavors into a compact, airy space featuring much less of Boeing than you would expect.

Left and **above**, Boeing exports more product than any other company in the United States.

count area hotels always seek, and the one force that looms over the region's healthy real estate market.

It sticks here because it's a stolid, lumbering giant that has spread itself across the metropolitan area like a blanket. Boeing's most visible sign is the ubiquitous presence of the company ID badges. You'll see them affixed to lapels and shirt pockets everywhere, sometimes the object of jests. Do Boeing workers really sleep with their badges? No, but Seattle itself has a Boeing badge. Bigger than life, it's just a little hard for outsiders to see.

The pioneers who first homesteaded the shores of Elliott Bay found steep slopes hidden by trees that strained the belief and stretched the necks of viewers: Douglas fir, hemlock and western red cedar towered 250 feet tall and measured 7 feet through at the base. They were magnificent and daunting, the world's greatest forest. They were also in the way, and with hand saws, axes and oxen Seattle's first residents cut them down, dragged them to shore and turned them into docks and storefronts, or sold them to trade ships that wandered by. For a while, at least, every Seattle settler was a logger.

Almost a century and a half later the technology had changed quite a bit when Washington's modern loggers came to call in Seattle, the city most consider the capital of the Northwest timber empire. On June 2, 1989, 125 contract timber haulers rolled into town in their log trucks, immense and forbidding machines whose trailer tongues, stored in travel mode, protrude above the tractor cab in a fashion that resembles nothing so much as a medieval catapult. The protest caravan's object was to remind urban residents that real people still make a living cutting down trees, just as almost all the residents of Seattle did 140 years ago.

Seattle police restricted the loggers' access to downtown streets, carefully counting the trucks that exited Interstate 5 and forcing 500 other protest truckers to parade north and south on the expressway. In town, the caravan rolled to the Seattle Center and back, through the skyscrapers which replaced those giant early trees, bearing messages almost plaintive in their earnestness: "Save Our Jobs." "Timber Is This Family's Living." The day before, a US judge had halted timber sales on federal land until the survival of a rare small forest owl was assured; one protest truck thus bore an effigy depicting the spotted owl strangling the timber indus-

try. After about an hour in town, the caravan headed off to the state capitol in Olympia. For loggers, it was an epochal event.

Orderly protest: For Seattle residents it was decidedly less memorable. A week later Seattle's police chief sent the protest sponsors a letter complimenting them on their orderly behavior, pleased he had not been forced to use the crowd control squads that were ready to clamp down on rowdy behavior. Even so – and despite the fact the

loggers carefully got in and out of town before the afternoon rush hour – what most urban residents noticed was just another traffic disruption in a city perpetually snarled.

Is Seattle a timber town? No. In a metropolitan county with more than 1 million residents, about 11,000 people are directly employed in the forest products industry. By comparison, the umbrella organization which represents most Washington state environmental groups claims about 50,000 members in the Seattle area, and the disparity is reflected in far more than numbers. Seattle is indeed the center of the US timber

Preceding pages: Tacoma sawmill with Mount Rainier in background. **Left**, old growth forest. **Right**, turn-of-the-century timber scene.

empire – if one can say such a thing exists – but that no longer means what it once did.

A century ago, distraught timber workers would have been embraced by townfolk well aware that the forest edge was the resource mine on which Puget Sound prosperity was based. Big trees brought civilization to the region; in fact, settlers did not really arrive until the need for wood spurred them. Gold was discovered in California in 1849, precipitating the greatest boom in US history, and lumber was desperately needed in San Francisco Bay. But there were no trees there, and while plenty of trees covered the north California and Oregon coasts, the latter ter-

capital of the Northwest timber industry.

Not the center: Although Seattle had its share of timber activity, it was by no means the leading port. There were never more than two or three major town mills, and by the turn of the century active timber processing in Seattle had diminished to cedar shingle manufacture in Ballard, north of downtown. The city itself became a trade and manufacturing center, and Tacoma turned into Puget Sound's premier timber town.

That's where a second irony came to call, in 1900. Frederick Weyerhaeuser sat at a table in the Tacoma Hotel that winter and with one stroke of a pen paid $5.4 million (an

ritory had no safe anchorages for clipper ships to load and unload. Puget Sound, however, is a 100-mile fjord with dozens of grand harbors, and the area's giant trees were practically falling in the water.

The result was the first in a long series of timber ironies still relatively misunderstood. The initial Northwest timber barons were from New England; they set sail from San Francisco, parked in Puget Sound, liked what they saw – and hired hard-bitten foremen to run their mills so they themselves could return to the balmier climes of the Golden State. For a while, California was the

almost unimaginable sum in those days) for 900,000 acres of timberland the Northern Pacific Railroad didn't want. But Weyerhaeuser wasn't a Northwest timber baron; he had made his fortune in the Midwest and, even though his company became the state's biggest timber firm, he never lived in Washington at all.

The name Weyerhaeuser is synonymous with the Northwest's timber giant – it owns 5.6 million acres of forestland, but almost half the company's operations are elsewhere (Arkansas, for example) and the headquarters were never in Seattle. The moss-draped edifice the company built in the 1970s for its headquarters sits astride a vale next to Interstate 5 in Federal Way, halfway between Seattle and Tacoma, and the item of greatest interest to visitors is a company-sponsored rhododendron garden which bristles with blooms from April to July. The nearest thing Seattle can claim to a timber giant is Plum Creek, a spin-off from Burlington Northern Railroad; or Simpson, one of the country's largest family-owned companies.

The urban/forest divorce that began at the turn of the century was solidified when Boeing became the mainstay of the Seattle economy around World War II, and final-

"The linkage between the industry and our metropolitan areas is not fully appreciated by current residents of these cities," he instructed the crowd. "There is not a person in Seattle whose quality of life is not dependent on a healthy timber industry." True, perhaps, but industry figures despair of convincing urban dwellers.

Attitude surveys consistently demonstrate a deep and abiding distrust among city residents for logging practices – especially the much-maligned clear-cut, which is the most obvious sign of the wood products industry to Seattle visitors who have flown in over the Cascades. Even the magnificent distractions

ized when Microsoft and the Bellevue high-tech explosion fueled the 1980s' computer boom. Still, timber is vital to the Northwest economy – it's third in Washington, behind aerospace and agriculture – and thus vital to Seattle. Forest products' loans are the second largest item of business for the state's largest bank (whose headquarters are in Seattle) so it's no surprise that a bank vice-president showed up at that 1989 logger solidarity rally to plead the industry's case with jaded city residents.

<u>Left</u>, log storage yards. <u>Above</u>, high-tech sawmill.

presented by the white spires of Mount Rainier, Mount Adams and Mount Hood can't obscure the patchwork appearance of the lower slopes, which have been scalped in piecemeal patterns. To the timber industry it represents crop rotation. To urbanites it represents land abuse; they do not believe industry explanations that every inch of forestland is replanted once cut and it will all grow back in 50 years.

It will. It won't be like the forest those first settlers found; today's lowland loggers are cutting second- and third-growth trees sometimes barely a tenth the diameter of the original firs, hemlocks and cedars. Visitors who want to see what the forest used to be like must journey quite a way; the best examples are preserved at Mount Rainier National Park, about two hours south of Seattle. Isolated original groves dot parks in the area; but the most popular wooded area in Seattle is the University of Washington Arboretum, an expansive park south of the campus whose trees were all planted by horticulturists enamored of creating a forest with dozens of non-native species.

Seeing the industry in action is even more difficult. There is just one active mill anywhere in the immediate Seattle area. It's at

Renton, on the southeast shore of Lake Washington, and the property is slated to become a massive office complex. The Seattle waterfront is founded on the timber trade, literally; clippers dumped their ballast along the shores of Elliott Bay when they took on lumber, and the waterfront rests on the result. But the Port of Seattle no longer depends on forest products.

Tacoma tide flats: It's somewhat different in Tacoma, whose port is the leading forest products shipper in the United States, approaching $1 billion in value; forest products represent 40 percent of the port's total ton-nage. A drive through the Tacoma tideflats north of Interstate 5 in Fife will take the curious visitor past acres of Weyerhaeuser logs awaiting export across the Pacific, the source of another controversy in the Northwest. Critics claim logs shipped overseas mean jobs shipped to foreign countries. Free enterprise, the industry answers.

Aside from protest demonstrations, one will see neither loggers nor log trucks in Seattle. Drivers in the metro area's outskirts can watch the log trade go by, especially on Interstate 5 in Federal Way, where log loads barrel down the road from 6am to 10pm. Active cutting takes place far from urban centers, although the burgeoning Seattle suburbs are beginning to encroach on timber lands, and new outlying residents periodically raise a fuss when they wake up to find the forest next door has been clear cut. Timber companies wonder, in response, whether area residents would rather see the only alternative: even more modern suburbs, stretching as far as the ancient forests once did. This is a somewhat disingenuous reply, because Weyerhaeuser has already turned so much of its Seattle land into suburbs that residents sardonically alter its nickname. The Tree-Growing Company? No, scoff critics: The House-Growing Company.

Timber companies claim they'd rather grow and harvest trees, but urban opinions make it impossible. The conflict typifies the estrangement between timber and city. A denouement occurred in the early 1990s, when mounting protests forced the City of Seattle itself to abandon its century-old practice of logging off the forests in its massive public watershed, southeast of the city along the Cedar River. Loggers working the stand shook their heads, wondering what the area had come to. "This is all I've ever done," said one. "It's an honest job. We help turn trees into homes. I guess all those people in their office buildings think wood just comes from the lumber yard." In the city limits of Seattle, uneasy capital of the timber empire, that's exactly where wood does come from.

Left and **right**, Washington State's economy depends primarily on timber, agriculture and the aerospace industry.

If landscape is character, then Northwestern-ers are most like water. We are shaped by the voluptuous shores and salt tides of Puget Sound, the deep currents of the Columbia, Salmon and Snake rivers; finally we are held back from falling off the proverbial edge of the world by a Pacific coastline whose rainforests and rocky peninsulas face the sea like guardians. So, surrounded by water, we cannot impose our own rhythms on nature as easily as a bulldozer does on a Southern California canyon or asphalt across a Southwestern desert. It is we who find ourselves subtly in synch with the rise and fall of tides, the ebb and flow of the natural world.

Slow motion: This distinction – that Northwesterners are more changed by their environment than it is by us – is crucial to understanding our character. Recently, a convention of New Yorkers visited Seattle. On the harbor cruise to Blake Island, birthplace of Chief Sealth, for a salmon feast (hosted by Native Americans to recreate the first salmon bake and potlatch ceremonies that defined tribal life here for thousands of years), the tourists commented that everything around seemed in slow motion.

"We've had to shift gears," said one New Yorker, somewhat anxiously. "Everything's so laid back. Maybe it's all those negative ions in the atmosphere."

Another visitor asked: "How do you stand traffic jams on those floating bridges? Can't they just pave a part of Lake Washington?"

Finally, a rather pensive, bespectacled literary agent was moved to remark: "Now I know why Seattle is single-handedly keeping the publishing business alive. You have to go inside from all this gray and wet. I feel like I'm dreaming."

"Must be why Seattle has espresso carts on every corner and some of the world's best coffee," someone laughed. "It's to keep yourselves awake!"

Northwesterners are a dreamy lot, in a fine

tradition of dreamers. According to the Wasco Indians along the Columbia River, the tribe knew well before the white men came to settle at Alki Point in 1851 that a change was coming. As told in Ella Clark's classic *Indian Legends of the Pacific Northwest,* one of the Wasco elders dreamed that "white people with hair on their faces will come from the rising sun." The strangers, it was prophesied, would bring with them "iron birds that fly" and "something – if you

just point it at anything moving, that thing will fall down and die." These strangers also brought modern new tools such as axes and hatchets; they even brought stoves to cook on. Along with this new technology, the white man brought a philosophy of individual ownership of the land.

The Native Americans knew that the land could never be owned, just as it was impossible to section off the vast, winding lengths of the emerald-clear body of Puget Sound. Even now, after a century of non-Indian dominance, Puget Sound property rights ebb and flow according to the tides, not the set

Preceding pages, Lake Union resident. **Left** and **right**, living with water.

boundaries of so-called land owners. If even our ownership of Northwest land is called into question by the changing and shifting of tides, how much more deeply are we affected by the water's relationship with us?

Physicists posit that by observing something, we subtly change it; does what we gaze upon then also change us? Northwesterners not only reckon with water shaping our physical boundaries; we must also learn to live most of the year as if underwater. Rain is a Northwest native. Our famous rainfall is perhaps all that shelters us from the massive population and industrial exploitations of nearby California. The rain is so

omnipresent, especially between late October and even into June, that most Northwesterners disdain umbrellas, the true sign of any tourist.

Widely-acclaimed Port Angeles poet Tess Gallagher tells it this way: "It is a faithful rain. You feel it has some allegiance to the trees and the people... It brings an ongoing thoughtfulness to their faces, a meditativeness that causes them to fall silent for long periods, to stand at their windows looking at nothing in particular. The people walk in the rain as within some spirit they wish not to offend with resistance."

One must be rather fluid to live underwater; one must learn to flow with a pulse greater than one's own. A tolerance for misting gray days means an acceptance that life itself is not black and white, but in between. If the horizons out of one's window are not sharply defined but ease into a sky intimately merged with sea and soft landscape, then perhaps shadows are not so terrifying.

After all, most of the year Northwesterners can't even see their own shadows cast on the ground... We live inside the rain shadow. We tolerate edges and differences in people and places perhaps because our landscape blends and blurs as it embraces.

Our Northwest character is flexible. There are not the rigid social stratas of New England or the South. There are not the climactic extremes that make for a sizzling summer race riot in Los Angeles or the violent cold of Chicago. Even the first Native Americans were known not as warriors so much as fishermen. While there were territory battles, there was also a diversity and abundance of food that was quite a different story from the Southwest tribal struggles over scarce resources. Amidst this plentitude Northwest art flourished – and so did tribal storytelling.

Shifting shapes: In keeping with the landscape's watery changes, native stories of the region are full of legends in which animals change easily into people and back again. For example, the Salmon People are an underwater tribe who also spend a season on land; the whales and seals can metamorphose into humans as easily as the ever-present mist and clouds change into different shapes. Many Northwest coast tribes tell of merpeople – part human/part mammal – who mediate between the worlds to keep a watery balance. One of the most respected native gods was named "Changer," a name perhaps explained by the local adage: "If you don't like the weather, wait five minutes and it'll change."

Many native tribes began their mythologies with water, floods and seas creating what we now call "the people." A Skagit myth details this beginning when Changer decided to "make all the rivers flow only one way" and that "there should be bends in the rivers so that there would be eddies where the fish could stop and rest. They decided that beasts should be placed in the forests. Human beings would have to keep out of their way."

Here in the Northwest it is we humans, not water, who must keep out of the way. We pride ourselves on living within nature's laws, on listening to our environment before it is irresponsibly lost and silenced. It is after all, here in the Northwest where the last nurturing old-growth forests still stand, fought over fiercely to preserve them for future generations of visitors. Here is also where the United States' last wild salmon

contaminations from industrial waste. And, as always, the old-growth forest debate rages between timber companies and those who struggle to conserve ancient trees.

Regional organizations such as the Puget Sound Alliance, a local program to protect that wondrous waterway, employs a fulltime Soundkeeper who patrols the shores checking reports of pollution. There is the highly acclaimed whale museum and its dedicated staff in Friday Harbor who have been studying the transient and resident pods or orcas in the San Juan Islands for many years. The organization called People in Puget Sound involves local volunteers in the education

still spawn. But for all its strong conservation of nature, there are signs that even the "Rainy-Day People" are facing growing environmental challenges.

Oil spills blacken our beaches and several species of salmon are endangered; gray whales are found on their migrating courses belly-up from pollution in Puget Sound. There have been major closures of shellfish beds throughout the region because of toxic

Left and right, Seattle residents tend to define themselves and their neighborhoods by their proximity to water.

and conservation of our beautiful inland sea.

There is a growing movement among corporations whose headquarters are in this area to give back some of their profits to protecting our wilderness: Recreational Equipment Inc. (REI) and Eddie Bauer are two such businesses which believe in investing in their own region's environmental resources. Such bio-regionalism runs strong in the Northwest. After all, many people moved to this area to be closer to the natural world. The urban sprawl of California, the East Coast penchant for putting nature in last place – this is the mindset most Northwesterners sought to escape and to guard against.

Respecting our roots: Just as Northwestern-ers claim closeness with their natural world so, too, are we close to our own history. Compared to the native tribes, we are young. Our history here is only 150-odd years compared with thousands of years of Skagit, Suquamish, Muckleshoot, Okanogan and multitudinous other tribal roots. Some of the myths favoured by Indians calmly predict that "the human beings will not live on this earth forever."

This is an agreement between Raven, Mink, Coyote and what the Skagits call "Old Creator." The prophecy predicts that human

hours of the failed coup in the Soviet Union, it was remarked that there were more fishing boats on Puget Sound than usual. It is typically Northwestern that this gone-fishing-while-the-world-falls-apart attitude prevails, while in New York City or Washington, DC a population is transfixed by CNN-TV. It is not that Northwesterners aren't involved, it's just that nature can be an antidote to such strong doses of terror. Nature can also remind us that there are other mysteries at work in the world which might hold more power than our own. And also more hope.

If water is our Northwest character and rainy reverie our temperament, it follows

beings "will stay only for a short time. Then the body will go back to the earth and the spirit back to the spirit world." The likelihood of this simple ebb and flow of our human tribe seems more possible here, where the animals interchange lives with the humans, where the mists can transform entire settlements and skyscrapers into low-hung cloud banks.

Our human worries carry less weight in this world surrounded by water. Perhaps this is why modern history fails to integrate: in the early 1990s, during the first days of the Persian Gulf War and also during those 72

that those of us who stay long in the Pacific Northwest have developed a deep inner life to sustain us through the flow of many changing gray days. This means that ambition is not only an outward thrust toward manipulating our environment; ambition may also be an inner journey, not to change, but to understand the often unexplored territory within, what Rilke called "the dark light." Are we a more mystical region and people? Let's just say the climate is here and so is the water.

Above, one in six Seattleites owns a boat.

WRITING ABOUT RAIN

Rain, or its absence, has always made the front pages in Seattle. It is the same story told with variations about a subject beloved by columnists and headline writers alike.

"This January, Wettest Ever, Getting Wetter" proclaimed the *Seattle Times* in 1953, announcing that a 40-year-old record for January 27 (9.8 inches in 1914) had been beaten that day. "Rainless Seattle: Will We Become Another Tucson?" asked columnist Don Hannula in June 1985, alleging misleading under-reporting of precipitation by the Weather Bureau. "Drop In the Bucket: That Splatter Didn't Matter" was a 1987 head in the *Times* after a long, dry spell.

In a city with only 50 totally clear days per year it is actually the lack of rain that seems to provide the most vivid stories. "How long, O Lord, How Long?" bemoaned columnist John Hinterberger in 1973, a year which clocked up only about half of the city's usual annual downpour. "What is giving us all this troublesome, lovely weather?"

Good – or at least exceptionally rainless – summer weather could indeed be troublesome for Seattle, lowering the level of the Cedar River up which 300,000 salmon travel from Lake Washington to spawn, and slowing the turbines to halfspeed at the Diablo Lake plant which supplies much of the city's power.

"(At present) there isn't enough water to cover all the gravel (in the river)," complained a spokesman from the State Fisheries Department.

But that was a rare year. Later in the decade people were once again calling Seattle "the rain capital of America," prompting a defensive story by writer Sharon Lane who quoted from the 1978 *World Almanac* to show that Seattle's annual rainfall of 39 inches had been exceeded in the previous year by at least 125 American cities including San Juan (64.2), Miami (59.8), Atlanta (48.3), Houston (48.1), Nashville (46) and New York City (41.6).

What seems to make the difference here is the rain's ubiquity, a sheer, steady saturation slanting down from what a 1902 columnist called "the humid vats of heaven." It rains so frequently yet so unobtrusively in Seattle that few people wear coats or even admit to owning umbrellas (although the Bon Marche department store alone sells 13,000 each year and the Metro system reports that more than half that number are left on buses). Almost a decade ago a *Seattle Weekly* writer commented poetically that "drizzle and gray become the badge of pride for those who stay, and the curse that drives others away."

Even the legendary Craig Cappuccino, credited with setting up Seattle's first outdoor espresso cart, waited in the rain week after week until the customers came, building up that mystic relationship between sipping and soaking that has become the hallmark of the true espresso aficionado.

This perverse affection for rain sometimes suggests overly macho if not masochistic overtones. "Here if the sun doesn't shine we don't consider the day lost," says Walter Rue, author of *Weather of the Pacific Coast.* "People here don't complain about a little rain."

And the *Weekly* quoted a visitor from Kansas:

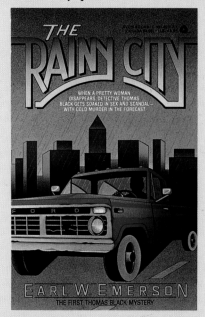

"People actually get nervous when it's sunny. They feel exposed.They like the gray days; they wrap up in them like a security blanket."

All this, of course, plays right into the hands of the Lesser Seattle Movement, a tongue-in-cheek campaign promoted by veteran *Seattle Times* man Emmett Watson who has repeatedly advocated a disinformation program to discourage would-be Seattleites. Fifteen years ago his fellow columnist Jean Godden gave his cause a helping hand with her playful list of 38 Things To Do In the Rain. "Write letters to all your friends," she urged her readers, "and tell them how horrible the weather is. Tell them this isn't even a nice place to visit…" ∎

Seattle is a city of distinct neighborhoods. They may not be defined by their ethnic populations, but the individual areas do characterize the city, and longtime residents are often as loyal to their community as to any cultural ties.

Residents of any one neighborhood chauvinistically tend to feel their local friends are more pleasant than those in other parts of the city, their views more picturesque and their local restaurant chefs more talented. Families with children are likely to label their neighborhood "a good place to raise the kids." If they are unmarried, they boast that it is exactly the right area for singles.

For the visitor, specific differences between neighborhoods are hard to pin down. The University District, surrounding the University of Washington, is understandably academic and student-oriented, the north Seattle Fremont area is labeled funky and the sprawling suburban neighborhoods in Bellevue and Redmond are called upscale. If one had any doubts that Ballard, north of downtown, was the city's Scandinavian center, you only need pick up a bottle of Ballard Bitter, made by Red Hook, the local microbrewery, and read the label: "Ya sure, ya betcha," it says.

Residents of Wallingford argue with Queen Anne residents about whose homes offer the most spectacular views over downtown. And residents of Magnolia and West Seattle offer similiar arguments about their views of Puget Sound, Vashon, Blake and Bainbridge islands and the Olympic Mountains to the west. But true distinctions are often more geographic than philosophic. Neighborhoods here are often named for dominant features such as Green Lake, Capitol Hill and Mercer Island. Geography offers more than names, however, as these physical characteristics also often define how residents spend their leisure time.

Because of the city's strong and diverse communities, some maintain, much of downtown Seattle is empty in the evenings because so many people find what they want closer to home. This is not entirely true. Pioneer Square has exuberant after-dark entertainment, and the reliable Pike Place Market bustles with activity every weekend.

But for visitors with time to spare, the real Seattle is best sought out in suburban parks, neighborhood restaurants and small shops. The city's excellent Metro bus system provides service to most communities from downtown, although traveling from one neighborhood to another is not always as easy as it might be. Weekend and non-rush-hour traffic are also quite manageable and the city has a number of good bike paths linking neighborhoods from the eastside to south Seattle.

Preceding pages: climbing the Kingdome; flagging the city; port of call. **Left**, mass transit.

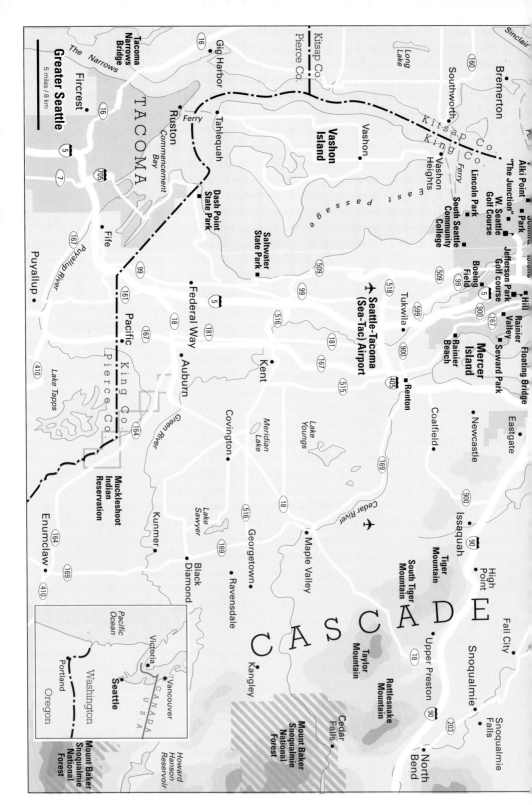

Greater Seattle

5 miles / 8 km

The Narrows

Tacoma Narrows Bridge

Fircrest

TACOMA

Ruston

Commencement Bay

Tahlequah

Ferry

Gig Harbor

16

16

5

7

705

99

167

Puyallup River

Puyallup

Fife

Pacific

167

Pierce Co.

161

Lake Tapps

410

Enumclaw

164

410

169

Kitsap Co.
Pierce Co.

Kitsap Co.

Long Lake

180

Bremerton

Southworth

Southworth

Kitsap Co.
King Co.

Vashon Island

Vashon

Vashon Heights

Lincoln Park

Alki Point
"The Junction"
W. Seattle

Jefferson Park Golf course

South Seattle Community College

Dash Point State Park

Saltwater State Park

Federal Way

18

181

5

509

99

516

Seattle-Tacoma
(Sea-Tac) Airport

518

East Passage

Tukwila

599

900

Boeing Field

Rainier Valley

Hill

Sinclair

Jefferson Park Golf Course

5

167

Rainier Beach

Seward Park

Mercer Island

Floating Bridge

Newcastle

Eastgate

Renton

405

Coalfield

900

Issaquah

90

High Point

Fall City

Snoqualmie Falls

Snoqualmie

North Bend

203

90

Upper Preston

18

Kent

Auburn

18

167

515

169

Covington

Meridian Lake

Lake Youngs

Lake Sawyer

516

Green River

164

Muckleshoot Indian Reservation

Kanner

Kummer

Black Diamond

169

Georgetown

Ravensdale

Kangley

Maple Valley

Cedar River

Cedar Falls

Taylor Mountain

Rattlesnake Mountain

South Tiger Mountain

Tiger Mountain

900

CASCADE

Mount Baker
Snoqualmie National Forest

Howard Hanson Reservoir

Mount Baker
Snoqualmie National Forest

Pacific Ocean

Victoria

Portland

Seattle

Vancouver

CANADA
U.S.A.

Washington

Oregon

Portland

112

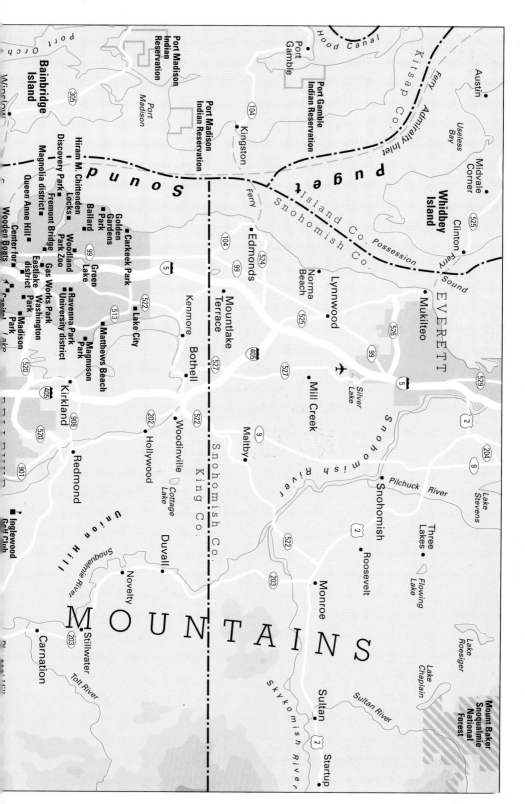

Port Orchard

Winslow

(305)

Bainbridge Island

Port Orchard

Port Madison Indian Reservation

Port Madison

Port Madison Indian Reservation

Port Madison

(104)

Kingston

Port Gamble

Port Gamble Indian Reservation

Hood Canal

Kitsap Co.

Austin

Useless Bay

Midvale Corner

Admiralty Inlet

Ferry

Puget

Possession

Whidbey Island

(525)

Clinton

Ferry

Island Co. Possession Sound

Snohomish Co.

Ferry

Ferry

Sound

Edmonds

(104)

(99)

(524)

(524)

Mountlake Terrace

Norma Beach

Lynnwood

(525)

(525)

Mukilteo

EVERETT

(526)

(529)

Hiram M. Chittenden Locks

Discovery Park

Magnolia district

Queen Anne Hill

Fremont Bridge

Ballard

Golden Gardens Park

Woodland Park Zoo

Green Lake

(99)

(5)

Carkeek Park

Kenmore

Bothell

(522)

(513)

Lake City

Ravenna Park

University district

Matthews Beach

Magnuson Park

Gas Works Park

Eastlake district

Washington Park

Madison Park

(520)

(405)

Kirkland

(908)

(202)

Woodinville

Hollywood

Cottage Lake

(527)

(522)

Maltby

(9)

Mill Creek

(527)

(5)

Silver Lake

Snohomish River

(99)

(2)

(204)

(9)

Pilchuck River

Snohomish

(522)

(2)

Roosevelt

Lake Stevens

Three Lakes

Flowing Lake

Center for Wooden Boats

Capitol

Madison Park

(520)

(405)

(901)

Redmond

Union Hill

Inglewood Golf Club

Snoqualmie River

Novelty

Duvall

King Co.

Snohomish Co.

(203)

Monroe

(2)

Lake Roesiger

Lake Chaplain

M O U N T A I N S

Carnation

Stillwater

(203)

Tolt River

Skykomish River

Sultan

Sultan River

(2)

Startup

Mount Baker Snoqualmie National Forest

113

SEATTLE CENTER AND THE WATERFRONT

Only one World's Fair has ever been the site of a movie starring Elvis Presley and that is the one held at Seattle in 1962. It brought more attention to this Pacific Northwest city than anything since the Klondike Gold Rush and not all the residents were happy about it. Most Seattleites are proud, however, of the Fair's long-lasting legacy: the **Seattle Center** with its internationally-recognized **Space Needle** and one of the only monorail systems in America.

The 605-foot Space Needle understandably offers some of the best possible views of the city: Lake Union, the immensely larger Lake Washington and the distant Cascade Mountains to the east; Elliott Bay opening into Puget Sound westwards with the Olympic Mountains fronted by verdant islands; and, southeast on any clear day, the snow-capped peak of Mount Rainier

Preceding pages: Space Needle and full moon. Left, Waterfront welcome.

(14,400 feet). If you go to the Space Needle Lounge at the top of the tower, ask for a "Spirit of the Needle" cocktail to sip while enjoying the view. This revolving restaurant makes a complete revolution every hour.

There's a **fun fair** in the 74-acre Seattle Center, also a **laserium, several theaters, arts and crafts centers,** an **amphitheatre** plus **flag-lined plaza** for events ranging from business exhibits to displays of old Studebaker cars. The enormous **Central Hall** contains a **Children's Museum,** 50 shops and restaurants all surrounding a **dance floor.** The **Opera House,** which was the origin of the whole project, is said to have some of the world's best acoustics. All of this plus the wonderful, larger-than-life shows in the IMAX **Theater** are quite enough to occupy the visitor for an hour or two, but what really takes time to do full justice to is the fascinating and imaginative **Pacific Science Center.** Riding a bike on a narrow rail 20 feet above ground, rolling a ball into a concave recess, spinning on a human turntable – all absorbingly simple demonstrations of natural forces such as centrifugal or gravity seem to be irresistible to adults and children alike. There are also well-stocked tidepools, holograms, IQ-taxing computers and a host of other participatory scientific and mathematical displays.

Leaving the Pacific Science Center, walk two blocks down Eagle Street to the harbor. Just to the southwest of the Seattle Center, the area known as **Denny Regrade** was once a hill whose removal provided much of the landfill that raised downtown's muddy streets. Today the former hill is covered with apartments, office buildings and two TV stations.

The Waterfront: At the foot of Eagle Street an old streetcar barn marks the northern terminus of the **streetcar route** along Seattle's 2-mile waterfront. Plying **Alaska Way** every few minutes from early morning until late at night, these green and yellow, 60-year-

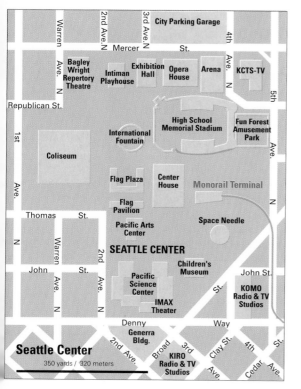

Seattle Center

350 yards / 320 meters

old Australian trams take 20 minutes to run down to the edge of the International District and offer easy access to most of the city's downtown attractions. The overhead viaduct along Alaskan Way has always been unpopular. As far back as 1970 *Seattle* magazine suggested that it be "scuttled," although of course it enables a lot of traffic to bypass the busy waterfront street.

Most of this part of the harbor, from Pier 70 here at the northern end to Pier 36 (now a Coast Guard museum) southwest of the Kingdome, is devoted to tourist activity although the **Washington State Ferry Line** (Pier 51) is possibly America's busiest waterbound commuter route. The 25 ocean-going boats of the Washington Transportation Department's Maritime Division each year carry 21 million passengers and almost 10 million cars, about half of them crossing Puget Sound to or from their island homes in under 35 minutes. The ferries run at a loss of a million dollars per week.

An inexpensive, short trip is across to Winslow on **Bainbridge Island** but try to avoid the crowded ferries before 9am and between 3 and 7pm. Whales are sometimes spotted on the crossing. The splendid **Joshua Green Fountain** outside the ferry terminal is named after the late centenarian who arrived in Seattle in 1886, operating steamboats on Puget Sound before helping to found one of the city's earliest banks. It is another of the fountains created by the redoubtable George Tsutakawa who was also responsible for the fountain outside the *Post Intelligencer* building further north along Elliott Avenue. Between the newspaper offices and Pier 70 another public sculpture can be admired: casually-arranged boulders in **Myrtle Edwards Park**.

Alaska boats: Though today it offers shopping, dining and covered parking, **Pier 70**, terminal for the sightseeing boats to Alaska, calls itself a "Gold Rush era" pier, harking back to that July day in 1897 when the steamer *Portland*

Seattle Center Mae West.

arrived with two tons of gold from the Klondike, setting off a rush that within weeks took thousands of Seattle residents (including the mayor) into the frozen north. The Gold Rush set off a boat-building boom too, and a great deal of office business for Moran Brothers shipyard which stood on the present site of the Kingdome.

Many of today's northbound explorers leave for Canada from Pier 69 by *Victoria Clipper,* an enormous hydrofoil which takes under three hours to reach the British Columbia capital of Victoria on Vancouver Island. Among other boats leaving from the waterfront are those of **Seattle Harbor Tours** from Pier 55; the **Tillicum Village** tour to dine with the Native Americans on Blake Island (Pier 56) and various Gray Line cruises from Pier 57. Because Puget Sound is so vast, it is easy to forget that the city is not on the Pacific Ocean but 125 miles from it, nestling on 54 miles of shore line in Elliott Bay. Despite its distance from the ocean, it is

actually two days shorter sailing time from Japan than are the California ports.

Many of the piers, particularly **Pier 55** and **Pier 56**, have been transformed into shopping centers and these and others sport restaurants of one kind or another, most offering views of the harbor. There is only one waterfront hotel, the 240-room **Edgewater Inn** on Pier 67. Under the development plan slated for this area, another hotel will be built in addition to a marina, housing a towering World Trade Center.

The **Omnidome**, on Pier 59, with its giant screen overwhelming viewers with stupendous images of erupting volcanoes and explorations beneath the Great Barrier Reef, may be the best show in town. It shares the pier with the delightful **Seattle Aquarium**, a visitor-friendly attraction that features 200 varieties of fish native to Puget Sound, plus environments that simulate the rocky reefs, sandy seafloor, eelgrass beds and tidepools.

Vividly striped lion fish, lethal elec-

Fountain at Center House, Seattle Center.

tric eels, chameleon-like flatfish, octopus, dogfish and salmon dart by to the enjoyment of visitors, all side by side with irresistibly entertaining otters and seals. The twice-daily oceanic tides that flood the Sound mixing with fresh water from ample rainfall has nurtured "an unequaled estuarine haven for plants, animals and humans," according to one of the many educational captions.

What was once Pier 58 is now **Waterfront Park**, a relaxing place to sit on weekends and watch the city's fireboats entertain by shooting tall streams of water into the air at the rate of 22,000 gallons a minute. It's a good place, too, to watch the sunset which is invariably spectacular. Green and white Foss tugs, of which there are 70, plus 200 barges ply the waters of the Sound hauling timber, sand and gravel as they have been doing for the past century since Thea Foss, a Norwegian immigrant, started the company with her husband by renting boats to fishermen. Thea was allegedly the model for Norman Reilly Raine's *Tugboat Annie*, portrayed by Marie Dressler in a series of 1930s movies, some of which were made in the region.

Pier 54 is the home of **Ye Olde Curiosity Shop and Museum** with its bizarre collection of carney attractions such as Siamese twin calves, mummies, shrunken heads, shark jaws and pins engraved with the Lord's Prayer. The shop/museum is still owned by the descendants of Joe Standley who opened it in 1899, later selling his ethnological collection to New York's Museum of the American Indian.

Sharing Pier 54 is **Ivar's Acres of Clams**; outside, a bronze statue by Richard Beyer of the late restaurateur Ivar Haglund feeding a seagull is a popular photo opportunity. A lovably irascible character who opened the city's first aquarium back in 1906, Seattle-born Haglund began his career playing guitar and singing on local radio and TV, and later made a fortune with his seafood restaurants which col-

Pacific Science Center.

lectively sell more than 200,000 clams each year (it takes a million and a half to cover an acre). Beyer, by the way, is also responsible for the city's most popular sculpture, a group at the north end of the Fremont Bridge called *Waiting for the Interurban*. Across the street from Ivar's, the tramcar stop is called **Clam Central Station**.

Pike Place Market: It started with half a dozen farmers bringing along their produce in 1907, moving into space the city had set aside for a commercial market in response to the public's demand for lower prices. Over the years the number of farmers has varied from a high of several hundred in the 1930s to a low of 30 by 1976. Developers wanted to demolish the market but Seattleites got the issue placed on the ballot and voted overwhelmingly to retain it. Since then the number of visiting farmers has stabilized at around 100, but **Pike Place** has become so famous for all of its other attractions that its role as one of the oldest (and probably biggest) daily produce markets in the country is sometimes sadly overlooked.

Most of the fruit and vegetable stalls, as well as those displaying all those gleaming banks of fish, are in the semi-open arcade along First Avenue centering around Georgia Gerber's giant bronze piggy bank **Rachel**, on whose back there always seems to be a child posing for a photograph. Rachel, who gets lots of fanmail, has collected almost $30,000 through the slot in her back for charities since her arrival at the market in 1986.

But not everybody comes in at the front entrance here; many approach from the waterfront, either via **Victor Steinbrueck Park** (named for the architect who revived the market in the '70s) or up the Hillclimb from the foot of Pike Street. Musicians tend to gather at this spot although there are a dozen places where musicians with permits (around 300 issued each year) are authorized to play. Many of the regulars – among them a classical music trio, a

Pike Place Market.

gospel singer who raises funds for his travels as a missionary and a man who wheels around his own piano – can usually be found somewhere near the **neon billboard clock**. Just north of here, around the uncovered stalls, crafts-people assemble each morning to be allocated a place for the day. Some of them have been attending the market for years and seniority plays a big part; there are hundreds of people on the waiting list who move up only if existing craftspeople turn up less than two days per week.

Eating at the market is a joy because there's so much choice. Stallholders favor the home cooking at Shane's Restaurant, two floors down; the funky, old Athenian Inn with its view of the bay; the stools at Jack's Fish Spot in the **Sanitary Market** or Burrito Express in the **Economy Market Atrium**. But there's everything from croissants at The Crumpet Shop (**Corner Market Building** on First Avenue) or over-stuffed sandwiches from the Three Girls Bakery or Philadelphia Deli in the Sanitary Market, to the more substantial cuisine of Il Bistro (**Lower Post Alley**), the Copacabana Café (**Triangle Building**) or the renowned **DeLaurenti's** combination bakery/deli. The Corner Market, Post Alley Market and Sanitary Market (no horses were allowed) are joined by walkways with eating spots on all levels. Artists sometimes hang out in the Corner Market's Café Counter Intelligence.

Don't overlook the **Soames Dunn Building** which houses Emmett Watson's Oyster Bar in a pleasant courtyard, as well as another deli, Vietnamese and Mediterranean restaurants and one of the Starbucks chain of espresso counters. These are only a few of the eating places: you'll find it helpful to have a map of the market which you can get at the information booth by the main entrance. The major fresh fish stalls are here; at one of them they are so used to visitors with videotape machines they'll borrow your camera and

Pike Place Market was established in 1907.

take some dramatic footage of the fish being thrown straight at the lens (into the safe hands of a colleague).

Home cooking: If you're virtually en route to the airport when you visit Pike Place, you could arrange to have your salmon packaged in dry ice for the journey home. Some visitors find it so frustrating to be unable to take the fresh produce home to cook that one local magazine recently ran a listing of Seattle accommodations with housekeeping facilities.

The problem has always been thus. Writing in *Harper's* in March 1925, Katherine Fullerton Gerrould commented: "Only the stern fact that food is perishable kept me from outrageous purchases; for the fish, the fruits, game, vegetables, cheese, butter, have an ambrosial look and a utopian price. Soberly speaking it is a shock to see the perfect lettuce head for eight cents, the big box of raspberries for ten… There is poetry in a market basket in Seattle; and what is more, the lean purse can fill it."

Under the **Main Arcade** is a labyrinth of corners, corridors and cubbyholes; shops, stalls, stairs and empty spaces. Magical tricks, old posters, talking birds, Australian opals, Turkish pastries, books, funky clothes… they're but a few of the thousands of items on display. No chain stores or franchises are allowed so everybody's an individualist and there's no shortage of characters. Even some of the tiles on the floor are eccentric. Locals were invited to pay $35 for their own design some years ago and one mathematician's wife listed all the prime numbers under 100.

There's an expensive but very popular 65-room hotel, the **Inn at the Market**, at the corner of First Avenue and Pine Street, and a branch of one of the best bookstores in town, **Shorey's**, one block south in the **Economy Market** (their main store is on Union Street). There is in this 6-block area, in fact, virtually anything that you might need. Except a parking space. Leave your car behind and come by (free) bus.

Going around in circles.

DOWNTOWN

Defined by the area in which daytime bus rides are free, downtown begins – at the southern end of town – beside the adjoining parking lots of what is now the Amtrak station and the unmistakable **Kingdome** (capacity: 74,000). In this sports palace with the world's largest freestanding concrete roof, the baseball Mariners and the football Seahawks play.

Highlight of the daily Kingdome tours is a visit to **the museum**'s collection of sporting memorabilia donated by sportswriter Royal Brougham. Among the exhibits are a pair of Muhammed Ali's boxing shorts, a University of Washington kimono – souvenir of a 1921 trip to Japan to play Waseda University – and the green shirt worn by Pele when his New York Cosmos beat the Seattle Sounders (2–1) during the stadium's first sporting event held in 1976.

Apart from a handful of patient souls (scarcely enough, one would imagine, to keep the espresso stand in business except at rush hours), the **King Street Station** is like a ghost town. Observant visitors will note the resemblance between its tower and the campanile of St Mark's in Venice after which it was modeled. Much of this terrain is reclaimed land from what was once the bay. As much as 60 million cubic feet of earth was used for new landfill and to raise the level of the old city.

Between the Kingdome and Pioneer Square, where Seattle historically began, is an area destined for development – a jumble of barren lots, obsolete signs, decrepit buildings and antique stores as well as new condominiums and sidewalk cafés. Irresistible to kids and adults alike is the **Iron Horse Restaurant**, a funky bar on Third Avenue, where, with suitable hoots, toots and whistles, a miniature train running on a track around three sides of the room

delivers cheeseburgers, shakes and fries right to your table.

Chic conversions: All around town modern skyscrapers contain attractive malls for shopping and eating, but one thing Seattle does with equal panache is the stylish conversion of older buildings. Two examples are the **Court in the Square**, a glassed-over atrium on Second Avenue almost opposite the station, and the splendid **Grand Central Building**, at First Avenue and Main Street. This began life in 1889 as an office building, became a hotel in the frenzied Gold Rush days, served a spell as an opera house and in the 1970s was restored with the attractive forecourt that exists today. Downstairs, off redbrick corridors lined with benches, are a group of upmarket stores.

Penetrating the enticing aromas of a bakery beside the rear door brings us out into **Occidental Square** whose curiously designed shelter seems to attract only the homeless. Nobody's quite sure what to do with the square although a

Preceding pages: "the last best city in America." **Left**, metal fatigue. **Right**, painting the trim red.

recent writer in the *Pioneer Square Star* suggested planting fruit trees and "discreetly" playing Jimi Hendrix tapes night and day. The **totem poles** came from Alaska at a time when native art combined with modern tools created something of a boom in production. (Along with carving tools, the new arrivals also introduced smallpox and missionaries, both of which played their part in eliminating both the natives and their culture.)

The four-cedar totems in Occidental Park were carved over a 10-year period by Duane Pasco, a Washington State master carver with an international reputation, and are sited to follow the traditional custom of having their faces to the sea and hollowed backs to the forest, the latter in this case being represented by the skyscrapers of the city.

The tallest one depicts the Raven with the moon in his beak bringing light to the world. Further down the 35-foot pole is the Chief of the Sky's daughter giving birth to the Raven, and the Chief himself holding the sun in his hands and the box that held "light." Snacking is possible at a few fenced-off tables beside the bakery, but savvy lunchtime brown-baggers walk one block up Main Street to the enclosed **Waterfall Garden Park** which must surely take the prize for the best miniature park in the country. It was funded as a tribute to the employees of the United Parcel Service, which commenced operations in Seattle in 1907.

The park's tables and snack bar are set amidst flowers and trees in front of a glorious waterfall, designed by Masao Kinoshita, which drops 22 feet onto huge boulders and recycles 5,000 gallons of water every minute.

Gold museum: Also on Main Street, across from Occidental Square, is the misleadingly named **Klondike Gold Rush National Park** which is actually a (free) museum filled with exhibits and photographs recounting the saga of the hectic 1890s when half the population of Seattle caught Gold Rush fever.

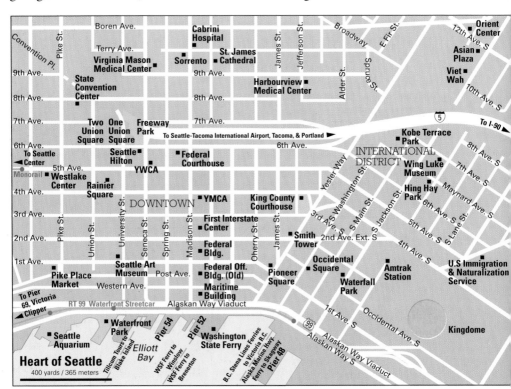

Thousands left their jobs to undergo the rigorous journey over forbidding mountains and up treacherous rivers 1,500 miles north to Alaska. Few of the spur-of-the moment adventurers struck it rich, most of the claims being already staked long before their arrival. Many of those who stayed behind in Seattle did better; at Canada's insistence, prospectors were obliged to take with them a year's supply of goods and provisions (400 lbs of flour, 25 cans of butter etc.) and many of the city's early businesses received initial impetus from supplying these needs.

One block north, the town of Seattle had begun 45 years before when, on February 15, 1852, Arthur and David Denny along with a score of other pioneers moved over from Alki Point, on which they had first landed only three months earlier. They named their new home Seattle after the Indian chief who was among the settlement's first visitors. The businessmen who came later were less respectful. A group from the Seattle Chamber of Commerce visited Alaska's Fort Tongass in 1899 and stole one tribe's totem pole while the Natives were out fishing.

For 40 years it stood at First and Yesler until it was vandalized. Shamelessly the city shipped it back to Alaska and asked for a replacement. When the Natives said it would cost $5,000, the city sent a check. The reply came from the Tlingit tribal chief: Thanks for finally paying for the first one; the second one will also cost $5,000.

Pioneer Square: The pole still stands in the square today close to James A. Wehn's bust of Chief Sealth. Wehn, who arrived in Seattle not long after the 1889 fire and lived until 1953, was also responsible for the fullsize statue of the chief at Fifth Avenue and Denny Way and later designed the city's seal which bears Chief Sealth's profile.

When the Chief died on June 7, 1866 he was buried on the Indian reservation at Suquamish. The text of Sealth's only known peroration has become disputed

The Kingdome has the world's largest freestanding concrete roof.

because a century later, a Texas screenwriter created a speech for a mythical Native American into which he dropped a few of the chief's words – and now some people aren't certain which lines are which.

Pioneer Square's southern end, where the street surface is genuine old cobblestones (unlike the moulded concrete fakes with which Tacoma has been experimenting), has long been dominated by an ornate **1905 pergola**. This once sheltered the patrons of the 1.3-mile cable car route which until 1940 ran between Yesler Way and Lake Union. Underground, but sealed off for more than half a century after flooding, is a spacious public toilet.

Behind the pergola is the **Merchant's Café**, the city's oldest restaurant, which in Gold Rush times served 5¢ beer to miners waiting their turn at the upstairs brothel. Seattle's great fire in 1889 wiped out most of the bar's neighbors in the 35-block Pioneer Square area but rebuilding began immediately.

Architect Elmer Fisher, responsible for at least 50 of the new buildings, set the predominant style, one example of his work being the elegant **Pioneer Building** whose turn-of-the-century tenants included several dozen mining companies above Doc Maynard's (now-restored) **saloon**. This is currently the headquarters of the unique Underground Tour – a 90-minute inspection of the shops and rooms that were abandoned when this part of town was rebuilt. To eliminate what had been persistent flooding, some of the buildings were raised as much as 18 feet and the unused subterranean city was sealed off until an enterprising newspaper columnist started to organize tours.

The Underground tour, which has been in business for decades, is an absolute hoot – a 2-hour performance by guides such as "Bruce" who offer a refreshingly irreverent and scatological survey of Seattle history. "Henry Yesler," Bruce announces, "had no moral or ethical values whatsoever;

Waterfall Park near Pioneer Square.

naturally he became our first mayor," and, on another occasion: "That's the true Seattle spirit – even if it's a lousy deal, we'll stick with it."

Beginning in the restored 1892 **Doc Maynard Saloon**, the tour descends two or three times into the warren of musty, debris-lined passageways and rooms that were at ground level. Passing under the glass-paneled sidewalk at First and Yesler, the tour ends in a tiny **museum** stocked with old photos, magazines, artifacts and scale models of the area when Yesler Way was three times as steep as it is today. On sale are books by columnist Bill Speidel who originated the tours. Funky old bars and restaurants dot this area, among them for example, the New Orleans, where the jazz is as good as the food.

Victorian architecture: Dating from before the fire is the **Maynard Building**, Washington and First Avenue, one block south on the site now occupied by the **Elliott Bay Bookstore** where once stood the hospital established by Doc Maynard. It was Dr Dave, in fact, who donated part of his land for Seattle's first industry: a steam-powered lumber mill built by an early arrival, German-born Henry Yesler, at the top of what is now Yesler Way. It began as Skid Road, the steep ramp down which the lumber was sped to the sawmill.

By the 1930s, Skid Row – as it became known – was a national term for an area frequented by the homeless, but in Yesler's day the mill ran day and night, employing almost half the people in town. Yesler's house nearby (in which he died in 1892) was on the site of what is now the **King County Courthouse**. The **Mutual Life Building** at Yesler Way and First Avenue went up in 1897 where Yesler's busy cookhouse once stood.

The city's first horsecar line began running along neighboring Second Avenue in 1884 and the electric car followed five years later. For at least a couple of generations First Avenue was renowned not only for its low-rent

Pioneer Square is one of the oldest parts of the city.

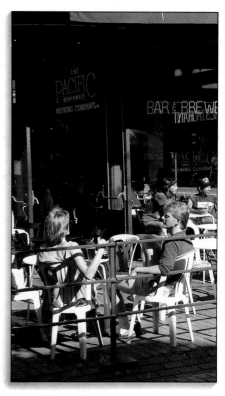

stores, hookers, X-rated bookstores and taverns, but also for pawnbrokers whose stock varied from jewelry and watches near Pike Place to more prosaic guns, radios and typewriters nearer to Pioneer Square.

On First Avenue at Cherry Street is the best place in the city to buy travel books and maps; a block away on Second Avenue is Ruby Montana's Pinto Pony with its amusing collection of kitschy souvenirs. This has a certain notoriety because of its co-sponsorship (with the Underground Tour) of an annual Spam Carving Contest. A plaque on the **Hoge Building**, Cherry and Second, identifies this as the site of Carson D. Boren's 1852 home, "the first cabin built by a white man in the city." Note the amusing sign denoting the New Museum of Hysteria and Indecision at Yesler Way and Third.

There are some sturdy, old structures around here but none more noteworthy than the **Arctic Building**, Third Avenue and Cherry, with its row of

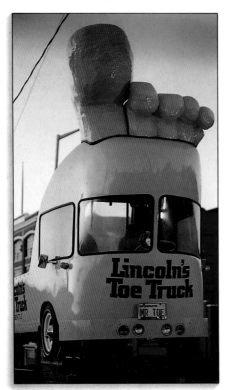

sculpted walruses adorning the upper levels. Believing the original terracotta tusks to be a potential danger to pedestrians below, the building's owners removed them some years ago later, replacing them with epoxy versions. On August 7, 1936, however, sidewalk strollers were more at risk from the falling body of Seattle Congressman, Marion Zioncheck. Zioncheck was sufficiently depressed one unhappy day to walk out of one of the building's 5th-floor windows.

Tallest building: Before the end of the century, Lyman Cornelius Smith arrived after his wife fell in love with the town while visiting an old friend. Smith, already wealthy from the sale of his gun company (later Smith & Wesson) and his revolutionary new typewriter (a subsequent merger created Smith Corona), promptly bought several blocks around Main Street and First Avenue and in 1901 erected the L. C. Smith building.

It was badly damaged by fire a year or two later and, although nobody in the building was killed, stocks of poultry feed and paper were destroyed. A pattern maker who had been stranded on the third floor was rescued by a daring spectator who climbed a telegraph pole to throw him a rope.

Smith at first announced plans for a 12-story replacement but, goaded by the plans of a business rival, ambitiously plotted the 42-story **Smith Tower**. When completed in 1914, this was the tallest building in the world outside New York. Gradually the distinction was whittled away until, at the time of the World's Fair, its last remaining title – that of tallest building in Seattle – was taken away by the 605-feet Space Needle.

But although nobody has ever been able to count all the supposed 42 storys, Smith Tower remains a sentimental favorite with Seattleites, and various attempts over the years to "modernize" the building have always been met with angry protests.

Feet and miles.

THE SMITH TOWER

When L. C. Smith's tower went up in downtown Seattle in 1914, it was widely touted as the tallest building in the West. Picture postcards depicting the 500-foot structure claimed that from "the world-famous catwalk surrounding the Chinese temple may be seen mountain ranges 380 miles in the distance." Well, not quite. The mountain ranges in view – the Olympics and the Cascades – are actually about 60 miles away. But 4,400 flocked to the opening anyway, paying 25¢ each to be whizzed past offices mostly rented by local government agencies and to admire the view from the observation deck.

"A work of art worthy of the builders of the awe-inspiring cathedrals of the Middle Ages," boasted the tower's historian Arthur F. Wakefield, who revealed that New York's American Bridge Company had taken 20 weeks to make the steel which had been transported cross country from their Pittsburgh plant in 164 railcars.

Smith spared no expense. The $1.5 million building's 600 rooms had steel doors (painted to look like mahogany), teak ceilings, walls of Alaskan white marble or tinted Mexican onyx, elevator doors of glass and bronze and, on the 35th floor, a $30,000 Chinese temple decorated with bronze lanterns, Oriental furniture and 776 semi-porcelain discs. A throne-like Chinese chair, reputed to have been a gift from the Empress of China, was actually obtained from a waterfront curio shop but did spawn its own legend. One year after Smith's daughter posed sitting in the chair she got married, convincing other would-be brides that to sit in the "Wishing Chair" would bring them a husband. Occasionally even today a couple will hold their wedding reception in the room.

One year after the tower's opening, some of the office tenants looked from their windows to see a one-armed parachutist go by, and a year or two later watched Harry "the human fly" scale the building. "I gave him a little help by hanging ropes over the cornices," recalled William K. Jackson, just before his retirement as building superintendent in 1944. Jackson, then 72, had worked in the tower since it opened, during which time Seattle had changed from "a friendly, clean little city to a town of strangers going so fast you can feel the tempo of wartime even in your own building." Recording the city's changes by what he'd seen in the harbor – first lumber barges and fishing boats, then liners, freighters and navy ships and now "mostly smoke" – he observed that the city "sort of grew up under me." The tower was still getting 300 visitors a day, was still the tallest building in the West and on most days still offered a clear view of Mount Rainier.

It was also the kind of user-friendly landmark that lent itself to stunts: in 1938 two high school students ran up stairs to the 36th floor in less than 10 minutes (and down again in four) to prove something or other; four years after that a proud grandfather named William R. Owen announced his new domestic status by running up a flag reading: "It's a girl."

Smith Tower was bought in 1985 by a San Francisco firm whose partners remodeled it with respect, even acquiring special parts and equipment to retain the original copper, brass and glass elevators. ∎

NO CHECKS CASHED

WA SA

INTERNATIONAL DISTRICT AND MIDTOWN

The blocks to the south of Smith Tower, across Yesler Way, are still somewhat of a Skid Row judging by the plethora of "No Loitering" signs. But a local food writer tagged it with a different name, **Seattle's Curry Triangle**, because of the many simple, cheap Thai, Laotian and Cambodian curry restaurants. This, after all, is the lower end of an area that has been the city's **Chinatown** for more than a century. Chinese were among Seattle's earliest residents.

A certain Wa Chong, credited with building – in 1871 – the third brick structure in the city, was also responsible for the first building to go up after the 1889 fire. The Wa Chung Tea Store, at the corner of Washington and Third, advertised in 1877 that contractors, mill owners and others requiring Chinese labor "will be furnished at short notice." And, as an afterthought: "The highest price paid for live hogs." A front-page announcement in that same paper by Tong Wa Shing & Co, dealers in Chinese Fancy Goods at 112 Washington Street, offered TEA... RICE... OPIUM.

By the turn of the century, Chinatown, riddled with secret passages and tunnels, had become a city within the city which saw few white faces except for the occasional adventurous opium smoker. Violent Tong wars were not uncommon. The mostly male population wore native garb with pigtailed hair and wooden-soled cloth slippers. A story in the *Post-Intelligencer* on December 14, 1902 talked about well-guarded Chinese gambling houses from which whites were barred.

Most of Chinatown's population spent summers working in local canneries later infiltrated by Japanese and Filipino workers. Long before World War II, the community became stabilized, largely because of the influence of such civic bodies as the Chung Wa Associa-

tion, of which all prominent Chinese were members. But the notorious gambling dens (in which the punishment for welshers was reputedly to "take a piece" – off the debtor's finger) survived until 1942, when the dens were closed after the military declared the Chinese city off-limits.

Named after the first elected Asian-American in the Northwest, the **Wing Luke Asian Museum** serves the entire community by rotating shows about different parts of the Pacific region. Its permanent collection includes historical photographs and such artifacts as a 50-ft dragon boat and a mock-up of an old Chinese apothecary, but its shows have ranged from exhibitions of Balinese masks to Japanese textiles or Persian miniatures.

Neighborhood gardens: To the west and north of the museum is what began as the Japanese area, denuded of most of its population by the shameful internment policies of World War II and then physically decimated by the Interstate 5

Preceding pages: Chinese take-away. Left, the International Festival. **Right,** market force.

freeway. Nihon-machi, as the area was called, centered around **Kobe Terrace Park** at the top of the hill. The park, from which there's a fine panoramic view, contains tiny gardens tended by low-income neighborhood residents and also a stone lantern donated by Seattle's sister city of Kobe. The redbrick **Nippon Kan Theater** began in 1909 as the Astor Theater and still displays a turn-of-the-century screen with its original ads for local businesses. It has been designated as a National Historic Site. Although some Japanese still live nearby, the area has seen a heavy influx of poorer Asians in recent years: Cambodian peasants, refugees from Laos and other lands and Vietnamese boatpeople. North of the freeway, the streets around the Japanese-owned shopping mall, **Asian Plaza** at Jackson and 12th, are sometimes referred to as Little Saigon and house a good proportion of the 450 Vietnamese-owned businesses now estimated to be in Seattle. The area is still expanding to the north.

Across from the **streetcar terminal** at Jackson and Third is a good spot from which to begin our tour of the International District, sipping an espresso and nibbling on a pâté pie at a pleasant Chinese coffee shop with the very un-Asian name of Maxim. Pick up a free copy of the *Seatown Crier*, Seattle's surprisingly interesting newspaper about the homeless. Just up the street, brightly colored figures from traditional Chinese legends cover the wall of **United Savings**, one of many banks which store family funds that in an earlier era might have gone into private safes. These would be shared by up to 10 individuals, each having a key that could be used only in conjunction with the other partners.

Asian shopping: Two fearsome white stone dragons guard the sidewalk outside Chung Kiu antique shop outside which unusual Chinese vegetables spill over from the neighboring grocery store. The **Bush Hotel** here might be a good choice for budget-minded visitors who enjoy being smack in the center of a genuinely authentic ethnic area. The hotel offers many services to the community as can be seen by the entrance off **Hing Hay Park** at the rear: a Chinese bakery, cheap cafeteria, pool room, Korean restaurant and various organizations are to be found in the hotel's basement. The park's ornamental arch dates from 1973 and was designed in Taiwan by architect David Lin. The No. 91 bus from downtown which runs along First Avenue past Pike Place Market terminates at the corner of Maynard and Weller, a block away, conveniently close to the region's largest Asian department store, **Uwajimaya**, which stocks everything from furniture to fruit and vegetables.

A common sight around here are the rows of jars displaying such herbs, flowers and roots as peony, honeysuckle, chrysanthemum, ginger, ginseng and especially licorice, which for centuries have been used to build **Natural** strength, "balance the body's energy" **defense.**

and prevent the re-occurrence of disease. Change is slow in coming to this area. True there are glittery new restaurants – both Chinese and Japanese – and a sleek **children's playground** with a humped bronze dragon overlooking the sandpit, but there are also 80-year-old grocery stores like **Yick Funglo** with its sign in the window still advertising the Blue Funnel Line, a British shipping company that plied between Yokohama, Hong Kong and Vancouver before folding in the 1940s.

Hilly terrain: Yesler Way slants northwards past the tower and the **Fire Museum**, crossing Fifth Avenue and the freeway by an overhead ramp. The King County courthouse is here on Third with the imposing **Federal Courthouse** a few blocks to the northwest opposite the Fifth Avenue entrance to the library. Hilly terrain this, and you might find it well worthwhile to wait for a bus which costs nothing to ride anywhere in the downtown area until 9pm. That, incidentally, is the time until which the superlative **Seattle Library** stays open each night, although budgetary restrictions may soon cause a cutback in hours. Outside the library's Fifth Avenue entrance is the **Fountain of Wisdom** by George Tsutakawa who taught at the University of Washington until 1980 and whose many other works include the Centennial Fountain at Seattle University. The library's terrace cafeteria is pleasant but better sandwiches are available at the Lime Green Café in the neighboring YWCA.

Possibly seeking the company of Seattle's most luxurious hotel, the refurbished **Four Seasons Olympic**, many of America's biggest hotel chains have located their local hostelries on Fifth and Sixth avenues only a block or two from the immense towers that have changed the city's skyline in the past decade. Under an agreement that goes back to the 19th century, as much as one quarter of the hotel's room rentals, plus an additional $400,000 per year, is paid to the University of Washington, whose

Community gardens in the International District.

10 downtown acres include this site as well as the ground under many of the adjoining buildings.

Seattle's tallest building, in fact the tallest in the West, is the 76-story **Columbia Center** which rises 1,049 feet above sea level and is served by 46 elevators. There is an observation room on the 73rd floor with an impressive but not panoramic view. However, the vista from the top floor (private) restrooms is reputed to be superlative. Below street level are carpeted, picture-lined corridors – one leading to the AT & T Gateway Tower next door – and an attractive mall lined with shops, classy snack bars and tables for eating.

The Starbucks flagship coffee shop here serves 500 customers an hour during its morning rush hour and claims to be the world's busiest espresso bar although doubtless other Seattle espresso counters would be in the Top Ten. Across from the library, the 1001 Fourth Avenue Building offers what some people consider to be the best free observa-

tion place in town; this from the 46th-floor foyer of the Mirabeau Restaurant.

Enormous skyscrapers began to rise in downtown Seattle in the late 1960s and early '70s but the really big boom didn't get underway until the following decade when the **Columbia Seafirst Center** was followed by the 62-story **AT & T Tower**; the 44-story **Pacific First Center**, Sixth and Pike; the 56-story Two Union Square, 600 Union; the 55-story **Washington Mutual Tower**, 1201 Third; and the recent **Second and Seneca Building** whose local nickname equates it with a brand of underarm deodorant. Aesthetic opinions about these structures vary a great deal but they have been a boon for sculptures under the city's 1973 1-percent-for-art ordinance which has resulted in some spectacular work. The Henry Moore sculpture, *Three Piece Vertebrae*, outside the Seafirst Center, predates the ordinance, however, and is only one of the bank's impressive collection of 12,000 artworks. This one was donated to the Seattle Art Museum when the bank changed hands some years ago.

Corporate collection: Seafirst's big art-buying spree peaked just before the bank moved into its new headquarters with its directors apportioning $200,000 for interior works to decorate the building's lower floors and a further $300,000 for public spaces, more than 50 percent of which was spent on the Henry Moore work. (The bank underwent some criticism for this, accused of making an unduly unconservative, even extravagant choice.) The offices were furnished both with works of local artists and such nationally-known painters as Karel Appel, Kenneth Noland and Jules Olitski, a policy that one local magazine approvingly dubbed "enlightened capitalism."

The five-story **Seattle Art Museum**, University and First, was designed by Robert Venturi, winner of architecture's highest award, the Pritzker Prize, who was credited with the wry observa-

Freeway Park: the sculpture is of both George Washington and Chief Seattle.

tion that "less is a bore." The $27 million museum is a recent addition to downtown, allowing the museum's former home in Volunteer Park to better display its incomparable collection of Asian art ranging from 4,000-year-old Japanese tomb art to 19th-century Chinese snuff bottles. About the new limestone and sandstone building, its exterior inlaid with richly-hued terracotta, Venturi says: "We think civic architecture should be popular; it should be liked by a range of people. It should not be esoteric."

The major hotel area is half a dozen blocks northwest with the two biggest – the twin-towered Westin and the 840-room Sheraton respectively – northeast and southeast of Westlake Center. The Sheraton is flanked by the **Washington State Convention Center**, which looks as if it's built from green-glass cubes and whose ground-floor tourist office is a good place to pick up maps and brochures. On the building's second level, hanging above an otherwise sterile

walkway to Pike Street, are a **series of bells** from schools, churches and other landmarks in each of the state's 39 counties. Controlled by an intricate computer system, the bells are played on the hour each day with special performances twice daily.

In the **walkway park** adjoining the center itself, is a remarkable aluminum sculpture by Seattle artist Buster Simpson combining silhouette heads of George Washington and Chief Seattle, the latter destined to "become a memory" as ivy gradually grows over it. Simpson has a reputation for this type of work. The convention center, airy, spacious and spotless, segues into the curious **Freeway Park**, an oasis of greenery and waterfalls straddling the busy Interstate 5 which runs undisturbed beneath trees and several feet of turf and concrete. Both projects span the freeway in an imaginative use of air rights. The park is delightful. Tree-shaded paths wind past a multi-level "canyon" in which invigorating cascades of water

Subterranean transportation.

pour down sheer walls into pools, spitting and gurgling before being recycled endlessly. Although the park's ingredients are little more than flowers, grass, trees, water and cement blocks, their imaginative placement results in one of the most restful oases in town.

Between Freeway Park and the Sheraton is **Two Union Square** with a pleasant, inexpensive cafeteria named D'Amico's. Higher up, huge 56th-floor windows look out over the freeway and an outdoor plaza with another waterfall. Across the street the **Pacific West Center** has comfortable chairs arranged inside an attractive atrium. (Cross at the crosswalk. Police issue an average of 10 jaywalking tickets citywide every day of the year.)

An underground walkway runs all the way down from **Union Square** to **Rainier Square**. The most accessible collection of photographs of old Seattle is to be found in the carpeted walkway running under the **Skinner Building** which forms part of the Rainier Square

complex. Here also is one of the 16 terracotta Indians that once adorned the White Henry Stuart building which it replaced in 1976. The rest of these 800-pound heads, each composed of 18 separate parts, have been distributed throughout the state. A picture of the White Henry Stuart building is among the collection here which also includes the Moran Brothers' shipyard in 1906, prospectors of the Alaska Gold Rush and collections celebrating the history of Boeing as well as the University of Washington.

Electric buses: Like many Japanese cities, Seattle seems to have a particular affection for subterranean activities. A submerged bus tunnel, which runs all the way from the Amtrak station under Third Avenue up into the center of town, not only reduces traffic congestion by diverting many buses from the main streets, but also provides stations sheltered from the wind. As in the rest of the downtown area, daytime bus travel around this part of town is free.

Seattle Art Museum.

THE ARTFUL BUS COMPANY

There probably isn't anywhere in the world where the locals don't complain about their bus system, but few visitors to Seattle go away without a good opinion of Metro. The city was among the first to introduce free transportation, an idea that has been a boon to downtown travelers and businesses alike. All stops display route maps and schedules, and drivers are refreshingly courteous and helpful.

Buses were introduced that would operate on both diesel *and* electricity, switching from the former to the latter on entering the $450 million Bus Tunnel. This runs for 1.3 miles under midtown and relieves street congestion to the tune of 18,000 passengers per hour as well as chopping almost two-thirds from the time it takes to negotiate the streets overhead.

Metro's outstanding achievement, however, has been to combine this tunnel with its sponsorship of public art: scores of artworks are distributed throughout the five stations of the tunnel and the passageways between them. Granite stairs are colored: white for north; south, black; east, green; west, red. As far as possible, artworks are appropriate to the specific station in which they are situated. In an attempt to make it obvious to travelers what part of the city they are in by what they see around them, the designers studied what was above ground before decorating underground.

At Convention Place station, for example, the adjoining Freeway Park is echoed by a concrete cliff and waterfall; the Paramount Theatre's musical past is celebrated with a silhouette of the Pacific Northwest guitarist Jimi Hendrix, the title of one of his songs edged into the steps.

At the University Street station, the streamlined surrounding architecture is reflected in the linear designs, glass railings and electronic art by Bill Bell; embedded in a wall are his randomly blinking "lightsticks" whose images are subtle enough to be invisible unless you study them carefully while moving your head.

The station at International District has tiles created from designs by children of the neighborhood and an enormous origami work created by Sonya Ishii from painted aluminum. The open plaza square is tiled with symbols from the Chinese zodiac.

Under Pioneer Square, engineers have placed a relic from the cable car system that used to run up Yesler Way, a huge cast-iron flywheel more than 11 feet in diameter – an artwork in itself. But this has been supplemented with such contemporary artwork as Laura Sindell's ceramic mural incorporating Native American baskets and a dugout canoe. The quotations here are from Chief Sealth and Seattle pioneers Arthur Denny and Doc Maynard.

Westlake, the biggest of the five stations, has been designed in such a manner that many of the customers passing through it from the adjoining department stores are barely aware that it is a station. Terracotta tiles are predominant here with one entire wall (by Jack Mackie) of vines and flowers symbolically echoing the park above. In the park, incidentally, is located what is probably the most accessible public artwork in town: Robert Maki's wonderful wall of water which encourages people to enter its cooling embrace. ∎

CENTRAL SEATTLE

At the eastern foot of Madison Street – Seattle's only waterfront-to-waterfront street, which runs from Elliott Bay to Lake Washington – sits the lovely, slightly quaint, unmistakably affluent waterfront community of **Madison Park**, once the western terminus of a passenger-boat line connecting Seattle to the east side of the lake. Here you can still find a charge-account grocery store, Burt's Red Apple, and until a year or two ago another local store delivered goods to customers' homes. Madison Park itself includes a pair of lighted all-weather tennis courts and a beach, populated on hot summer days by an interesting urban mix from surrounding neighborhoods. In the past 10 or 15 years, a steady influx of younger people has moved into Madison Park to join the more settled older residents in a comfortable enclave of lakefront apartments, new condos and townhouses and increasingly expensive, but very pleasant, single-family homes.

The village itself boasts a fine bakery, long a Madison Park hangout and still the best place to catch up on local gossip. A trendy hot spot, Cactus, draws raves – and customers – for imaginative Southwestern dishes, a snappy tapas menu and generally upbeat atmosphere. Lola, the proprietor of Madison Park Hardware and the unofficial mayor of Madison Park, is a tireless, tenacious advocate for preserving the community's genteel charms.

Upscale area: Just up the hill from Madison Park reigns the wealthy – on some blocks, extravagantly wealthy – neighborhood of **Washington Park**. Particularly noteworthy in this residential area of stately homes and doted-upon lawns is the majestic thoroughfare of **36th Avenue East**, extending south between Madison and East Mercer streets. Towering trees on both sides of 36th Avenue arch toward each other high above the street to form Seattle's most magnificent natural cathedral, a sight that on its own makes it worth a special trip. Washington Park is also a presidential neighborhood: the handsome brick mansion of the president of Washington University is here, at 808 36th East, with (one hears) a lovely rose garden, although you would have to be an invited guest to see it.

Nearby, arguably the most striking residential structure in the city dominates the southeastern corner of 36th Avenue East and East Ward Street, extending a full block along Ward Street to 37th Avenue. Traditionalists in the neighborhood, and there are many, were not amused when this house began to take shape in the early 1980s, replacing a longstanding, more conventional mansion. But somehow, perhaps partly because it's on a corner, the house, though radically different from any of its neighbors, does achieve a kind of harmony with its surroundings.

Opposite 36th Avenue on the north

Preceding pages: living on Queen Anne Hill. **Left** and **right**, turning over a new leaf.

side of Madison Street is the private residential community of **Broadmoor**, complete with golf course. Here, behind gatehouses and armed guards at both entrances, bank presidents, corporate lawyers, financiers and the like take refuge from urban clash and clatter.

Madison Valley, the area west from Lake Washington Boulevard to 23rd Avenue East along both sides of Madison Street, underwent a transformation in the past decade. Two-story retail complexes now anchor the intersection of Madison and Lake Washington Boulevard, replacing a group of four gas stations.

A consistently top-rated restaurant (with the unlikely name of **Rover's**), the expansive **City People's** gardening store and several delis and cafés, along with numerous new condominiums lining the hillside, signal the resurgence of this formerly overlooked neighborhood. Other arrivals in the area include **Le Sommelier**, which doubles as both a wine shop and a wine bar, and a health

club that is popular with the locals.

Leschi: A sparkling waterfront neighborhood south of Madison Park along the western shore of Lake Washington, Leschi is named after a Nisqually Indian chief who liked to camp here and was said to have been among those who gathered in 1856 to plan an attack on Seattle. The first automobile ferry, *The Leschi*, started regular service from here to the eastside of Seattle in 1913.

At one time considered a "hot spot for romping, mixing and romantic recreation," Leschi is today a quiet neighborhood of waterfront homes, condominiums and apartment buildings, with a public beach, a small-sailboat marina and the lushly green **Leschi Park** – once an amusement park at the terminus of the Yesler Street cable car line. There are a couple of attractive restaurants that offer waterfront dining.

Capitol Hill gets its name not from the seat of government in Washington, DC, but from a neighborhood in Denver, Colorado. Real estate promoter James A. Moore, whose wife was from that city, came up with the name in 1901. The area, which lies just east of downtown, is culturally, economically, racially and sexually mixed with the hill being home to a substantial gay and lesbian population. A heavy concentration of apartment buildings supplements the mansions of "Millionaires' Row" (14th Avenue East, between Mercer and Prospect streets).

Broadway (Pine Street to East Roy Street, Metro bus No 7 from downtown) is the neighborhood's leading thoroughfare and commercial district; it is also one of the few places in town where you can still find casual strollers out on the street as late as midnight even on weeknights. B & O Espresso (Olive Way at Belmont Street) dispenses good coffee drinks and irresistible desserts until even later on weekends. Other nocturnal dessert and coffee establishments include Dilettante, a chocolate-lover's paradise located on Broadway, and Harvard Espresso Gallery on East

Seattle is "a city that likes itself."

Roy Street opposite the Harvard Exit moviehouse.

In an age of multiplex cinemas in shopping malls (there's one here, too, in the **Broadway Market**), the **Egyptian** on East Pine and **Harvard Exit** are handsome survivors from an earlier era of individualistic movie theaters. Both specialize in first-rate foreign films and the Egyptian hosts some shows of the annual **Seattle International Film Festival** each May. Another distinctive neighborhood movie theater, the beloved Broadway, recently gave way to a Pay 'n' Save store, which retained the theater's marquee; now, instead of first-run films, the sign beckons passersby with promises of sale prices on mini fans and lawn chairs.

Traffic is heavy on Broadway at almost any time of day and parking is all but impossible to find except extremely late at night, when nothing remains open. But with its ever-changing assortment of shops and restaurants, the street is a good one for strolling. You can even practice (or learn) some traditional dances by following sculptor Jack Mackie's bronze footsteps embedded in the sidewalk, which is part of the public art program.

The metal-tech Gravity Bar, at the main entrance to the new multi-level **Broadway Market**, is worth a stop for the decor alone. But it's an interesting restaurant, too, offering imaginative veggie dishes, wheatgrass juice and espresso drinks. This may also be the premier people-watching place in town. Here, it's fun to check out everybody: the passing parade on the sidewalk, fellow Gravity Bar patrons and, without question, the staff behind the counter.

Going green: A block east of Broadway on the corner of 11th Avenue and Pine Street is the flagship store of **REI** (Recreational Equipment Inc.), the country's largest co-op. The specialty here is the outdoors, with everything from down parkas, bicycles and running gear to heavy-duty climbing equipment, canoes and kayaks. Despite

St Joseph Church, Capitol Hill.

having grown to big-business size – there are stores up and down the West Coast and some 2 million members nationwide – REI continues to be a forceful, outspoken advocate for environmental responsibility.

Fifteenth Avenue East (Metro bus No.10 from downtown) north from Pine Street hosts another Capitol Hill shopping district, one that's less congested, and less flamboyant, than Broadway. Here can be found a quintessential used-book store complete with a pair of cats, a fine organic-food grocery store, a handful of good restaurants representing varied cuisines and the City People's Mercantile with the obligatory espresso cart out front.

A few blocks north of the retail district on 15th Avenue lies one of Seattle's largest and loveliest parks, the 45-acre **Volunteer Park**. Originally a cemetery for the city's pioneers, the land became Lakeview Park when it was decided, in 1887, to put a reservoir (which now holds 20 million gallons of water) at the southern part of the property. The bodies were moved a few hundred feet northward to what's now called Lakeview Cemetery. In 1901, the park was renamed Volunteer Park in honor of the two companies of Seattle men who served in the Spanish-American War of 1898.

With an elevation of 445 feet, the park offers magnificent views of the Space Needle, Puget Sound and the Olympic Mountains. The park's major attractions are the 1932 Art Deco building which houses the **Seattle Art Museum**'s **Asian Collection**, and the **Volunteer Park Conservatory** with its three greenhouses.

Eastlake: Cut off from the rest of Capitol Hill by Interstate 5, the Eastlake district, north of downtown along the east side of Lake Union (Metro buses No. 70, 71, 72), is a lively mix of historic homes, multi-family dwellings and a thriving houseboat community sharing the neighborhood, uneasily at times, with ever-changing commercial and in-

Hydrangea blossoms.

dustrial properties. The Boeing Company got its start here in 1915, when William Boeing began building – in a hangar at the foot of Roanoke Street – seaplanes which he tested on the lake. Boeing moved his company to the south end of the city two years later but the hangar survived until 1971, when it was demolished to make way for a projected, but aborted, condominium project, defeated after a fierce 13-year legal battle fought by a coalition of determined neighborhood groups.

The south end of Lake Union, which used to be exclusively an industrial area, has seen an explosion of development in recent years. Some residents see this as disturbing evidence of the advancing "Californization" of Seattle. A small group of restaurants rings the south end of the lake, most of them with outdoor decks overlooking the water and docking facilities. More are planned for the future.

The Volunteer Park Conservatory was built in 1910.

The **Residence Inn-Marriott**, a 234-room, $25-million hotel complex, opened in the early 1990s. And Seattle's world-renowned **Fred Hutchinson Cancer Research Center** is erecting a massive, multi-phase complex of research buildings which is scheduled for completion by the end of the decade.

The Center for Wooden Boats at the south end of the lake is a nostalgically charming maritime museum with some 75 sailboats and rowboats, many of which can be rented. Indeed, rowing or paddling around the lake is by far the best and most enjoyable way to appreciate the lake's diversity of activity, as well as being the only way to admire from nearby the multi-styled houseboats lining the northeast and northwest shorelines.

Northwest Outdoor Center on Westlake Avenue offers canoes and kayak rentals. A planned South Lake Union Park awaits negotiations between the city and the United States Navy, whose **Naval Reserve Station** currently occupies the intended park site.

Lake Union is also home to several

commercial seaplane services which offer flights to the San Juan Islands, as well as to Vancouver, Victoria and other destinations on Vancouver Island over the border in Canada.

Miniature mountain: Queen Anne Hill, in the words of Seattle photohistorian Paul Dorpat, "is cleansed by winds, girdled by greenbelts, and topped by towers and mansions." Sometimes called "Seattle's miniature mountain," **Queen Anne Hill** rises sharply on all four sides to a summit of 457 feet, the second-highest elevation in the city (35th Avenue SW in West Seattle reaches 514 feet).

Seattle pioneer Thomas Mercer, who arrived in 1853, filed the first claim on Queen Anne Hill and had to cut through a virtual forest in order to build. The hill got its name when the Reverend Daniel Bagley referred to it as "Queen Anne Town," a jocular reference to the lavish mansions some of the city's prominent citizens built on the hill during the 1880s in an American variation of the Queen Anne style of architecture.

Bounded by Mercer Street on the south, Lake Union on the east, Lake Washington Ship Canal on the north, and Elliott Avenue on the west, the Queen Anne district (Metro buses No.1, 2, 3, 4, 13) is home to 27,000 residents. Because of its great height, the hill offers spectacular views in all directions: Puget Sound, the Olympic Mountains and dramatic sunsets to the west; Lake Union, Capitol Hill and the Cascade Mountains to the east; Elliott Bay, the downtown skyline and Mount Rainier to the south; the Ship Canal and Mount Baker to the north.

Queen Anne boasts some of the loveliest residential streets in the city. For a good look at one of them, head west on Highland Drive from Queen Anne Avenue, about halfway up the hill. After passing gracious apartment buildings on both sides of the street, you'll come to **Kerry Park**, a narrow stretch of green with wide-open views of the Space Needle, downtown office towers,

The Queen Anne district has 27,000 residents.

the Elliott Bay harbor and, if you're lucky, Mount Rainier. The views from here are just as good at night as during the day.

West of the park, stately mansions line both sides of **Highland Drive**, which ends in beautiful Parsons Garden, a tiny, secluded public park which is perfect for a quiet interlude. A worthwhile viewpoint at the end of Highland Drive offers a commanding sweep of Puget Sound and the towering Olympic Mountains.

The area's main shopping district runs along Queen Anne Avenue North from Galer Street at the top of the hill north to McGraw Street. The 5 Spot Café, Pasta Bella and Ristorante Buongusto lead the list of hilltop restaurants. At Queen Anne Thriftway, the city's first and best upscale supermarket, you can have your car washed while you're shopping. La Tazza di Caffè and Starbucks are the best stops for coffee. The avenue also has a couple of bakeries, a fine wine shop and a good book-store for buying and for browsing in.

On the south side of Queen Anne, at the bottom of the hill, real estate values drop along with the elevation. It's apartment country down here, with none of the grand homes that grace the hilltop. But there's an interesting assortment of shops, coffeehouses and restaurants along Roy and Mercer streets and on Queen Anne Avenue just south of Mercer. Without question, the most eye-catching structure in this neighborhood is on the north side of Roy Street just east of First Avenue North. Nicknamed "the blob" by Seattleites, the building sat empty for years after the failure of a Mediterranean restaurant it was built to house. The place is now a lively Greek restaurant, with an interior as soothing as its exterior is jarring.

Magnolia: This district gets its name from the madrona trees that line its southern bluff overlooking Puget Sound. Sounds confusing? Well, seems that in 1856, the US Coast Survey named the bluff for the magnolia trees

Magnolia homes.

growing along it. The only problem was they turned out to be madrona, not magnolia, trees. The community liked the name "Magnolia," however, and decided to keep it.

Magnolia, which is north and west of downtown, is an affluent, well-ordered, conservative neighborhood of mostly single-family homes resting on expansive lots. There are magnificent waterfront properties – protected from view by vegetation and long driveways – along the western edge, south of Discovery Park.

At 527 acres, **Discovery Park** is Seattle's largest. In 1964, the US government declared 85 percent of this land, which had been the site of the Fort Lawton Army base, to be surplus. Eight years later, after Congressional legislation (initiated by Washington's Senator Henry M. Jackson) made it possible for cities to obtain surplus federal property at no cost, the city of Seattle acquired the land. The park was named for the ship of Captain George Vancouver, who, during his 1792 exploration of Puget Sound, spent several days with the *Discovery* at anchor within sight of this land.

A 2½-mile loop trail around the park winds through thick forests and crosses broad meadows and high, windswept bluffs with spectacular views of Puget Sound and the Olympic Mountains. One of many branch trails leads down to the beach. Wildlife is abundant here: bald eagles are often seen in the treetops and in 1982 a cougar was discovered in the park. A major attraction is the **Daybreak Star Arts Center**, which sponsors Indian events and exhibits of contemporary Indian art. Discovery Park also has numerous playfields and picnic areas, plus tennis and basketball courts.

Fishermen's Terminal, West Thurman Street on Magnolia's north side, provides an opportunity to admire the boats of a major fishing fleet. You can sample the day's catch at one of the restaurants in the complex or purchase some at the fish market to cook at home. One of Seattle's few remaining tobacco shops is here, too.

Commodore Park, west of Fishermen's Terminal on the south side of the **Hiram M. Chittenden Locks**, is a great place to watch the boat traffic passing through the locks. By visiting the fish ladder here you can see something rarely glimpsed in the open water: countless fish jumping all over the place. The park is an attractive one, its cool, grassy slopes offering a welcome breeze on sultry days.

Magnolia Village, the neighborhood's shopping district (West McGraw Street between 32nd and 35th avenues), has recently undergone some dramatic changes after remaining much the same for years. In addition to the usual banks and real estate offices, there are now several trendy shops and eateries. It's worth stopping at the **Village Pub**, on 32nd Avenue, a longtime neighborhood favorite for lunch. The conversation is good and the service is very democratic.

Left, Uncle Sam shakes. **Right**, heavenly music on Capitol Hill.

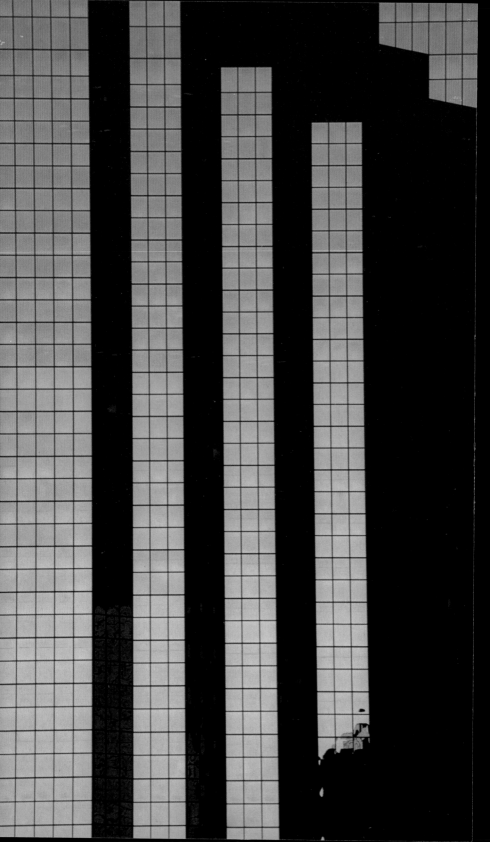

EASTSIDE PLACES

Stroll along the Kirkland waterfront, latte or espresso in hand. Stop for an outdoor lunch on a sunlit deck overlooking Lake Washington. Head to downtown Bellevue for an afternoon at the Bellevue Art Museum. Visit the velodrome in Redmond's Marymoor Park and see world-class cyclists. Drive into Issaquah for an evening of professional theater or head out to Woodinville for an afternoon of wine tasting and music at the delightful Chateau Ste Michelle Winery.

While these scenarios increasingly are being taken for granted by Eastsiders and Seattleites alike, they can be inadvertently overlooked by visitors intent on seeing the city's sights. It wasn't long ago that, to most people in Seattle, visiting the Eastside meant packing a picnic lunch and going for a drive in the country. Most urban dwellers were familiar with the Eastside mainly as a place to get through on their way to the Cascade Mountains.

Today all that has changed and Seattleites zip back and forth across Lake Washington to the east side of the lake (20 minutes one-way, if the traffic gods are with you, over an hour if they're not) without feeling the need to pack a first-aid kit or a canteen. In fact, increasing numbers of them pack up and move to the Eastside each year and then make the trip across the lake twice a day as dedicated commuters.

It's **Lake Washington** that provides the frame of reference for the term Eastside, a designation that applies to the very individual cities, towns and rural areas that dot the hills and valleys to the east of the lake.

A generally accepted definition of the Eastside includes the cities of Bellevue, Mercer Island, Kirkland, Redmond, Issaquah and Woodinville. As escalating house prices push acceptable commuting times to the outer eastern limits,

cities such as North Bend, Fall City, Duvall and Carnation start to turn up in conversations about the Eastside.

Navigating the waterways and highways of the Eastside requires a few main reference points. The bridges that run east and west across Lake Washington are the **Evergreen Point Floating Bridge** (SR-520) that connects downtown Seattle, just south of the University district, to Kirkland and continues on to Redmond.

The **Mercer Island Floating Bridge** (Interstate 90) connects southern Seattle with south Bellevue via Mercer Island, a residential community about midway across Lake Washington. The main north-south route on the east side of the lake is Interstate 405 which runs the length of Washington State and goes directly through Bellevue, Kirkland and north on to Bothell and Woodinville. The road eventually ends up in Vancouver, about three hours north across the Canadian border.

By the late 1880s Seattleites were

already referring to the area that would later become Bellevue and Kirkland as "East Seattle." An influx of population after the Great Fire of 1889 was supplemented by new homesteaders coming to the shores of Lake Washington from many other parts of the country.

As the decades passed and the population grew, agriculture, logging and mining gave way to housing and the Eastside increasingly took on the role of bedroom communities. Today many Eastside cities are discovering identities of their own as financial centers (Bellevue and Redmond) or as increasingly sophisticated regional recreation centers (Kirkland and Woodinville). More and more companies previously based in Seattle are making the leap across the lake and choosing to locate on the Eastside. Bellevue, for instance, has the distinction of attracting numerous financial, electronics and computer companies to its city limits.

In many ways the Eastside owes its development to the bridges that connect it to Seattle; truly a love-hate relationship. These bridges can be the scenes of some of the most horrendous traffic and some of the most spectacular scenery imaginable. In fact, one could probably make a good case that the scenery causes some of the traffic problems. Area residents never seem to grow blasé about the beauty of Lake Washington. A boat skimming the water on a sunny day can still clog traffic on the bridges as motorists slow down to cast envious glances at the scene.

Public boat launches in both Bellevue and Kirkland make the lake accessible to all kinds of floating vehicles from sailboats to motorboats, cabin cruisers to canoes. There are sunny days in the summer when the waterways are so populated it seems like offices everywhere must have simply given up and shut down in honor of the weather.

Bellevue: Given the beauty of Lake Washington and the finite aspect of its waterfront, it's no surprise that, from Bellevue north to Bothell, waterfront property is prime real estate. Properties with private docks, private beaches and multi-level houses cascading down the hills can be seen from the highways. They look even more spectacular, unsurprisingly, from the vantage point of a cruiseboat on the lake.

One cruise that leaves from Kirkland's Carillon Point near the northern border of Bellevue is D'Elegant Cruises' "Champagne Fleet." Another company which offers year-round cruising on Lake Washington, including late-night cruises, is The Islander.

While cruising, keep a lookout for the mega-mansion on Mercer Island built by Bill Gates, the billionaire founder of Microsoft *(see page 201)*. Among many other luxury features, the house has a 30,000-sq-ft library.

Bellevue's **Meydenbauer Bay**, an area of luxury homes and condominiums on Lake Washington, to the west of Bellevue's downtown is named for William Meydenbauer, a Seattle baker. North of Meydenbauer Bay, the exclu-

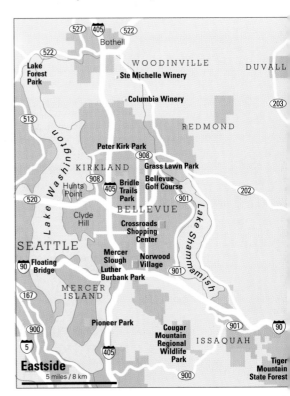

sive communities of **Medina**, **Yarrow Point** and **Clyde Hill** are other prominent Bellevue area waterfront places. Public beach access to Lake Washington in Bellevue is limited but **Chism Beach** offers swimming, trails and picnic facilities. Other good beaches in Bellevue include **Meydenbauer**, **Newcastle** and **Enatai**.

Aside from Lake Washington, the strongest attraction in Bellevue for visitors is **Bellevue Square**, known to locals as Bel Square. Among the teen set, a day of shopping at Bel Square is known as "squaring off." Opened in 1946 as one of the first suburban shopping centers in the country, Bellevue Square doubled in size in the early 1970s and today includes more than 200 shops and one million square feet of space. Three major department stores anchor the enormous mall – Nordstrom, J C Penneys and the Bon Marché.

One of Bellevue's most popular annual events, the **Pacific Northwest Arts and Crafts Festival**, began the same year the shopping center opened. What started in 1946 with a few paintings on display on the sidewalk is now one of the largest outdoor art shows in the western United States. Always slated for the last weekend in July (one of the weekends of the year when rain is least likely to fall), the show attracts artists, exhibitors and visitors who travel from all over the country.

Plan some extra time at the square or, better yet, plan a separate visit and take the glass elevator to the top floor where the **Bellevue Art Museum** is open seven days a week. A delightful surprise to find in a shopping center, the museum specializes in the decorative arts and frequently features traveling national art exhibits.

Bigscale park: Across the street from the southern side of Bellevue Square is Bellevue's **Downtown Park**, a 17½-acre site in the heart of the shopping district. It includes a 10-ft high waterfall, a canal enclosing a 5-acre meadow and a 28-ft wide promenade. The park is

Bel Square has more than 200 shops.

the location of the annual **Bellevue Jazz Festival**, where spirits run high.

Just south of the park is **Old Bellevue**, the city's main shopping district before the advent of Bel Square. Highlights of the two-block area are a Christmas shop open year-round, Cucina del Puerco, a cafeteria-style Mexican café, and several art galleries. Also in Old Bellevue is The Fountain Court, a delightful restaurant serving elegant lunches and dinners in an older home complete with picturesque courtyard and fountains. Keep in mind that, in Bellevue, "old" means dating to about 1940.

Head east across town and at 156th Avenue NE you'll find **Crossroads Shopping Center**, a mid-size center whose claim to fame is a smorgasbord of ethnic eateries bordering a center courtyard of tables, giant chess and checker games (pieces are about three feet tall) and a domed skylight. One of the best newspaper and magazine stands in the area, **The Daily Planet News**, is smack in the middle of everything. A cinema complex offers 10 screens with a variety of movies, and Crossroads stages free musical entertainment on most Friday and Saturday evenings.

At Bellevues's **Kelsey Creek Farm** pigs, horses, chickens and rabbits can be admired up close and there are trails, picnic tables and plenty of room to roam. A Japanese garden dedicated to Bellevue's sister city Yao is also located at the farm.

Mercer Island: Named for Aaron Mercer, one of the first two homesteaders in Bellevue, this island sits directly to the west of Bellevue, about midway between Bellevue and the southern part of Seattle. A thriving community of 21,000, it was incorporated in 1960. There are still people around who remember when **Mercer Island** was a summertime vacation land accessible only by ferry. The floating bridge section of Interstate 90 that linked the island to the Eastside and to Seattle changed all that.

Today, it's a residential community known for some incredible luxury homes

Kirkland's marina park.

162

and an excellent youth theater. Definitely worth a stop on Mercer Island is **Luther Burbank Park**. Originally a private estate, today the park features 77 gorgeous acres of lake front, tennis courts, an outdoor amphitheater and a playground for kids. Picnic tables, barbecues and a swimming area with a sandy beach add up to a great spot for summer fun. If you're traveling west on Interstate 90, take the Island Crest exit and follow the park.

Kirkland: Just north of Bellevue, with much of its shopping, restaurants and commercial areas hugging the shore of Lake Washington, is the city of Kirkland.

This city of 40,000 has more public access to waterfront through parks, open space and walkways than any other city in the state of Washington; public access to the waterfront has been a priority here since the city was first incorporated in 1905.

A walk along **Lake Street** passes by a series of grassy lakeside parks providing public access to the lake and to numerous waterfront restaurants. The tiny Red Duck Café, about 100 yards from the dock, serves breakfast, lunch and dinner, and the popular Foghorn provides its very own dock for restaurant patrons.

A central part of Kirkland's downtown is **Peter Kirk Park** with tennis courts, a ball field, one of the few public outdoor swimming pools on the Eastside and a children's playground. On summer evenings, the lighted baseball field is a big draw.

Parkplace Shopping Center offers movie theaters, gift shops, a bookstore, **Pinocchio's** toy store and a variety of places to eat. Downtown, the **Antique Heritage Mall** displays the merchandise of many dealers.

Art walks are periodically scheduled when galleries stay open late and invite the public to meet the artists whose work is on display. The **Kirkland Creative Arts Center** offers classes and exhibits for children and adults. There are numerous outdoor art works, which are

Seattle is a city dominated by water.

listed in a brochure produced by the Chamber of Commerce.

Carillon Point, a waterfront complex completed in 1991 which includes a luxury hotel, restaurants, waterfront walkways and docks as well as shops and restaurants, is a mile or two south of downtown. Two large office towers and a hillside of condominiums caused some initial complaints from nearby residents but the view from the hotel, the restaurants and the docks is spectacular. The Kirkland Downtown Association operates a **free trolley car** to carry people from Kirkland Parkplace through the downtown shopping district and on to Carillon Point.

A few miles north of downtown (from the northern end of Lake Street turn left onto Central Way, right onto Market and then left onto Juanita Drive) is **Juanita Bay Beach Park**, a county-run beach complete with summertime lifeguards, roped-off swimming areas and a snack bar. The park is open year round but without lifeguards. There are picnic

areas, a children's playground and a series of piers into the lake. Other Kirkland beach parks include **O. Denny**, **Waverly** and **Houghton**.

Bridle Trails State Park, right in the middle of residential neighborhoods, is a heavily wooded haven for horseback riders and hikers who don't mind sharing their trails with horses. The park is located in south Kirkland near the Bellevue border and can be accessed off 132nd Avenue NE.

Redmond: In the past two decades Redmond tripled its population to 37,000 and shows no signs of slowing. Fortunately, there's still enough open space in parts of the city for one of its signature activities to continue: hot air ballooning. Look out toward the northern part of the city along the Sammamish River area on just about any summer or fall evening and chances are you'll see colorful hot air balloons drifting peacefully in the sky. Balloon rides are available from several companies and in varying styles: some offer "red carpet" romantic rides complete with champagne and gourmet lunches or dinners; others offer family prices. One longtime company is The Balloon Depot.

The **Sammamish River** (often called the Sammamish Slough) winds its way south from Bothell to Marymoor Park, passing through Redmond and Woodinville. An asphalt pathway alongside the slough makes a perfect course for bicyclists and on weekends the place gets quite a mix of visitors with widely varying skills.

Toward the south end of Redmond, the Sammamish River travels past **Marymoor Park**, a 486-acre county-operated park that includes a museum housed in an old mansion, plus bike and hiking trails. Marymoor is also the home to the **Redmond Velodrome** – one of only six of its kind in the country – a banked racing course that attracts professional bicyclists from around the world. Every Fourth of July weekend, Marymoor is the site of the very popular **Heritage Festival**, an event featuring

Native carver in Issaquah.

an abundance of good food, live music and arts and crafts from many different ethnic heritages.

Woodinville: There are a couple of interesting sights in Woodinville, the main one being the **Chateau Ste Michelle Winery**, just west of the Sammamish River, a frequent stop for bicyclists on the slough route. The internationally acclaimed winery, the largest in the state of Washington, has 87 acres of picnic grounds, a pond with ducks and swans, a tasting room and test vineyards. Musical concerts are staged here each summer. Tours of the winery's operations (its main vineyards are in Eastern Washington) are offered daily, along with free wine tastings.

Across the street in a large, recently built, gingerbread-style building is **Columbia Winery**, formerly housed near downtown Bellevue. Also in the Woodinville area are the **Tegaris**, **Salmon Bay** and **French Creek** wineries, all of which welcome visitors with an interest in wine.

From Woodinville you can catch the **Tolt Pipeline trail**, either westward to Bothell or eastward to the Snoqualmie Valley. Its wooded and open terrain makes it a popular hiking spot.

Molbak's Greenhouse and Nursery is probably the most popular downtown stop. Thousands of varieties of plants, a greenhouse, fountains and flowers are the attractions. At Christmas, when the greenhouses are filled with seemingly endless rows of blooming poinsettias, it's a local holiday tradition to head for Molbak's to be photographed against the colorful background.

Small antique shops dot the roads throughout Woodinville, one larger mall called **Emerald City Antiques**, being not far from Ste Michelle Winery. Next door is Pacifica, a restaurant that, naturally, has a good wine list.

Issaquah: Southeast of Bellevue nestled in a valley between Squak, Tiger and Cougar mountains is the little town of Issaquah whose developers decided on a village theme for its shopping center.

Sammamish Slough.

They scoured the area for old clapboard-style homes, moving them into a village setting at the edge of downtown. Then they built wooden boardwalks, planted flowers and set to work attracting a special kind of retailer.

The result is Gilman Village, a "destination shopping center" of specialty shops and restaurants that draws people from many miles away. Antiques, home decorating items, boutique clothing, art, books, toys and gourmet kitchen items are just some of the merchandise offered at Gilman Village. During the Christmas shopping season, costumed carolers entertain shoppers. Also downtown is the Village Theater on Front Street, which puts on regular dramatic performances that are very popular.

A few blocks east of Gilman Village you'll enjoy touring Boehm's **Candy Kitchen**, a family-owned candy-making operation that has been in Issaquah since 1956. Delectable Swiss-style chocolate candies are still made here the old-fashioned, hand-dipped way. Samples are delicious and sometimes free.

Wildlife enthusiasts can enjoy the **Washington Zoological Park** and the **Issaquah State Salmon Hatchery**, where in the fall the salmon head up Issaquah Creek via a fish ladder. The Salmon Days Festival, usually held the first week in October, celebrates the return of the salmon.

Lake Sammamish State Park, just north of downtown Issaquah, provides access to the south shore of Lake Sammamish with its trails, baseball fields, picnic tables and barbecue spots. Lake Sammamish is a popular boating spot in the summer, although the incessant engine noise from the boats of water skiers tends to aggravate some visitors seeking peace and quiet.

Outer areas: Continuing past Issaquah on Interstate 90, the farther east one travels, the more rural the experiences become. In the Carnation and Fall City areas there's enough to merit at least one full day's visit, if not an entire weekend. Snoqualmie Falls *(see pic-* **Surburban living.**

ture on page 74 and text on page 228) is a dramatic sight that is worth visiting.

In the heart of the scenic Snoqualmie Valley, **Carnation Farms** is open to the public March through October. Known as the home of the contented cows, Carnation Farm is a 900-acre working dairy farm. Free, self-guided tours lead visitors through the maternity and calf barn, petting area, milking parlor and formal gardens. The tour takes about 40 minutes and can be topped off by making use of the picnic facilities in the nearby **Tolt River/John A. MacDonald Memorial Park**.

One mile south of the town of Carnation is **Remlinger U-Pick Farms**, a great place to stop and prove to the kids that there really is some connection between the land and the food they eat. Here during summer months you can pick berries and take them home in buckets. Remlinger offers fruits and vegetables aplenty, a restaurant, a viewing and petting farm and frequently a new litter of kittens or puppies that will soon be looking for good homes.

Herb eaters: Not far away in **Fall City** is the **Herbfarm**, a combination of working herb farm, gourmet restaurant, country store and nursery. Highlights include the 16 herbal theme gardens, and special events keyed to major holidays (including a hayride to a pumpkin patch on Halloween). Proprietors Carrie and Ron Zimmerman have created a gourmet restaurant so popular (focusing on edible herbs and plants grown on the premises) that reservations for lunches and dinners must be made well in advance. There are also regular classes on the farm in cooking, growing and crafting with herbs.

Duvall, the outer limits of the Eastside, celebrates its rural atmosphere with Duvall Days every spring, the weekend after Mothers' Day. The one-street downtown area sports several antique stores and Duvall Books, a popular bookstore selling used books. A street fair, parade and pancake breakfast highlight the annual celebration.

Carnation, home of the contented cows.

SOUTH OF
THE KINGDOME

It was on the windswept shores of what is now Alki Beach that Seattle's pioneers first built a community. The area's original residents, led by Arthur Denny, came from the state of Illinois seeking a better life. After one blustery winter on Alki, however, most of the Denny party moved away from the beach's winds to the shelter – and superior anchorage – of Elliott Bay.

Today, West Seattle's oldest landmark is a concrete column marking the beach as the "Birthplace of Seattle." It was presented to the city in 1905 by Arthur Denny's daughter, Lenora Denny, and stands at 63rd Avenue Southwest and Alki, having been moved from its original location on the other side of the street in 1926. At that time, a piece of the actual Plymouth Rock, the Massachussetts boulder towards which the Pilgrims sailed in 1620, was embedded in its base.

West Seattle: West Seattle is situated on a peninsula, separated from downtown Seattle by the Duwamish River. The West Seattle bridge, which connects the area to the rest of the city, arcs over busy **Harbor Island** and the **Duwamish River** like the back of a brontosaurus, its tail the Spokane Street Viaduct, its neck the sweep of the freeway up a tree-covered hill. Harbor Island, at the river's mouth where it empties into Elliott Bay, is a man-made industrial island and storage depot for much of the equipment serving the busy Port of Seattle.

The present high-level bridge, still called the "new bridge" by longtime residents although it was completed in 1984, replaced a pair of bascule bridges that too often stopped traffic when they opened to let sailboats and freighters down the river.

"Downtown West Seattle," as it is occasionally – if facetiously – called, is best known as **The Junction**. It is

centered around California Avenue and Alaska Street. This central shopping area has had its ups and downs; a number of businesses have made passing appearances while several others have stood almost unchanged for more than 50 years. Neighborhood institutions, such as the doughnut shop on California where oldtimers congregate to reminisce and discuss politics, adjoins a corner shop that has changed from a drug store to a shoe store and (currently) a record store.

Popular local establishments include Northwest Art and Frame (frames, gifts, books and art supplies), Husky Delicatessen (great sandwiches, locally made ice cream, imported food and beverages) and the Coho Café (salmon dinners and fine dining).

The Junction's display of murals is remarkable: more than half a dozen wall-sized paintings decorate the exteriors of retail and business buildings, most of them depicting the area as it looked in the 19th century. The best of

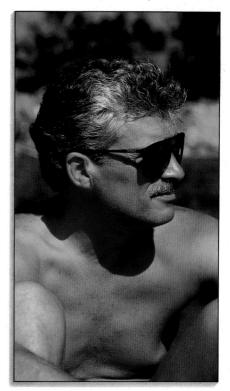

Preceding pages: Hat 'n' Boots, a defunct gas stop near Boeing Field. **Left,** West Seattle. **Right,** Alki Beach.

these murals, on the wall at California and Edmunds, looks as if you could walk right into a turn-of-the-century street scene.

North of the junction on California, just past West Seattle High School, is the **Admiral District**, named for **Admiral Way**, which arcs over the hill from Alki on the west to the West Seattle bridge on the east. The district is home to the last of West Seattle's movie theaters, the Admiral Theatre, which for many years sported a ship's mast.

West Seattle is located on two hills, **Gatewood** and **Genesee**, which gives it an abundance of properties with views. Homes on the west sides of both hills overlook Puget Sound and the Olympic Mountains; those on the east overlook downtown and Harbor Island. At the top of Genesee Hill are a number of scenic outlooks including **Hamilton Viewpoint**, at the north end of California Avenue, and **Belvedere Viewpoint**, on Admiral Way.

Alki Beach: The closest thing Seattle has to a Southern California strand is **Alki Beach**, which, for many years, was the summer place teenagers headed for in their cars. Anti-cruising laws passed in the 1980s restrict drivers to one pass along the beach every four hours, thus cutting down considerably on the noise and traffic that plagued local residents. The park is closed between 11pm and 6am, mid-April through September. In summer, however, Alki still attracts a fair share of shiny cars, bronzed bodies in bikinis and teenagers out to see and be seen. Volleyball courts are usually filled with players and lined with spectators. A trail along the beach is popular with bikers, joggers and skaters.

In the fall, winter and spring Alki is still a wonderful place for a beach stroll under swirling clouds amidst squawking gulls. And when the wind and rain that drove the Denny party to the other side of the bay get to be too much, the area also offers plenty of places to eat. Popular local restaurants include Pegasus Pizza and Pasta, where there's

Alki Beach is Seattle's answer to Southern California.

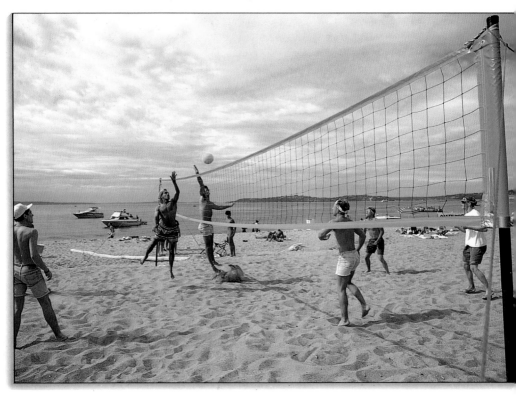

usually a lineup outside even on week-nights, the Alki Bakery and Spud Fish and Chips, said by regulars to be the best in town. Farther along the beach is Salty's on Alki, one of a chain of trendy seafood restaurants, and one that offers a great view across Elliott Bay of downtown Seattle.

At the southern end of the beach – just before it becomes residential, is the **Alki Point Lighthouse**, first established in 1881 and marking the southern entrance to Seattle's harbor. The present lighthouse, standing on a small reservation between apartments and condominiums, dates to 1913. The lighthouse is open to visitors for regular tours on weekends; group tours can be arranged Tuesday through Friday.

Beautiful parks: Continue along the waterfront road which becomes Beach Drive, passing beachside homes both extravagant and funky, as well as apartment buildings and open spaces such as **Emma Schmitz Memorial Park**. **Beach Drive** culminates in the lower part of Lincoln Park, at the foot of Gatewood Hill. Alki may be the most visible of this area's city parks, but it is certainly not the least of them. Most prominent is 130-acre **Lincoln Park** (designed by the Olmsted brothers, creators of New York's Central Park) with miles of wooded and waterfront trails, and **Colman Pool**, a heated 50-meter Olympic-size outdoor pool open only from June through Labor Day. Filled partly with chlorinated freshwater and part saltwater, Colman Pool is accessible only on foot; the roads are restricted to park vehicles.

One of the city's few parks to offer overnight facilities, **Camp Long**, just off 35th Avenue Southwest at Dawson, is 68 acres of wilderness. Open to organized groups for camping and wilderness-skills programs, Camp Long is a popular site for weddings and also features a rock wall for climbing practice and instruction. **Schmitz Park**, just east of Alki, is a 50-acre nature preserve with narrow trails through thick woods,

but with no picnic areas or playgrounds. Just off 35th Avenue Southwest, the hillside **West Seattle Municipal Golf Course** offers views of downtown Seattle, Elliott Bay and the Duwamish Waterway. This 18-hole, par-72 course was built in 1940.

Just east of West Seattle is **White Center,** which was named in the early 1900s for George W. H. White, a partner in the railway that served West Seattle. White Center was then a rugged logging area. Government housing projects went up after World War II and, later, taverns were built here – just outside the city limits – earning White Center in the 1960s the nickname Rat City. Nowadays, White Center is one of the few nearby places left with affordable real estate for first-home buyers, partly owing to its placement adjacent to a low-income housing development.

At the south end of Lincoln Park is the **Fauntleroy Ferry Dock**, where you can catch a boat for Vashon Island or Southworth. Either place makes a

pleasant day trip. Vashon, just 20 minutes from the dock, is a charming rural area far from the rush of city life. Many residents farm as a hobby and make the daily commute to Seattle or Tacoma via ferry; others have found work on the island itself, working in such industries as ski manufacturing, orchid growing or food processing.

The region immediately south of the Kingdome, which marks the southern edge of downtown, is mainly industrial. Shops here often sell carpeting, building supplies and reduced rate furniture, though a few landmarks remain, including Andy's Diner in an authentic railroad car.

One brilliant beacon in south Seattle, however, is a glowing red neon "R," visible from Interstate 5 and often accompanied by the strong smell of brewing hops. It marks the **Rainier Brewing Company**, once locally owned but now part of an Australian conglomerate that includes J. Heilemann Brewing. Rainier's strong local

reputation is based mostly on its earlier advertising campaigns which included the Brews Brothers (a takeoff on the Blues Brothers) and a herd of running beer bottles. Many drinkers prefer the more distinctive flavor of popular local microbrews, including West Seattle's own California and Alaska Street Brewery. Like some of the microbreweries, Rainier offers tours of the premises. The free, afternoon tours include a tour of the beer house, an orientation film and taste testing in the taproom; those younger than 21 are served root beer.

Harbor Island, between downtown Seattle and West Seattle, is home to the city's shipyards as well as loading facilities for freighters. It is composed of more than 25 million cubic yards of sludge pulled from the Duwamish River. At the time of its completion in 1912, it was the largest manmade island in the world. Shortly after the island was created, the meandering Duwamish River was straightened, allowing plenty of room on its banks for industrial development. On its way south from Elliott Bay, past busy Harbor Island and through Seattle's industrial corridor, the river passes salvage ships, commercial shipping lanes, Boeing Field and the city of Tukwila.

The Big Lake: On the other side of Beacon Hill is **Lake Washington**, flanked on the west all the way to Seward Park by the boulevard that begins at the University of Washington Arboretum in North Seattle. Along the way, the road offers eastward views of the Cascade Mountains as it meanders past the Lake Washington parks, a string of grassy beachfronts along the lake's western shore. An adjacent bike path follows the road for some miles.

The stretch of lake shoreline from just south of the Mercer Island Floating Bridge to Andrews Bay is hydro heaven during the Rainier Cup Hydroplane Race in August. The races, part of the city's Seafair celebration and first staged in 1950, have become a Seattle tradition, drawing thousands of specta-

Rowing along the Thea Foss waterway, Tacoma.

tors despite the horrendous noise of engines on 150-mph boats. Seafair's official viewing beach is **Stanley Sayres Memorial Park** (where the hydro pits are located), but many fans watch from homes along the lake and hundreds pay a per-foot charge to tie their boats up to log booms along the challenging course.

The Lake Washington parks culminate in **Seward Park**, 277 acres of greenery, trails and waterfront, home to a pair of breeding bald eagles. The park has an art studio, a fish hatchery, an outdoor amphitheater and a 2½-mile lakeside trail for cyclists and runners. Like Alki, and several other Seattle parks, Seward Park closes at 11pm each night because of citizen and police concerns about drug and gang activity.

In **Rainier Valley**, named for the vistas of Mount Rainier it offers, once stood the old Sicks Stadium, home successively to baseball's Seattle Rainiers and the Seattle Pilots, but now an industrial park. Neighborhoods near the Duwamish River as it winds south from Elliott Bay include Holly Park, Highland Park, South Park, Beverly Park and, farther to the southwest, Burien. To the east on the edge of the lake is **Rainier Beach**. Limited real estate in the city's International District prompted some Asian immigrants to seek other areas for development, including the area just south of the Kingdome which now has a substantial Asian population, mostly Vietnamese, and several good ethnic restaurants.

Many more Asian restaurants can be found on Pacific Highway South, one of which is The Orchid, which offers Thai food at reasonable prices.

Southcenter, at the southern confluence of Interstates 5 and 405, is one of Seattle's largest covered shopping malls. This 92-acre shopping complex houses some 125 stores, anchored by department stores Nordstrom and the Bon Marché. Specialty apparel and gift stores, plus a busy food court sell everything from toys to tacos.

Tacoma means "Mother of Waters."

The region south of Seattle is Boeing country. The aerospace firm's test field, at the south end of Lake Washington, is flanked by plants in Renton, Auburn and Kent.

Flight path: The city of Sea-Tac was incorporated in 1990, its main claim to fame being the **Seattle-Tacoma International Airport**, from which it gets its name. There are many ways to get to the airport from town, the most economical being via Metro; several buses make the trip from downtown. Watch out for the defunct gas station in the form of a giant western hat and boot, a couple of miles out of town. There are inexpensive motels along Pacific Highway South near 140th Street.

Near Sea-Tac, rent a canoe or kayak at Pacific Water Sports and put in at one of several spots along the Duwamish River to follow the river back to its source. South of Sea-Tac, the Duwamish becomes the **Green River**.

Whether or not you have any ongoing interest in the jet that brought you to

town, no visit to Seattle is complete without a stop at the **Museum of Flight**, an impressive collection representing the entire industry, not just the local influence on it. Occupying the original Boeing building, the **Red Barn** – built in 1909 as part of a shipyard along the Duwamish – and the adjacent **Great Gallery**, built in the 1980s, the museum offers a history of man's fascination with flight.

Inside the Red Barn are a few restored early planes, historical photographs and drawings. The gallery features a main hall with 30-foot ceilings from which hang an assortment of flying craft ranging from hang-gliders to fighter jets. Visitors can admire the craft from below or take an elevator to see them at eye level from viewing decks. Other interesting objects in the museum include an airplane car that looks like (and is) a shiny red sportscar with wings. From the museum, visitors have a clear view of Boeing's runway, where commercial aircraft are detailed and tested prior to delivery. The museum's souvenir gift shop has plastic models for kids and complex wooden ones for adults.

Renton, a city of 43,000 at the south end of Lake Washington, just east of Southcenter, is home to two Boeing facilities and a municipal airport. Among its attractive city parks is **Liberty Park** beside the Cedar River, which serves as the site for the annual Renton River Days, and **Gene Coulon Memorial Beach Park**, on the lake. The **Renton Historical Museum**, not far from Liberty Park, recounts the city's birth as Black River Bridge, a coal mining community. On view are a number of historic photographs and mining equipment as well as maps showing the mining shafts that crisscross under the expensive contemporary homes on Renton Hill.

The **Kent Valley** south of Renton, which used to produce much of the Puget Sound area's agriculture, has more recently turned to trade and is fast becoming one of the world's largest

Go for great eats at Art's. This is Art.

trade distribution centers. Farther south are the cities of Normandy Park (where many Boeing employees live) and Des Moines (a big marina), named by a founder from Des Moines, Iowa, who persuaded friends in the Midwest to finance his venture in 1887.

Federal Way, south of Seattle along Interstate 5, named for federally funded Highway 99, was incorporated in 1990. It is home to **Dash Point State Park** and **Wild Waves Water Park and Enchanted Village**. The latter is a popular summer attraction for children and one of the few water parks still operating in the area. Also in Federal Way are the Rhododendron **Species Foundation Display Gardens**, at Weyerhaeuser Corporate Headquarters. The 24-acre botanical gardens feature 2,200 labeled and classified varieties of rhododendrons, Washington's state flower. It is one of the world's largest collections of rhododendron species. The gardens include an array of such other plants as heathers, lilies, ferns and maples.

City of destiny: About an hour's drive south of Seattle, residents of Tacoma (pop. 158,900) contend with the "Tacoma aroma," produced by the local pulp mill, while quietly building a number of excellent local restaurants and a strong arts scene. Like many cities in the shadow of larger ones, it tends to be the butt of sometimes unfair jokes, such as the one about how you can tell a car is from Tacoma – it fails the emissions test with the engine off.

The aroma is produced by the Simpson Tacoma Kraft mill, which makes cardboard and other products – principally liner board used in frozen food boxes, yogurt containers and milk cartons. So many other products are packaged in liner board that the substance is one of the items tracked by the government as part of its monthly index; by measuring the amount of liner board produced, statisticians can guage how the economy is doing overall. This distinction might not make the smell of pulp any sweeter when the wind carries

it inland, but there have been commendable recent efforts by the proprietors to clean up their mill.

Tacoma, originally called Commencement City due to its position on Commencement Bay, was renamed Tacoma in 1869 – the name derived from the Indian word "Tahoma," meaning "Mother of Waters."

Tacoma was tagged the "City of Destiny" by city fathers in 1855 to help boost its growth, but the city has had trouble realizing that destiny and has played second fiddle to Seattle most of the time. Tacoma was chosen as the western terminus for the Northern Pacific in the 1870s, but Seattle became the terminus for the Great Northern Railroad in 1893 and soon pulled ahead.

The local arts scene includes a number of solid theater companies, a fine art museum and modest musical companies. The **Pantages Theater** is a restored 1,100-seater hall dating back to 1918. It has been remodeled and is well suited for dance, music and stage pro-

shot at he slot.

ductions. The **Tacoma Art Museum** hosts a number of good traveling exhibitions and houses an impressive collection of works by Northwest artists. The **Washington State Historical Museum** has a large collection of pioneer, Native and Alaskan exhibits.

The Tacoma Dome: At 152 feet tall and 530 feet in diameter, this is the world's largest wood-domed structure, a multipurpose entertainment facility offering better acoustics than the larger Kingdome in Seattle. A popular venue for visiting rock acts, the $44 million arena, completed in 1983, seats up to 27,000 and has hosted events ranging from the Billy Graham Crusade and the US Figure Skating Championships to truck and tractor pulls and home shows. The city is also home to AAA baseball's Tacoma Tigers who play outdoors at **Cheney Stadium**.

One of Tacoma's most appealing landmarks is 700-acre **Point Defiance Park**, located on a finger of land that juts out into Puget Sound. This 700-acre wilderness park, one of the largest urban parks in the US, is maintained by the Tacoma Metropolitan Park Service with a policy that enables it to absorb heavy use without heavy damage.

Within the park the **Point Defiance Zoo and Aquarium** displays performing elephants, a polar bear complex, Pacific walruses and penguins. The aquarium specializes in safeguarding marine mammals and the zoo is a world leader in breeding rare animals. **Ruston Way**, along the south shore of Commencement Bay, has trails, parks and piers as well as enough restaurants to earn it the nickname Restaurant Row.

Shootings and gang activity in the Tacoma's Hilltop area in the past decade spread fear throughout the Puget Sound area, but do not necessarily reflect the whole city any more than violence in parts of other cities makes them entirely unsafe for tourists. Nevertheless, it is not a part of town where it is advisable for tourists to be late in the evening, although community and po-

Former Northern Pacific HQ and the old City Hall.

lice efforts to clean up the area have been somewhat successful at decreasing the drug trade and violence.

Other local recreation attractions include **Fort Nisqually**, on a cliff, and **Camp Six**, featuring original loggers' bunkhouses and an operating 1929 steam train that chugs around the camp.

Puyallup: Pronounce this place "Pewallup" if you don't want to sound like a foreigner. Adjacent to Tacoma, Puyallup is best known for its annual fall event, the Western Washington State Fair, better known locally as just the **Puyallup Fair**. One of the 10 biggest fairs in the country, the Puyallup is the largest of Washington's state and county fairs. Every September, more than 1 million people "do the Puyallup" for two and a half weeks, enjoying everything county fairs are known for: demonstrations of multi-purpose kitchen gadgets, displays of 4-H Club-raised rabbits, heifers, horses and pigs, carnival rides and scones with raspberry jam. The city is also home to the largest amateur-owned and operated observatory in western Washington, the **Pettinger-Guiley Observatory**, run by the Tacoma Astronomical Society. Numerous daffodil farms contribute to the annual Daffodil Parade every April.

On the west side of the city, the **Tacoma Narrows Bridge** is the fifth-largest suspension bridge in the world. The original bridge, constructed in 1940, was dubbed "Galloping Gertie" because of its tendency to undulate in the winds that whipped through the Tacoma Narrows spanned by the structure. Gertie galloped too much, however, and just a few months after her opening collapsed. Sections of the old bridge and the marine life that it attracts now draw scuba divers to the cold waters far below the present 5,979-ft-long bridge, which has been firmly in place since 1950.

Just across the Narrows Bridge is **Gig Harbor**, a lovely harbor town with old-fashioned shops and restaurants and several bed-and-breakfast inns.

Tacoma Dome: the world's largest wooden dome.

NORTH SEATTLE

The hulking specters of a bygone industrial age dominate **Gas Works Park**, situated on a knob of land jutting boldly into Lake Union, the front door to north Seattle. Once a working factory, the recycled gas works is now the most popular park in the Northwest.

The Seattle Gas Light Company manufactured heating and lighting gas on the 20-acre knoll from 1906 until 1956, fueling a rapidly growing city and earning a reputation as a filthy, foul-smelling killer of vegetation and wildlife. Once the plant closed its doors for good, Seattle scorned it as an eyesore and a nuisance. When the site was proposed as a park in the early 1960s, the City Council hired landscape architect Richard Haag to create a lush, arboretum-type park. Instead, the Haag submitted a plan incorporating much of the old gas plant. His design triumphed after a storm of controversy. The world's first industrial site conversion park was opened in September 1975.

A medley of kites fly high over the **Grand Mound**, a natural grass amphitheater built west of the park's core from abandoned industrial waste. Picknickers and joggers share the space along an incline and at the crown, visitors admire an autognomonic sun and moon dial, created in 1976 by local artists Chuck Greening and Kim Lazare. The crest offers a panorama of inner Seattle – downtown, Queen Anne Hill, the Aurora Bridge to the west and Capitol Hill to the east. To the north, the unique park gives way to the University of Washington and the residential houses of Wallingford and Fremont.

The 8-mile-long **Lake Washington Ship Canal** separates the northern neighborhoods from the city core. Completed in 1917, the man-made water route winds through the Ballard, Fremont, Wallingford, University and Montlake districts linking the salty Puget Sound and Shilshole Bay with the fresh waters of Salmon Bay and Lakes Union and Washington. Six bridges cross the canal leading into a cluster of neighborhoods that make up North Seattle. These districts, born as independent townships in the 19th century, mostly maintain their individuality.

Starting at Gas Works, the **Burke-Gilman Trail**, a 12½-mile biking and hiking route, swings along Lake Union, winds through the University of Washington campus and courses north on the left bank of Lake Washington. The innovative and scenic track follows the course of the lakeshore railroad which connected these communities a century ago, an imaginative "recycling" which gave the impetus to what has become a national "rails to trails" movement.

University district: Find your way to the **U District**, an eclectic commercial center thriving on the cultural, educational and athletic amenities afforded by the adjacent University of Washington. **University Way North**, affection-

ately called "the Ave" by locals, is a bustling strip of shops, theaters, news-stands, bookstores, pubs and eateries. Seattleites regard this animated district with caution. Increasing numbers of panhandlers, rebellious youth and the homeless who hang out here bring with them a sometimes shadowy sub-culture. But the diverse community of students, business people, academics and vagrants indisputably creates an endearing vitality.

The Avenue is dotted with inexpensive eateries. You can get a slice of cheese and a cola at Pizzeria Pagliacci, a good pizza joint with walls lined in contemporary Italian film posters. Idlers linger over lattes at the tacky Café Roma, deeply mired in their latest existential crisis. The slogan at Shultzy's Sausage reads "The Best of the Wurst." Nooks and hideaways specialize in Indian, Ethiopian, Thai, Italian, English and even the land of Timbuk-tofu.

The **University Bookstore**, a resident of the Ave since 1925, carries a huge selection of contemporary fiction as well as textbooks, school and art supplies and UW tee-shirts. Down the street is Beauty and the Books, a used bookstore occupied by lolling black cats. For import shopping, find an exquisite collection of imported instruments, clothing, and jewelry at La Tienda Folk Art Gallery. Pop singer Elton John once told somebody he might have worked at Tower Records had he missed his calling as a rock star.

Locals queue up for the latest Hollywood hit at the **Varsity Theater**, or for animation festivals at the **Neptune Theatre** around the corner. The spacious **Big Time Brewery and Alehouse** brews four traditional American ales and sports the only shuffleboard table in the neighborhood. Apartment developers almost demolished the **Blue Moon Tavern** a few years back, but this smoky, seedy den of glory won historical landmark status and a 40-year lease. The University Bar and Grill and Lox, Stock and Bagel both offer live music on weekends, and Lox, Stock opens its front window to the street on sunny days. The Unicorn serves premium English meat pies, puddings, and beers to the accompaniment of folk musicians playing Celtic ballads.

A few blocks to the east is the 694-acre **University of Washington** campus. Started on a 10-acre plot which it still owns (and from which it generates huge rents) in downtown Seattle in 1861, it moved to its present site in 1895. More than 33,000 students and 17,000 faculty and staff come here to what has been recognized as one of the elite universities in the nation. Pick up a self-guided walking tour from the **Visitor's Information Center**.

Classy designers: Much of the original campus – one of the most beautiful in the world – was designed by the Olmsted family, famous for Central Park in New York City. Drumheller Fountain sits at the top of the Rainier Vista Mall, the gateway to the Gothic-style **Liberal Arts Quad** where, in

Lake Washington Ship Canal.

April, rows of cherry trees burst into pink and white blossoms. The **Allen Library**, completed in 1990 with a $10 million donation from Paul Allen, one of the founders of the Microsoft Corporation, expands by 40 percent the capacity of the **Suzzallo Library**, a Gothic-style cathedral-like hall opened in 1927 and dubbed "the soul of the University" by then-president Henry Suzzallo. The adjoining red-tiled plaza from 1969, known to all as **Red Square**, serves as a mid-campus rendezvous for demonstrations and celebrations.

On summer evenings at the **Observatory**, near the north campus entrance, you can stargaze through a 6-inch telescope. The **Burke Museum** houses a superb collection of Native art of the Northwest Coast tribes and the nearby **Henry Art Gallery** features 35 exhibitions each year. To the southeast rises **Husky Stadium**, the largest in the Pacific Northwest, with a capacity to hold 72,000 spectators. Just below, on Union Bay, weekend water warriors rent row-

boats or canoes at the **Waterfront Activities Center**. One mile north of the stadium, the **University Village Shopping Mall**, known for its speciality food shops, offers ample free parking along with hardware, clothes, groceries, furnishings and garden supplies.

The city of Seattle is young enough that residents still wistfully imagine the land as it was a century ago – a wilderness of virgin forests and crystal waterways. Just north of the university lies lush **Ravenna Park**, an unspoiled deep wooded gorge far from the hustle of cosmopolitan life. Standing in silence next to a towering tree or a spill of green fern, it is not hard to envision one's ancestors meeting a bear on the track or gathering herbs for healing. Both the town and the park were named Ravenna, after the Italian hamlet which stands on the edge of an ancient forest. The land was sold to the city in 1911.

In the neighborhoods bordering Lake Washington, large contemporary homes built on landscaped hillsides

NASA view of Seattle taken from 12,000 ft.

capture sweeping views of the Cascades and Mount Rainier. On the southern stretch of the Sand Point Peninsula, at least 87 species of birds and numerous kinds of wildlife frequent the recontoured terrain of **Magnuson Park**, once an air strip and now filled with bluffs, sports fields, trails and long, serene stretches of beach. On the same delta extending into Lake Washington, Bill Boeing flew his first airplane and, in 1921, the first around-the-world flight began and ended here.

Public art: In 1974, the city of Seattle granted the National Oceanic and Atmospheric Administration (NOAA) the northern 114 acres of what had been a naval air station for its new **Western Regional Center**. It is now this country's largest federal center engaged in atmospheric and oceanic research. Visitors are invited to saunter down the **Shoreline Walk** to see five publicly-funded artworks, which have proven to be so successful that the project has set a nationally admired example for public art. Earth, wind and water are the artists' media: a concrete spiraling dome with views in every direction; a viewpoint over the lake with chairs and sofas made from cut boulders; a bridge lettered with excerpts from *Moby Dick*; a multi-surfaced berth lapping up waves on the curve of the shoreline; and a sound garden of lacy towers and tuned organ pipes that make music from the wind. Have lunch overlooking the lake at the delightful and inexpensive NOAA **Cafeteria**, whose employees are mostly people with disabilities. About a mile to the north is Seattle's largest freshwater bathing beach (lifeguard on duty) at **Matthews Beach Park**, just off of the Burke-Gilman trail. At the south end, cross the footbridge above Thornton Creek to a little wildlife refuge.

Traversing west, you may want to stop in the **Roosevelt** neighborhood, a largely residential area of early 20th-century homes known for its antique shops and ethnic cuisine. The corner of 65th and Roosevelt may yet become

Green Lake skating situation.

known as "New Age Alley." Among the three or four competing booksellers in the vicinity, Zenith Supplies carries crystals, music and massage tools as well as an extensive stock of manuals for awakening the inner self; East West Book Shop stocks a comprehensive Jungian collection. Across the street the Sunlight Café serves up hearty whole-wheat sesame waffles and a stick-to-your-ribs dinner of stir-fried veggies in yogurt sauce. The Kirsten Gallery down the street completes the cultural package with frequent cutting-edge exhibits exploring alternative aesthetics.

The recreational center of North Seattle lies a few blocks west. The shimmering waters of **Green Lake** ripple against grassy shores amidst the high-density neighborhood of the same name. It's a bonus lake in a city surrounded by water, an algae-tinged reservoir born of glacial gougings 15,000 years ago. Locals take their leisure time very seriously; a flurry of joggers, bicyclists, walkers and roller skaters zip along the busy 3-mile perimeter path in all weather. Rent a pair of rollerblades or elect to feed the (sometimes agressive) ducks at the **Waldo Waterfowl Sanctuary**. Cast off the banks for a fresh rainbow trout or play nine holes at the Pitch 'n' Putt Golf Course. A community center and its environs include such facilities as football fields, tennis courts, a swimming pool, gym, beach and rowboat and canoe rentals. On West Greenlake, local thespians perform at the **Bathhouse Theatre**. And once or twice each century, the winter cold creates ice thick enough to draw crowds of skaters.

Spud Fish and Chips across the street is a favorite summer spot. Choose from the Northern Italian menu at Saleh al Lago or grab a gourmet burger with creole-spiced fries at Duke's Chowder House. Alternatively, check out the chow at the Outrageous Canoe Club where the young and restless are known to cavort or take in local microbrews and jazz at the friendly Latona by Green

Contemplating life in North Seattle.

Lake. The **Honey Bear Bakery** steals the heart of this laid-back district, serving up pastries, steamed milk, conversation and live music on weekends.

The neighborhoods of **Phinney Ridge** and **Greenwood** blend easily together into an area known as "The Ridge." Here, Greenwood Avenue, once touted as Seattle's **Antique Row**, mixes traditional antiques and second-hand stores with modern merchants such as Metropolis, a brilliant card shop; Ken's Market, a specialty food mart; and the Cellar Wine Shop. Enjoy contemporary Northwest art at **Francine Seders Gallery** or get your aesthetics instead at the **Ridgement Theater**, a pioneering venue for art films, where the decor has not changed much since the 1950s. The chicken-fried steak and mashed potatoes at Buddy's Homesick Café aim to take you back to that very same decade of Americana. As you may have noticed, Seattleites rate their pubs by how many varieties (preferably from the micro-

brewery kingdom) flow from the taps. The 74th Street Alehouse pours 16 drafts while at La Boheme, established in 1934, assorted strains of golden suds spill from 19 spigots.

User-friendly zoo: Almost 300 animal species dwell in the hills tucked between Phinney Ridge and Green Lake at the **Woodland Park Zoo**. The former wilderness estate of Guy Phinney, a leading Seattle real estate developer in the 1880s, this 92-acre park pioneered the concept of creating naturalistic habitats for animals. Though many of the exhibits still imprison dispirited and sullen creatures behind iron bars, the zoo demonstrates a true commitment to a cageless future. By 1997, eight bioclimatic zones will be in place to provide greater comfort for the animals and encourage natural behavior. Already the Asian Elephant Forest and African Savanna have earned international recognition. Just outside of the 300's southeast exit, take time for the magnificent and free **Rose Garden**, originally laid out in the 1890s by old man Phinney himself. The adjoining **Poncho Theatre** offers children's productions, films and special events in a cozy milieu.

Swinging back north, in the tiny hamlet of Pontiac, a railroad worker once hung a sign that said "Lake" on a shed near the tracks of Northern Pacific Railroad. The name stuck and **Lake City** was annexed by Seattle in 1954. Here, as in the surrounding neighborhoods, reasonably priced starter homes can be found relatively close to the urban core. Even though the blur of chain restaurants, car lots, gas stations and supermarkets lining Lake City Way NE won't make an impressive mark in the annals of history, there are a few spots worth noting: Cooper's Northwest Ale House has on tap 22 beers, mostly microbrews; the Italian Spaghetti House and Pizzeria dishes up a convincing old-country-in-the-new-world pasta and sauce and there is good curry at the Taj Mahal India Restaurant, ginger and raw fish at Toyoda Sushi and

Detail from a Phinney Ridge café.

188

marinated duck at New Peking. A flagpole dedicated to World War II veterans sits in what is the smallest official city park. The **Lake City Community Center** is the only Seattle Parks Department facility built and maintained entirely by local citizens. A **Will Rogers Memorial** honors the Oklahoma-born wit and philosopher who spent one of his last days playing polo in Lake City.

Every week, 500,000 conspicuous consumers stride down the indoor sidewalks of **Northgate**, the West Coast's pioneer shopping mall. Opened in 1950 as the first mall west of the Mississippi River, it finally got a roof in the early '70s and now houses several major department stores and 118 specialty shops. Up the street, more than 8,000 students attend **North Seattle Community College**. Also in the neighborhood is the 18-hole Jackson Park Municipal Golf Course.

If access to the jeweled shores of the Puget Sound means prosperity, then Seattleites are rich indeed, for yet another urban wilderness, the 216-acre **Carkeek Park**, winds and plunges down into a maze of wooded pathways, over the Burlington Northern Railroad tracks and onto an unfettered stretch of beach. Locals are laboring to re-establish the park's **Piper's Creek** as a salmon spawning site, once a stable run now destroyed by development.

Heading south: Follow the railroad south and you're on your way to proud-hearted **Ballard**. The tracks run through **Golden Gardens Park**, neatly dividing it into two distinct sections: a forested hillside and a golden beach stretching along **Shilshole Bay**, Seattle's coast-of-blue. Sunbathe, scuba dive, dig for clams or watch the sailboats breezing out toward the Puget isles. Wind up Golden Gardens Drive and go south until a "Scenic Drive" sign at NW 77th denotes the aptly-named **Sunset Hill**. Have some great seafood with your setting sun at Ray's Boathouse, burned down in 1987 but now happily restored.

After developers discovered this re-gion in the mid-1880s, Scandinavian immigrants were drawn here by the abundant fishing, lumber and boat-building opportunities to be found in a majestic and watery region much like their homeland. Thickly-accented Scandinavian tongues can still be heard in local coffee shops. When downtown Seattle was rebuilt after the Great Fire of 1889 and Washington entered the Union as the 42nd state, Gilman Park, now a community of nearly 2,000 residents, hurried to be the first to incorporate, naming their boomtown Ballard. At the turn of the century it was known as "Shingleton USA," the largest producer of red cedar shingles in the United States. It may as well have been dubbed "Saloon Town" for early Ballard was a bastion of pioneer revelry, said to hold 27 saloons on a 4-block strip.

The thriving community of 15,000, highly coveted by Seattle officials for its major industrial district and access to water routes, was annexed to the city in 1907 and has served as a major com-

Giraffe from Woodland Park Zoo.

mercial fishing port throughout the 20th century. The "Dream of America," a major exhibit at the **Nordic Heritage Museum**, tells a graphic story of the immigrants' travel to a new land and five Ethnic Rooms survey the legacy of every Nordic country: Sweden, Norway, Iceland, Finland and Denmark. Pick up a self-guided walking tour of Old Ballard at the **Chamber of Commerce** office on NW Market Street.

Incidentally, Ballard still sports its share of saloons and plays a key role in Seattle's hot music scene. One of the oldest bars, the **Owl Café**, established in 1902, features late-night blues. The Old Ballard Firehouse has a spacious dance floor and books big names in Cajun, blues, rock and reggae. The very progressive **Backstage** bills the best artists from the region and international headliners. Folksy music and dancing brings all ages to The New Melody Tavern, while Spinnaker's on Shilshole draws a younger, disco-esque crowd.

Get out of the clubs and into the fresh salt air down by the ship canal. Every year, about 100,000 commercial and pleasure vessels navigate through the 1917 **Hiram M. Chittenden Locks**, two masonry gates which raise and lower boats between fresh and salt water. About 500,000 sockeye, chinook, and coho salmon use the same channel to get to their spawning grounds, climbing a 21-level **fish ladder** built in 1976 to preserve the migrating runs. Watch their passage upstream through six lighted underwater viewing windows, a moving portrait of creatures driven by a mandate of nature and against all odds back to their birthplace. The terraced lawns and rose bushes of the waterside **Carl S. English Jr Ornamental Gardens** make a fine picnic spot.

No bridge on the planet opens more often than the **Fremont Bridge**, built in 1916 for the completed ship canal. Since then it has opened its arms in a 3-minute prayer to the clouds more than 500,000 times – every 10 minutes on a busy summer day. You can watch boats **Fremont Library.**

go under the two-toned drawbridge from a peaceful overlook at the **Fremont Canal Park**, a walkway on the north side of the Fremont which features work by local artists.

Artists' haven: The close-knit community of **Fremont**, strategically located at the Northwest corner of Lake Union, was once a busy stop on Burke-Gilman's SLS&E Railway which carried lumber, coal and passengers between downtown and Ballard. (The Edgewater station at the foot of Stone Way Avenue can still be seen today.) During Prohibition, Fremont's thriving taverns and hotel saloons were closed down, though the basement speakeasies flourished despite police raids. The new **Aurora Bridge** opened in 1932, bypassing Fremont. Family-oriented residents trickled out of the town when "bikers, brawls and busts" arrived. By the 1960s, hippies and unemployed drifters had taken over the Fremont and Triangle hotels but the 1970s brought a long-awaited local renaissance – a food

bank, a public association, grants to restore the area and the first **Fremont Fair**. Artists moved into the cheap brick studios in lower Fremont, setting up the kind of eclectic galleries, shops and cafés that define the neighborhood today. Fremont got funky.

In fact, nary a tale is told of Fremont without the alliterative descriptive "funky." Funky vintage collectibles are sold at the Daily Planet, whose business hours vary according to how much of the day the sun hits this side of the planet. ("We're not into time. We're into light.") Wonderful locally-crafted and yes, funky, furniture can be found next door at Frank and Dunya, a store named after the owners' dead dogs. Dusty Strings sells handcrafted acoustic musical instruments not commonly found anywhere else, like hammer dulcimers, folk harps and the didgeridoo, an aboriginal drone instrument. Around the corner, the **Still Life in Fremont Coffeehouse** draws zealous followers of the café scene from adjoining

Zesto's, a Ballard classic.

neighborhoods, all bespectacled and scribbling, funkily, in notebooks.

As in Ballard, Fremont's tavern life has survived intact throughout the century. Bikers still hang out at The Fabulous Buckaroo and actress Ann-Margret played a waitress for the movie *Twice in a Lifetime* on location at **Poor Richard's Saloon.** The Red Door Alehouse rates high with 22 beers on tap and, just on the south side of the Fremont Bridge, the 318 Tavern proffers pool tables and a hefty and delicious hamburger. Red Hook, Wheat Hook and Ballard Bitter are celebrated Seattle beers brewed at the **Red Hook Brewery**, a state-of-the-art facility with its own taproom in the same restored brick trolley barn. The Trolleyman, a clean and cozy non-smoking bar, bills local talent every Monday night.

Fremont also has some excellent restaurants. The Swingside Café in upper Fremont serves an impressive *huevo ranchero* breakfast. Indulge in pizza and pasta at the Fremont Classic or go

across the bridge to Ponti's for a continental menu and a lookout onto the canal. The view may even be more impressive at Costas Opa, a popular Greek dining room, for it looks out at "the funky Fremont statue that has come to represent the city's soul." *Waiting for the Interurban* is artist Rich Beyer's sculpture of five life-size adults, a baby in arms and a dog (said to have the face of a former mayor), all supposedly waiting for the electric trolley which until the 1930s ran north to the town of Everett. Although some art critics are aghast over this sculpture, it is beloved by the general public. A few blocks northeast, the 15-ft high one-eyed *Fremont Troll* hunkers down under the Aurora Bridge clutching a Volkswagen, its trunk a time capsule of memorabilia (*see picture on page 72*).

The last stop is **Wallingford**, whose residential history is mired in memories of the sounds and stench that rose from the gas plant at the bottom of the neighborhood. The district attracted working-class folk who took special pride in their schools. The earliest school in the area, Latona, was founded in 1889. The Home of the Good Shepherd, a girls' orphanage started in 1906 by the Sisters of Our Lady of Charity, is now a cultural and community center.

In 1907, Wallingford gained Seattle's respect with the opening of Lincoln High, called "the little red schoolhouse" even though it served almost 3,000 students. Interlake Elementary, built in 1902, was transformed 80 years later into the **Wallingford Center**, now the heart of the district. Shops such as the Yazdi Fine Clothing import boutique and the Metropolis stationery shop line the worn hardwood floors of the halls. Outside, the **Garden Spot** nursery serves as a backdrop to the courtyard, where locals sit on balmy days with a *buono punto* (good spot) from the Spot Bagel Company and an espresso cart latte. Other landmarks include the Irish-style Murphy's Pub, the Guild 45th Theatre and the Beeliner Diner.

Left and right, the city's high rainfall lends itself to an interior life.

NORTH OF THE CITY

After Seattle was named America's "most livable city" by *Money* magazine in 1989, much of Puget Sound's young and affluent population settled in the suburbs outside of the city limits, searching for that emblem of prosperity known as "quality of life." Indeed, from the northern frontier of Seattle at 145th Street to the city of Everett, 25 miles north on Gardner Bay, a stretch of satellite communities with award-winning parks and progressive public schools seem to offer the culmination of migratory dreams.

Now, these bedroom communities on the northern tip of King County and the southern stretch of Snohomish County are some of the hottest growth regions in the nation – rapidly developing expanses of verdant rolling hills, tiny lakes and major streams. The entire Puget Sound area, encompassing King, Kitsap,

Preceding pages: Clifford's Restaurant above Kenmore Air Harbor. **Left,** high-tech shadows. **Below,** Microsoft's headquarters.

Pierce and Snohomish counties, grew more than 20 percent from 1980 to 1990. Snohomish County grew at almost double that rate and remains the fastest-growing county in the United States. Its population of 500,000 is still rising.

The earliest settlers – millowners, homesteaders and developers – relied on a steamship line known as the Mosquito Fleet to transport them up and down Puget Sound, but railroads and electric trolleys soon speeded up the flow of goods and passengers. Today's commuters head to their jobs in downtown Seattle or, more likely, to any of the seven business parks on **Technology Corridor**, a path of commercial communities stretching along Interstate 405 between Bothell and Everett. More than 250 electronic, telecommunications and computer businesses cluster on quadrants, campus-like neighborhoods where high-tech execs walk along groomed bike paths at lunch or work out in the company weight room after hours.

The Technology Corridor marketing group began working together in 1985 to create a series of business parks that would be ideal for high-tech companies. It is estimated there are approximately 50,000 jobs located within and around the corridor, and during the past few years the parks have gained national and international recognition. The best known of the corridor's resident companies is Microsoft, founded and run by college dropout Bill Gates, the youngest person to top the Forbes 400 list of richest Americans. In a recent year Microsoft sold about $1.5 billion worth of computer software, while Gates' personal fortune is estimated at $6.3 billion. (*See box on page 201*).

Bothell is the gateway to the corridor, a town of 12,500 people northeast of Lake Washington and nestled in the winding Sammamish River Valley. Only 30 minutes' drive from Seattle or to the Boeing plant in Everett, families settle here for the top-rated Northshore School District, the envy of many regional schools for its high level modernization

and extensive programs for children with special needs. The **Sammamish River biking and hiking trail** joins the Burke-Gilman Trail in Bothell and curves along 33 acres of wetlands south of the river – a natural habitat for wildlife – and continues uninterrupted to the **Marymoor Park** on the east side of Lake Washington. The trail connects by a pedestrian bridge to the north side of the river where **Bothell Landing** serves as a focal point for the community, housing the Northshore Senior Center as well as the local **historical museum**.

Dine on Wedgewood china at **Gerard's Relais de Lyon**, a well-known four-star restaurant, where you'll feel you just beamed down into the French countryside. Downtown Bothell was recently renovated for shopping and the quintessentially quaint **Country Village** shopping center, just north of Bothell, features a select blend of more than 40 shops and restaurants, including European pastries, collectables, Northwest and Amish quilts and a children's

book safari. The quality of the merchandize is exceptional; the atmosphere tranquil and rural.

Also in the vicinity is **Kenmore**, best known for its watersports, its spectacular view of Lake Washington (check out the **Lake Washington Grillhouse and Taproom**) and the **Kenmore Air Harbor**, the country's largest seaplane base. **Mill Creek**, especially affluent, began as a contained community when, in 1976, almost 3,000 homes were developed around a country club and private 18-hole golf course, tennis courts, swimming pools and nature preserve. It was incorporated as a city in 1983. The **Mill Creek Café** draws a large cocktail crowd and well worth sampling are the smoked salmon at **Larry's Smokehouse** and the exquisite oriental feasts in an elaborate Chinese gardens setting at **Imperial Gardens**.

The National Park Service awarded a gold medal to the town of **Mountlake Terrace** for its parks and recreation system, a lavish sprinkling of little neighborhood parks, pocket parks and a 9-hole golf course on Lake Ballinger. The largest and one of the fastest growing commercial and manufacturing centers in the north is **Lynnwood**, sporting a huge middle class, 40 percent of whom are commuters. About 300,000 cars per day pass through the intersection at 196th Street and 37th Avenue, which is rated in traffic terms as Level F ("beyond gridlock"). The **Alderwood Mall** is one of the largest in the state, streets attracting shoppers from Canada and Eastern Washington as well as Puget Sound. Not surprisingly, shoplifting accounts for 75 percent of the criminal offenses reported in Lynnwood. The only truly rural community around here is **Briar**, a small town of fewer than 1,000 citizens whose no-growth policy has kept the town at two grocery stores, one café and occasional horse traffic on the main street.

Flower boxes and hanging planters dot the main street of **Edmonds**, the self-proclaimed "Gem of Puget Sound,"

Flying fish.

a modern community of more than 30,000 on the shore 15 miles north of Seattle. Property values here are such that probably few people under 40 can afford the taxes, much less the mortgage payments, in this growth-resistant town and thus few big business interests bother with the area. But Edmonds, aiming to be the artsy/craftsy town of the Northwest, doesn't mind. Residents know that their prestigious Amtrak station, ferry terminal, waterfront shops, restaurants and stylish parks will continue to draw weekend visitors.

One of three waterfront parks in Edmond's **Brackett's Landing** features the oldest and most popular **Underwater Park** in the state of Washington. It was dedicated as a marine preserve in 1971. Divers can explore the 300-foot long DeLion dry dock which dropped to the sandy bottom in 1935, and numerous other sunken structures. The dock creates a maze-like haven for schools of fish and plant life. Visitors are encouraged to feel the texture of leaves, needles

and tree bark at **Sierra Park**, innovatively designed with the aroma and fragrance of plants in mind. The park provides paths and braille signs for sight-impaired visitors. The Edmonds Beach Rangers lead free guided beach walks during low tide in the summer. Views from **Marina Beach** include the Unocal oil refinery loading dock at Edwards Point just off the beach to the south and the port of Edmonds to the north. At **Olympic Beach**, you can inspect the sea lion sculpture and observe activities at the **Edmonds Fishing Pier**, open year-round to fishermen. Other parks along this stretch of waterfront include the woodsy **Meadowdale Beach Park** and the high, sandy cliffs of **Norma Beach Boathouse**.

At the center of Edmonds is **Old Mill Town**, a living museum with historic mementos, shops and the prosperous **Edmonds Antique Mall** built in the old shingle mill, a wood building with plank floors and looming timbers with many individual sales booths. Everyone

Kenmore is the US's largest seaplane base.

recommends Anthony's Homeport for fine seafood on the waterfront, with Fishhouse Charlie's coming in a close second. Among Edmonds' cultural attractions is a community theater featuring the Driftwood Players and the Cascade Symphony Orchestra.

Even the affluence of Edmonds can't match the opulence of its southern neighbor **Woodway**, where homes are built on lots of at least one acre. The 900 Woodway residents live in grand estates selling for a minimum of $250,000 up to $6 million. Narrow roads lead to gateways from which little can be seen.

Everett (pop. 70,000) was where Tacoma lumberman Henry Hewitt hoped the Great Northern Railroad would site its western terminus. He persuaded investors to develop an industrial timber site on Port Gardner Bay, but although the town boomed in 1891 it went bust almost immediately afterward during the national Panic of 1893. This cycle continued to haunt the town through the next century. Eventually

the city's emphasis on lumber and shingle mills shifted to an economy based on high-technology operations.

In 1966, the Boeing Company constructed the world's largest building in Everett and now employs 23,000 workers in its aircraft plant on a parcel of land next to **Paine Field**, a fog-free commuter airport. Between five and seven of the widebody air carriers fit inside of the structure, and the company has plans to double that capacity during the next few years. Construction of **Homeport Navy**, US Naval Air Station Puget Sound, is slated for completion in Everett during the early 1990s, and is expected to draw an additional 100,000 people into Snohomish County within the next decade. The southern suburbs of Everett, such as the area adjoining **Everett Mall,** have recently been expanding while the downtown core sits empty, awaiting the expected boom. **Colby Square**, a new 16-story city-block long retail and office complex, is designed by city planners to save the downtown area regardless of the cycles of boom and bust.

The late Senator Henry "Scoop" M. Jackson, 1976 presidential candidate, spent most of his life here until his death in 1984; the pristine **Jackson Mansion** remains the pride of the city.

Perhaps the city's most popular tourist stop is the 90-minute tour of the **Boeing Assembly Plant**, followed by the **Heritage Flour Mills** with its inspection of stone grinding mills and an adjacent country store. The Pacific Northwest's largest coffee roasters, **Millstone Coffee Company**, offer a 20-minute tour of their roasting plant. And don't miss the historic **Mukilteo Lighthouse**, built in 1905, or the **Firefighters Museum** on the Everett dock, built for through-the-window viewing. Restaurants abound in the area.

For some quality-of-life-seeking residents, peace of mind comes from knowing that Everett is home to the **Everett Giants**, a minor league baseball team who play under the summer sky on real grass at **Memorial Stadium**.

A Sound knowledge.

BILL GATES: THE MAN BEHIND MICROSOFT

Tom Swift should be as accomplished as Microsoft chairman Bill Gates. Seattle's most heralded resident virtually invented an entire industry that brought him billions of dollars, unparalleled acclaim, fame and all the options success brings. Who wouldn't want to be able to build their 37,000-sq-ft dream house in the lakefront confines of an exclusive enclave in a city that tops the country's most livable polls?

Bespectacled and lanky, droopy-clothed, a shock of hair slipping down the side of his forehead, William H. Gates III, son of a successful Seattle attorney, gained his first programming experience at the city's posh Lakeside School in 1968, when he was 12; at the age of 19, having dropped out of Harvard, he founded Microsoft, which he has since built into the world's leading computer software company. Almost everyone who uses personal computers utilizes his disk operating system (MS-DOS, in its various versions), standard of the IBM-compatible industry. Computers are just humming chunks of electronic equipment until you add the functions software provides. It was part of Gates' genius to realize that software, not hardware, would ultimately dominate.

Gates' success is built on a 1981 coup in which he won IBM's contract for the operating system in Big Blue's new line of personal computers. He also won the right to license DOS to other makers, and today the system is installed in 85 percent of the world's PCs. The rewards: billion-dollar revenues for Microsoft; an almost fortress-like position from which to launch its other software products and a run-up in Microsoft stock value which has put Gates' net worth at $6–7 billion, said to be the 23rd largest fortune in the world, and making him the richest man in America.

The rewards of success are considerable. Gates' $10 million house features a movie theater, underground parking, and a dining pavilion for 100 people. Computer monitors in each room display images from his electronic collection of art, and he indulges his other vice, fast cars, to the maximum.

Fame brings attention from all quarters. The *Wall Street Journal* called Gates "the single most influential figure in the computer industry." *Playboy* splashed him across one of their issues, sandwiched between the Barbi Twins, and purred: "He's the biggest, he's the baddest, he's the ultimate power in software." And a month or two later, devoting six pages to "Mr Software," the *New York Times Magazine* painted a picture of a man whose awed staff believe him to be a technological wizard.

There are detractors. IBM and Microsoft have parted ways, the former allying itself with erstwhile enemy Apple to take on Gates. The federal government has pondered anti-trust allegations, and other software magnates accuse him of running roughshod over the industry. Seattle's biggest celebrity even earned a four-day exposé in one of the papers that painted a sour, gawky portrait of a bumbling bachelor genius.

He claims he's a regular guy. He likes pizza and F. Scott Fitzgerald. He flies coach class. Then off he goes to wander the Microsoft halls, looking to drop in on one of his programmers playing with a new system. He's just an ordinary guy who dominates an entire industry. ∎

One of the main reasons people choose to live in Seattle is, ironically, the ease with which they can go elsewhere. Escaping the urban bustle can be as easy as a brief trip on a ferry to nearby Bainbridge Island, or as bracing as a trek lasting several days across the majestic Olympic Mountains.

Toss a slightly mashed hat into the waters of Puget Sound, claims one writer, and it resembles the Olympic Peninsula. The tip of this peninsula is Mount Olympus, which towers 7,965 feet over the surrounding mountains. The crown is the 922,000-acre Olympic National Park, with glacial rivers that roar down the folds to empty into the Pacific Ocean, the Strait of Juan de Fuca and Puget Sound itself. This park encompasses what may be the last remaining wilderness forest on the United States mainland. Wildlife, both in the mountains and on the shore, is abundant. Among the animals common to the area is the Olympic short-tailed weasel, found nowhere else in the world.

A good measure of rain and fog, coupled with a mild coastal climate, are the essential ingredients of a temperate rain forest. Sitka spruce are the dominant trees in Olympic National Park, and record-sized specimens are much in evidence. The overall impression is one of 80-ft high trees draped in moss, shot through by hazy sunlight. One of the first expeditions to cross the Olympic Mountains on foot took nearly six months, but now, over 100 years later, you can do it in four or five days.

On the way to the peninsula are picturesque towns, one of which, Port Townsend, was designed to be the city Seattle has become today. In the mid-19th century, Port Townsend was set to become the great port of Puget Sound. But when Union Pacific's transcontinental railroad failed to connect to the Port Townsend Southern Railroad, this community faded into elegant obscurity. It has been revived only in the past few decades.

The jewels of Puget Sound are the San Juan Islands. This archipelago gets more sunshine than the surrounding area, so in winter the weather is pleasant; in summer it's even better. Commercial ferries stop at four of the San Juans, which, if time allows, you should definitely explore.

Jagged mountain peaks, temperate rain forests, Victorian towns and remote, sandy islands: all of these are just a few hours from downtown Seattle. "We'll take you to someplace special," is the boast of Washington State Ferries' ads. But, in fact, you may just be there already.

Preceding pages: sailing the Sound; Crescent Lake, Olympic Peninsula; a Northwest anemone field. **Left,** seals off Lopez Island in the San Juans.

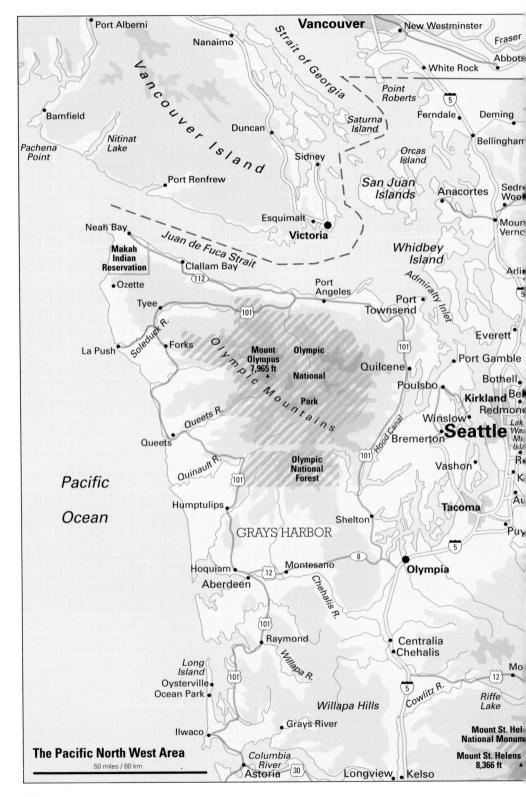

The Pacific North West Area

50 miles / 80 km

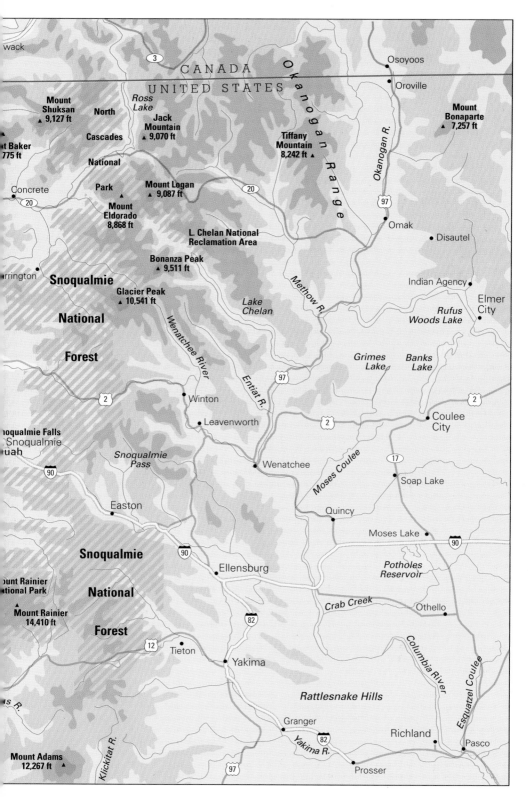

wack

3

C A N A D A

Osoyoos

U N I T E D   S T A T E S

Oroville

Mount
Shuksan
▲ 9,127 ft

North

Ross
Lake

Cascades

Jack
Mountain
▲ 9,070 ft

Tiffany
Mountain
8,242 ft ▲

Mount
Bonaparte
▲ 7,257 ft

t Baker
775 ft

National

Okanogan Range

Okanogan R.

Concrete

20

Park

Mount Logan
▲ 9,087 ft

20

97

Mount
Eldorado
8,868 ft ▲

L. Chelan National
Reclamation Area

Omak

Disautel

rrington

Snoqualmie

Bonanza Peak
▲ 9,511 ft

Glacier Peak
▲ 10,541 ft

Lake
Chelan

Methow R.

Indian Agency

Rufus
Woods Lake

Elmer
City

National

Wenatchee River

Entiat R.

97

Grimes
Lake

Banks
Lake

Forest

2

Winton

2

Coulee
City

noqualmie Falls
Snoqualmie
uah

90

Leavenworth

Snoqualmie
Pass

Wenatchee

2

Moses Coulee

17

Soap Lake

Easton

Quincy

Moses Lake

90

Snoqualmie

90

Ellensburg

Potholes
Reservoir

unt Rainier
tional Park

National

Crab Creek

Othello

▲ Mount Rainier
14,410 ft

Forest

82

12

Tieton

Yakima

Columbia River

Esquatzel Coulee

s R.

Rattlesnake Hills

Granger

Richland

Pasco

Mount Adams
12,267 ft ▲

Klickitat R.

82

Yakima R.

97

Prosser

THE OLYMPIC PENINSULA

A good ferry system, a few artfully placed bridges and excellent roadways link Seattle to the nearby mountains, peninsulas and network of waterways that surround the city. Day trips can easily extend into longer excursions, as each point of interest leads to another. All roads – and ferries – lead in a scenic route back to Seattle.

The Olympic Peninsula lies directly west of Seattle, separated from the mainland by the Kitsap Peninsula.

Catch one of the frequent ferries from the waterfront terminal at the foot of Yesler Way to Winslow for a pleasant 35-minute ride across Puget Sound to **Bainbridge Island**. Infrequent buses run from the ferry dock here but you'll really need a car to do this route justice. Head about 15 miles north on Route 305 over the Agate Pass Bridge onto the **Kitsap Peninsula**, where a quick right on Suquamish Way leads to the grave of Chief Sealth, the Salish Indian chief for whom Seattle was named. Nearby is the **Suquamish Museum** with its excellent collection of Salish Indian artifacts.

Along route 104 is **Poulsbo**, a charming Scandinavian fishing village nicknamed "Little Norway" because of its fjord-like setting on Liberty Bay and the Nordic families who emigrated here a century ago. Famous throughout the state is Poulsbo Bread, baked fresh daily at Sluys Bakery. At certain times of the year Bainbridge Island is redolent with another aroma – that of the strawberries grown here, some of which go to flavor one of the products of the **Bainbridge Winery** just north of Winslow's ferry dock.

Before crossing the bridge over Hood Canal – a channel really – a worthwhile diversion is to **Port Gamble**, one of the last lumber towns to boast a fully operational mill, the oldest in North America. Built by the Pope and Talbot timber families, who arrived by clipper ship from Maine in the 1850s, the town's original trading center serves today as **The Country Store**. Passing over the immense Hood Canal Floating Bridge puts travelers on the **Olympic Peninsula** and into **Port Ludlow**, another timber town which was transformed into a bustling recreation and retirement community in the 1960s: this is the Resort at Port Ludlow, on the site of the original mill, a 148-unit complex against a backdrop of the verdant Olympic Mountains.

To the Strait: Follow the signs north toward the Strait of Juan de Fuca, where picturesque towns dot the shoreline west to the Pacific Ocean. Paradise Bay Road leads to historic **Port Townsend**, Washington's "Victorian City," settled in 1850 and the main port of entry into Puget Sound until the town went bust in the 1890s. Filled with Victorian architecture, elegant inns and restored hotels, the charming shops that line historic Water Street and the Uptown Business District (originally built so that refined ladies did not have to go down to the rough waterfront) make for a delightful afternoon browse. This is a town with a few claims to fame: the Port Townsend Jazz Festival, which draws people from all over the country in July, nearby **Fort Worden State Park**, where *An Officer and a Gentleman* was filmed, and **Manresa Castle**, a 40-room medieval-style castle built by a Prussian baker for his young wife in 1872 from the proceeds of his business of supplying the outgoing ships with bread. Later it was to house Jesuit priests and is now an imposing inn with an excellent kitchen. A ferry service connects Port Townsend and Whidbey Island, making Port Townsend a convenient place from which to island-hop.

Follow Route 20 south to regain Highway 101 at **Discovery Bay**, then look for the giant wooden hamburger that sits in front of Fat Smitty's restaurant, a testament to the Pacific Northwest's penchant for chainsaw art. Grab one of Smitty's "obese burgers," then

Preceding pages: above Olympic's Anderson Glacier. **Left,** Hoh Valley Rain Forest, Olympic National Park.

head for sunny **Sequim** (pronounced *skwim*), famous for its peculiar name and because it sits in the middle of a rain shadow cast by the Olympic Mountains (which means that the sun actually shines here). Six miles northwest lies **Dungeness Spit**, the longest sand spit in the country and famous for its Dungeness Crab, a delicious hard-shell crab available in many of Washington State's restaurants. Stop at the **Olympic Game Farm**, where a few movie star animals now reside: Ben, from *Grizzly Adams*, Charlie, the lonesome cougar, and other animal matinee idols.

Continue on 101 to **Port Angeles**, the largest port city on the northern Olympic Peninsula and the spot either to hop a ferry to Vancouver Island or enter Olympic National Park. Port Angeles boasts a huge harbor and the Clallam County Historical Museum, housed in an historic Georgian-style courthouse; a spectacular view of the Strait of Juan de Fuca and Victoria Island lies to the north, of the Olympic

Mountains to the south. To enter the park, take Race Street to the well-marked **Hurricane Ridge Road** to begin the steep 17-mile ascent to the Ridge, 5,200 feet above sea level.

From here is the best view of **Mount Olympus**, the glaciers and the high country, with the Strait of Juan de Fuca and Canada's Vancouver Island in the distance. No roads lead into Mount Olympus, only hiking trails; in winter months, Hurricane Ridge is the only place in the Olympics from which to cross-country and downhill ski. Mount Olympus towers 7,965 feet over the surrounding mountains.

Follow 101 for 5 miles beyond Port Angeles as it curves south around **Lake Crescent**, an immense cobalt-blue glacier lake surrounded by tall-timbered forest; Lake Crescent Lodge, on the southern shore, is where Franklin D. Roosevelt stayed in 1937, immediately before he signed the act to create the 922,000-acre **Olympic National Park**. Head west along 101 and south down Soleduck River Road to Sol Duc Hot Springs and resort where, for a minimal fee, the Olympic-size pool or hot (102–109° F) mineral pools are open to guests and non-guests. A lovely 1-mile hike through the rain forest leads to **Soleduck Falls** and another none-too-fancy geothermal spring, Olympic Hot Springs. Rocks dam up the waters to form soaking pools, many of which are so shallow a person must lie completely flat to benefit from the springs.

Neah Bay: Seventy-two miles west of Port Angeles along route 112 at the northernmost tip of the state lies the remote Indian fishing and whaling village of Neah Bay on the **Makah Indian Reservation**. Ivan Doig's *Winter Brothers*, the journal of a man who lived with the Makah Indians during the 1800s, offers modern readers fresh insight into the ancient Makah culture. Today sportsfishing for sturgeon and shark is a big attraction, while non-fishermen can enjoy whale-watching during the spring months. Nearby

Port Townsend was once wealthier than Seattle.

Tatoosh Island hosts elephant seals.

Neah Bay is renowned for its Makah Cultural and Research Center and the $2 million museum filled with Northwest Indian artifacts, such as a replica of a longhouse that served as the hub of Makah village life and photomurals from turn-of-the-century pictures by Edward S. Curtis. Most of the Indian artifacts, more than 55,000, were discovered on the archaeological dig at nearby **Lake Ozette**. Considered one of the most important archaeological finds in North America, the original village was buried by a mudslide more than 500 years ago when the clay soil sealed the contents of the houses remarkably, preserving them for posterity. The dig has, sadly, been closed since 1981 because of a lack of funding.

Head south to regain 101, which ambles down the coast on the western edge of the Olympic National Park. Here a long lineup of beautiful rugged beaches and coastal resorts make easy jumping off points into the park. The only sizable community on this side of the peninsula is **Forks**, which lies at the midpoint of the Olympic Peninsula and boasts more rainfall than any other town in the United States, around 140-inches per year. Thirteen miles west of Forks lies **Rialto Beach**, a favorite spot for international fashion photographers to capture their lovely models trying not to shiver in the winter winds. Notable along this stretch of beach is **La Push**, a Quileute Indian village known for its jagged rock-lined beach, interesting offshore rock stacks and famous 16-mile beach walk, certainly one of the finest in the world. It is a favorite spot for those in search of Japanese glass floats (which come in with the tide!). Any of the resorts along this stretch make for an easy drive to the rain forests that line the Hoh, Bogachiel, Queets and in Quinalt rivers.

Only three rain forests exist in the world: in Chile, in New Zealand and on the western side of the Olympic Peninsula. The helpful **Hoh Rain Forest**

Visitor Center, about 19 miles into the park just south of Forks off 101, offers a vast amount of information on the wildlife, botany and history of the rain forest, with three trails (and a wheelchair-accessible paved mini-trail) leading directly into the rain forest. Elk, deer and other animals are often seen off the roads or while hiking the trails. One way to experience the rain forests that surround Lake Quinalt, just south of the Hoh River along 101 and often referred to as "the other rain forest" (the more popular one the Hoh River), is to drive the 25-mile loop around this beautiful glacial lake. **Lake Quinalt Lodge**, a huge old-fashioned cedar hotel built in 1926 on the southern shore of the lake, is a landmark. Several trails lead from the lodge into the awesome rain forest. Try a short hike to **Big Acre**, a grove of huge old-growth trees, or the 10-mile hike to **Enchanted Valley**, where a cozy log chalet awaits weary travelers.

Ocean beaches: Head south on 101, then turn west at colorfully-named

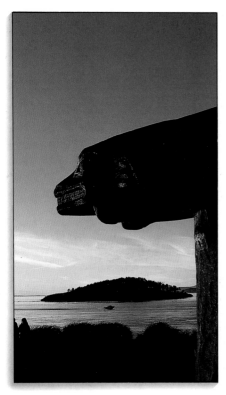

Humptulips to Copalis Beach and on to route 109. Ocean beaches dot the shoreline to the north and south. Moclips boasts both a beautiful stretch of beach and the Ocean Crest Resort, which occupies the spot where tourists in the early 1900s once gathered for beach holidays. Follow the highway south to **Ocean Shores**, which lies on a 6-mile peninsula called **Brown's Point**, entering through the city's peculiar but imposing stone and cement gateway.

Originally homesteaded in the 1860s, Ocean Shores did not become an incorporated city until 1970 when investors, including singer Pat Boone, got the town under way. Today Ocean Shores is considered one of the major recreational spots in the state for beachcombing, fishing in both freshwater and surf (27 miles of freshwater canals are left over from the town's original Venetian concept) and clamming during the summer months; winter storm watching is high on the list of activities. At the tip of Brown's Point sits the marina, from which a small passenger ferry travels back and forth to the coastal town of **Westport** on the peninsula at the other side of **Gray's Harbor**. (Westport is also reachable from Aberdeen at the inland end of the harbor.)

Take 109 from Ocean Shores (or 105 from Westport) to the adjoining Grays Harbor communities of Aberdeen and Hoquiam, twin lumber towns that lie at the base of the harbor. Discovered by Captain Robert Gray in 1792 (just days before Vancouver sailed into the harbor to claim unsuccessfully the land for Canada), **Aberdeen** and **Hoquiam** share a rich history of fishing and shipping timber from the harbor which continues today; Grays Harbor, the only deep-water port on the outer Washington coast, is a major terminal for transporting lumber to international targets. Through the Seaport Authority's Tall Ships Project, the tall ship *Lady Washington*, a reconstruction of the ship sailed by Captain Gray now docks in the **Grays Harbor Historical Shipyard**, a

Whidbey Island can be reached from the Olympic Peninsula.

working shipyard that constructs and maintains these ships. A later ship, the *Columbia*, became the first American vessel to circumnavigate the world. The *Lady Washington* makes frequent cruises, two or three times a week April-June, twice as often in July and August.

Long Beach Peninsula: A sidetrip south on 101 to route 6, then south again along Willapa Bay leads to one of the nicest stretches of beach in Washington State, the Long Beach Peninsula. A 3½-hour drive from Seattle, the freeway turns into a wonderful span of timbered highway just past the state capital of Olympia, then winds south through the many small towns that dot Willapa Bay. Long Beach Peninsula is a 28-mile stretch of ocean beach. The lively town of **Long Beach** is a mini-Coney Island: the main drag filled with huge chainsaw art sculptures (a near-naked mermaid, the Louis and Clark duo and more) and Marsh's Free Museum, where nothing is actually free. The historic town of **Oysterville** had its hey-day during the Gold Rush with a booming oyster trade, shipping oysters to San Francisco at $1 each. The lovely old homes still standing here were made from redwood shipped from California in oyster boats.

To close the loop around the Olympic Peninsula, follow route 12 east to 108. Go north 12 miles to regain 101, a winding road that hugs the western edge of Hood Canal. The area is renowned for its oysters and rocky beaches – at the northern tip lies **Quilcene**, home to the world's largest oyster factory, where fresh oysters and clams can be had to steam or to bake later; in fact, most of the stores in the area carry copies of *Oyster Cookery* just for this purpose.

Back to Seattle: Several routes lead back to Seattle. North of Quilcene, catch 104 to take the route over the Hood Canal Bridge and return to Seattle via the Winslow Ferry, the fastest way back to the city unless ferry traffic is backed up. Or bypass Poulsbo and catch a ferry from Kingston to Edmonds, only 20 minutes north of Seattle.

The Elwha River is colored by glacial flour.

ISLANDS AND PEAKS

Between Seattle and Tacoma in the Puget Sound is **Vashon Island**, an easy 20-minute ride on the Fauntleroy Ferry from West Seattle and a perfect island to explore by bicycle, although the uphill walk from the ferry dock is not for everyone. Originally a counterculture retreat, this woodsy little island has gradually become interesting to mainlanders and tourists and many island-based companies – Stewart Brothers Coffee company, one of Seattle's most popular coffees roasters, and K-2 Skis, Inc., which supplies the world's top skiers with equipment – are based here. Drive the length of the island to the southern tip and catch a ferry to Tacoma for a stop at Point Defiance Park, right on the water's edge, complete with a zoo and aquarium.

Easily accessible from Seattle (and from the Olympic Peninsula) are the **San Juan Islands**, nearly 200 islands in Washington State's northwest corner (in the Strait of Juan de Fuca) that are always a memorable journey – whether you arrive by float plane, by chartered sailboat, by the *Victoria Clipper* passenger ferry that leaves Seattle daily, or by the most common route: the Washington State Ferry that stops at four major islands at least five times daily on its rounds from the mainland to Canada's Vancouver Island.

The islands vary in size – as small as a pinpoint, like the Peapod Rocks, which barely break the surface of the water, or as large as lung-shaped **Orcas Island** with its 2,407-foot high **Mount Constitution**. The green-and-white ferries, some of the oldest and most picturesque in the Washington State fleet, are perfect for a first visit to the San Juans: the boats are comfortable, with big windows and spacious observation decks, and the coffee is hot.

Traveling through narrow fjord-like channels on their 3-hour journey through the islands, the boats pass by sandy beaches, shallow bays, curving sand spits, grassy estuaries, broad fir-forested slopes and then past the arching red-barked trunks of madrona trees that cling to the basalt branches and rock balustrades above the clear saltwater. The islands are most notably home to a handful of residents: large pods of Orca (killer whales), hundreds of seabirds, harbor seals, otters, bald eagles and thousands of brown rabbits. The air is salt-braced and sometimes misty, but it doesn't often rain in the San Juans. Blocked by the Olympic Mountains, water-laden clouds dump most of their load on the Pacific coastline of Washington State. The islands, however, lie in what is called a rain shadow, receiving a sprinkling of about 22 inches a year.

Each island is unique, but the flat rural terrain of **Lopez** (30 sq. miles), **Shaw** and **San Juan** islands (55 sq. miles) are best for bicycling. Orcas Island, dominated by Mount Constitu-

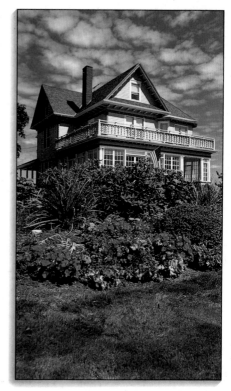

tion, is more difficult for bicyclists: rolling hills, narrow shoulders and hairpin curves. All islands are resplendent with meadows, farms, forests, fields and outcroppings of rock covered with soft yellow grasses.

Minimal facilities: The ferry landings on Lopez, Shaw and Orcas Island have few if any tourist facilities. (Lopez has none at the landing, but a few inland.) Shaw Island has a small esoteric grocery store at the dock, maintained by nuns from Our Lady of the Rocky priory, and a campground on the south shore. Orcas has a well-stocked grocery store, hotel and several restaurants near the dock. On San Juan Island, the ferry docks at the foot of **Friday Harbor**, a small village of quaint restaurants, hotels and shops. (Reservations for overnight accommodations on all islands, particularly during the summer, must be made months in advance.)

Of the four islands, San Juan and Orcas hold the most interest for tourists. San Juan Island is the site of a territorial dispute between Great Britain and the US over 100 years ago with the camps of the opposing armies now state parks. At the island's north end, visit charming **Roche Harbor**, once mined for limestone (the quarries and kilns are still visible). A 100-year-old log cabin and 1850 hotel, with its delightful flower garden at the harbor's edge, stand side by side. Luncheon guests frequently arrive here by chartered planes that land on a nearby grass field. In Friday Harbor, be sure to visit the **Whale Museum** at 62 First Street North, three blocks from the ferry landing.

Orcas Island was not named after the black-and-white Orca whales that sometimes surface just offshore. It was named in 1792 by explorer Francisco Eliza after his patron, the viceroy of Mexico: Don Juan Vincene de Guemes Pacheco y Padilla Orcasiteos y Aguayo Conde de Revilla Gigedo. (There's an Orcas in there somewhere.) Since the 1890s, when the first passenger ferries came to the San Juans, Orcas has been a

Rosario Resort, Orcas Island.

tourist destination. Today, the tiny villages of Orcas Landing, Eastsound, West Sound, Deer Harbor and Olga have minuscule grocery stores, restaurants and shops. Charming bed-and-breakfast inns are scattered throughout the island with the only establishment resembling a destination resort being **Rosario**, the 1904 estate of shipbuilder Robert Moran.

Nearby **Moran State Park** was named after him following his gift of more than 3,600 acres of forested land, mountain lakes and streams surrounding Mount Constitution to the state of Washington. A paved road and hiking trail both wind to the top of the mountain where, on a 50-foot high stone lookout tower, is "a facsimile of military fortifications built by mountain tribes in the Caucasus Mountains of Russia during the twelfth century," say Marge and Ted Mueller in their thorough guidebook, *The San Juan Islands*. Up the stone steps visitors have a 360-degree view of the islands and, on a

clear day, of the volcanos of the Cascade Mountain Range on the mainland. The islands are a popular subject with writers; at least two dozen books dealing with the region are still in print.

Also easily accessible from the Olympic Peninsula and Seattle is **Whidbey Island**, the longest contiguous island in the United States, which sits northwest of Seattle in Puget Sound and boasts a colorful history, rolling hills, fertile farmlands and rocky beaches. From Seattle, take Interstate 5 north 45 minutes to **Mukilteo**, where a 15-minute ferry crosses the channel to **Clinton**. If starting from the peninsula, take the Keystone Ferry from Port Townsend. Follow the signs to **Langley**, a lovely town perched on a cliff overlooking Saratoga Passage. Spectacular Sound and mountain views provide a picturesque backdrop to the stylish century-old shops, restaurants, art galleries and inns. Historic **Coupeville** is the other town of note on Whidbey, with its Victorian homes and quaint

Snoqualmie Station.

shops that include the **John Alexander Blockhouse**, built in the mid-1800s to keep hostile Indians at bay.

At the northern tip of the island lies **Deception Pass State Park**, the most visited park in the state of Washington. More than 3 million people visit here each year and cross the enormous bridge that spans Whidbey and the adjacent Fidalgo Island. **Anacortes**, at the tip of **Fidalgo Island**, is the largest town on the two islands and is known primarily as the place to catch a ferry to the San Juan Islands or to Canada. Anacortes is also home to totem-pole carver Paul Luveram, whose totem poles are displayed all over the world and can be seen in a colorful line-up adjoining his home on E Avenue.

Friendly LaConner: Cross Route 20 to the mainland and head for the bustling tourist town of **LaConner** (only an hour's drive from Seattle north on Interstate 5), a fine example of what energetic townspeople can accomplish by promoting their history and staging an-nual events to restore a dying town. Tourists arrived in droves, far exceeding the wildest dreams of local entrepreneurs in the 1970s, who had filled their tiny shops on First and Second streets with art galleries, antique stores, restaurants, boutiques and country stores. Now the best known town in the **Skagit Valley**, LaConner's claim to fame is tulips as busloads of flower-happy tourists make treks here each April for the Skagit Valley Tulip Festival, then head into town for the parades, flower shows, streetfair and dances.

Because of the area's beauty, Northwest artists like Morris Graves, Mark Tobey and Guy Anderson chose to live here and paint remarkable landscapes of the area. Several of the in-town eateries offer waterfront dining and surely there must be more ice cream here than anywhere else in the state. The **town hall**, built as a bank in 1880, and the 1869 cabin of Magnus Anderson vie with the 1891 22-room **Gaches Mansion** on Second Street for most popular old

Morning dew in the Cascades.

structures. The mansion is a wonderful example of Victorian architecture right down to the widow's walk that overlooks the Skagit Valley. Just over the **Rainbow Bridge** outside town is **Hope Island**, with one of the most pristine beaches in all of the Pacific Northwest – Sneeoosh Beach.

LaConner makes a perfect jumping off point to many of the nearby attractions. Cross Swinomish Channel by the Rainbow Bridge to visit one of the earliest Indian communities built by Christian missionaries. Back on the mainland head through the Skagit Valley to Chuckanut Drive, a fairly famous piece of roadway once part of the old Pacific Highway and now one of the most scenic drives in the state. The roadway curves north and follows the water up to **Bellingham**; along this stretch are several top-notch restaurants mostly specializing in oysters and sea food; Teddy Bear Cove nudist beach (no signs, just look for the cars) and pretty **Larrabee State Park** located south of Belling-ham, Washington's first state park.

The North Cascades, which lie east of Seattle and divide the Eastern and Western parts of the state, are 700 miles in length and run from Northern California, where they join the Sierra Nevada Range, to the Fraser River just south of Vancouver, BC. Visible on clear days to the east, the **North Cascades'** towering peaks are so reminiscent of the Alps that they have been nicknamed the "American Alps." Five hundred miles of scenic highway loop through the 505,000-acre national park, traversing snow-covered mountains, rushing rivers and the many pretty towns scattered along the way.

Leave Seattle on Interstate 405 north to highway 522, then take the Woodinville exit to the Northwest's largest winery, **Chateau Ste Michelle**. (The state's oldest winery, the Columbia Winery, is just across the street.) A clever replica of a French chateau, Chateau Ste-Michelle offers daily wine tastings and tours, plus summer con-

One-stop shopping, LaConner.

certs featuring big-name entertainers (*see page 165*).

Follow Highway 2 to Highway 9 and into the town of **Snohomish**, once an active logging town (founded in 1859, it is one of Washington's oldest communities) and now the self-proclaimed "antique center of the Northwest." Its downtown historic district is loaded with antique stores, most within a 4-block radius. Head east on Route 2 and follow the Skykomish River through the conifer forests of the **Mount Baker-Snoqualmie National Forest**; the jagged peaks of the Cascade Mountains loom ahead.

The road is especially scenic in the fall, when vine maples lend a distinctive scarlet color to the landscape. At **Wallace Falls State Park**, a 7-mile roundtrip trail leads to the impressive 365-foot cascade, and a view of an imposing **Mount Index**, nearly 6,000 feet high. Kayaking, fishing and river-rafting are popular activities along "the Sky," and many trailheads originate

along the route. Stop at the United States Forest Service Ranger Station in the town of **Skykomish** for local maps and information. In winter, downhill and cross-country skiing are enthusiastically pursued at **Stevens Pass** (elevation: 4,061 feet), near Leavenworth, and at **Mission Ridge**, located 13 miles southwest of Wenatchee.

Twin Peaks country: Highway 20 west through the beautiful Methow Valley intersects Interstate 5 west of Burlington and, from there, it's an hour's drive back to Seattle. Interstate 90 bisects the Cascade range east of Seattle and heads into Eastern Washington. The valley surrounding the base of the mountains is rich dairyland and Highway 203 leads through several charming small towns, especially Duvall, the original Northwest counterculture town (that still boasts the Silver Spoon Restaurant, famous in its hey-day for folk music and bean sprouts) and Carnation, home of the Carnation Research Farm, where self-guided tours reveal the mysteries of the pasteurization process.

Well worth a visit is sensational **Snoqualmie Falls**, a 268-foot avalanche of water (100 feet higher than Niagara), above which sits the internationally famous **Salish Lodge**, known world-wide for its appearance in the *Twin Peaks* television series, but better known locally for its fabulous Paul Bunyan-size country brunches. The small town of **North Bend** on Interstate 90 is where much of the series was shot and its **Mar-T Cafe** has seen the demand for cherry pies escalate dramatically. **The Alpine Blossom** gift shop in North Bend carries more than a score of *Twin Peaks* items including T-shirts emblazoned with cherry pies, log ladies, "I Know Who Killed Laura Palmer" and the logo of the Twin Peaks sheriff's department. In addition are mugs, Laura's diary, the "autobiography" of FBI Special Agent Dale Cooper and numerous calendars.

While fall-gazing is about the only pastime here, a bit further on lies **Sun and daughter.**

Snoqualmie Pass, a good place for finding trail heads into the mountains or skiing at the three easily accessible winter ski areas near the Snoqualmie Summit. Seattle is about 30 minutes away on Interstate 90.

The Mountain: While Seattleites refer to other mountain peaks by name, 14,000-ft Mount Rainier is called "The Mountain." Visible for more than 200 miles in every direction, its cone rises thousands of feet higher than any of the other peaks in the Cascades as it looms up southeast of the city.

First named Tahoma by the Indians, then renamed Rainier in 1792 by Canadian explorer Captain George Vancouver, the mountain has inspired artists, mountain climbers and entrepreneurs alike with its monumental and breathtaking beauty. One single road loops around the mountain, through miles of national park and timbered canyons. During the winter months, Cayuse and Chinook passes are closed; between May and October the loop trip and the road to Sunrise are open. Climbing Mount Rainier is a challenge and all but experienced climbers must undertake the ascent with a professional guide service, because Mount Rainier, for all its majesty, is dangerous and many people have been killed trying to scale its snow-covered heights.

To reach Mount Rainier and the **Mount Rainier National Park**, leave Seattle heading south on Interstate 5. Curve around **Puyallup** (pronounced Pew-allup), site of the Puyallup Country fair each September, then continue on Route 161 with a stop at **Northwest Trek** (just outside of the timber town of Eatonville) for an open-air bus tour through the 600-acre wildlife park: moose, bison and caribou can be seen in their natural habitat.

Follow the **Nisqually River** south to the tiny town of **Elbe**, the only train town this side of Strasberg, Pennsylvania. Here a cluster of cabooses, coaches and an antique steam engine sit in the **Elbe trainyard** – the cabooses are actu-

Mount Rainier from Reflection Lake.

ally a motel and the **Mount Rainier Scenic Railroad** is a working train that chugs into the lush mountain forests three times a day, then transforms into an old-fashioned dining car on weekends. Just behind the depot is the "tiniest church in the world," according to *Ripley's Believe It or Not*.

Only two hours from Elbe is **Mount St Helens**, the active volcano that erupted with unexpected fury in May of 1980. Follow Highway 7 south to Morton and stop for travel information. The volcano's peak is now a gaping mile-wide crater, 2,000 feet deep. Several roads lead to views of Spirit Lake and the volcano itself; the volcanic landscape is spectacular and makes for a wonderful diversion from Elbe.

Follow 706 out of Elbe to **Ashford**, a small town just outside the Longmire entrance to the park and the most convenient place to find lodging outside of the park. **Alexander's Country Inn**, an imposing 1912 hotel turned bed-and-breakfast establishment with an excellent dining room, or **Mountain Meadows Inn**, a rambling 14-acre bed and breakfast property complete with pond, pigs, a nightly campfire with toasted "smoors" and the (remote) possibility of encountering Bigfoot, once heard nearby in the woods, are comfortable places to stay.

From here it's only 6 miles into the park and to **Longmire**, just inside the southwestern border, where the modestly-priced **National Park Inn** is the only lodge open all-year, a simple rustic inn and restaurant, with wildlife museum containing stuffed animals on display. Longmire is the only place in the park to buy gas. Follow the road for a few miles where a short hike into the **Grove of the Patriarchs** leads to the tallest trees in the park. **Paradise**, the most popular destination point in the park, lies ahead (at 5,400 feet) and has paved parking, a controversially-shaped visitor center (that offers guided hikes and slide shows), gift shop and cafeteria. There are spectacular views of the **Narada Falls** and **Nisqually Glacier**, as well as of Mount Rainier from the observation deck.

Paradise Inn, a massive structure on the hill above the visitor's center, is open May through October, with 125 surprisingly inexpensive rooms and a full-service restaurant. Up the highway is **Sunrise**, the closest spot to the mountain (at 6,400 feet); the lodge here offers no accommodation, but has a snack bar, exhibits and dozens of trails.

Up ahead, just off the road on the western edge of the park, is **Crystal Mountain**, where some of the best ski slopes in Washington entice avid skiers to down-hill and cross country throughout the winter. In the summer, chair lifts are used to catch a glimpse of Mount Rainier, while tennis, horseback riding and easy park access all lure tourists. Head out of the park to **Greenwater** with a stop at the **Naches Tavern**, the perfect place for après ski. A fireplace, homemade food, comfortable chairs, a jukebox and pool tables await.

Left, moving up mountains. **Right**, branching out.

TRAVEL TIPS

GETTING THERE

Unless otherwise stated, all telephone numbers are preceded by the area code (206).

BY AIR

Seattle-Tacoma Airport, known as Sea-Tac, is located midway between Seattle and Tacoma. For information on the airport, its services, parking or security, call the Skyline information line, tel: 431-4444. Airport Public Information also has information on services available at Sea-Tac, tel: 433-4645. For information regarding the status of flights, call the airline directly.

Major airlines calling at Sea-Tac include:
Air BC: tel: 1-800-663-8868
Air Canada: tel: 467-7928
Alaska Airlines: tel: 433-3100
America West: tel: 1-800-228-7862
American: tel: 1-800-433-7300 or 1-800-223-5436
British Airways: tel: 1-800-247-9297
Continental Airlines: tel: 1-800-231-0856
Delta: tel: 433-4711
Hawaiian Airlines: tel: 1-800-367-5320
Horizon Air: tel: 1-800-547-9308
Japan Airlines: tel: 1-800-525-3663
Korean Air: tel: 1-800-421-8200
Luftansa: tel: 1-800-645-3880
Northwest Airlines: tel: 433-3500
Qantas: tel: 1-800-227-4500
Scandinavian Airlines: tel: 1-800-221-2350
TWA: tel: 447-9400
US Air: tel: 587-6229
United Airlines: tel: 441-3700

Check the *Yellow Pages* under "Airline Companies" or tel: 1-555-1212 for more information.

AT THE AIRPORT

There are many services available at Sea-Tac to ease the transition from air to ground; some are especially helpful to foreigners. Aside from restaurants, rest rooms, gift shops, and a resort-wear clothing store, there is a foreign currency exchange located on the second level behind the American Airlines ticket counter. Hours: 6am–9pm seven days a week.

At the **US West Communications Center**, located in both the main and north terminals, fax (outgoing only) and copy machines are available as are desks,

telephones and even a small conference room (on a first-come, first-served basis). There are also telephones for the hearing impaired here.

A **nursery** with an enclosed carpeted play area for children, a crib and a nursing room with rocking chairs, will provide relief for travel-stressed parents and children.

A **beauty salon/barber** shop offers not only haircuts and manicures, but also showers. There is a **meditation room/chapel** with services held daily on the mezzanine level. For chaplain, tel: 433-5505.

On the second level of the terminal, **Traveler's Aid** offers an escort service at the airport for children, the elderly or handicapped for a fee. It also has information on transportation from the airport and tourist attractions in the area. Tel: 433-5288.

Operation Welcome provides **interpreters** fluent in 21 foreign languages to aid passengers through customs and immigrations. They also provide assistance in setting up transportation or hotel accommodations by phone at two information booths in the baggage claim area. Tel: 433-5367.

The **Seattle-King County Convention and Visitors Bureau** operates a tourist information booth near the baggage claim area. Tel: 433-5218.

The **lost and found** is located on the mezzanine level. Tel: 433-5312.

Last but not least, **Ken's Baggage**, on the baggage level, room G42B, will take care of all the odds and ends for travelers, like keeping a salmon catch fresh, storing coats and boots, dry cleaning, UPS and Federal Express package services, notary public, ticket and key holding service and much more. Hours: 5.30am-12.30am, seven days. Tel: 433-5333.

BY BUS

Transcontinental bus lines providing services throughout Seattle and the US include:
Greyhound, 811 Stewart Street (corner of Eighth Avenue and Stewart Street). Tel: 624-3456. Greyhound offers the most comprehensive service of scheduled bus routes from Seattle throughout the continent.

BY RAIL

Amtrak, Third Avenue and S. Jackson Street. Tel: 1-800—USA-RAIL. Amtrak connects Seattle with the east via the "Empire Builder" from Chicago and the "Pioneer" from Denver, and with the south via the "Coast Starlight" from Los Angeles. The "Coast Starlight" is the most popular route with beautiful coastal scenery and stops in Tacoma, Olympia, and Vancouver, Washington and Portland along the way. In summer early reservations are essential. **Lost and Found**: tel: 382-4128.

BY ROAD

Major land routes into Seattle are Interstate 5, known as "I-5," which stretches from the Canadian to the Mexican borders; and Interstate 90, or "I-90," which links downtown Seattle eastward to the cities of Chicago and Boston.

Federal and state highways are well-maintained and policed, with refreshment areas and service stations at regular intervals. There are no bridge tolls or highway fees around Seattle.

TRAVEL ESSENTIALS

VISAS & PASSPORTS

To enter the United States you must have a valid passport. Visas are required for all foreigners except Canadians and Britons. Vaccinations are not required for entry unless the visitor is from or has passed through an infected area. In this case, a health record may be necessary. Visas for three months are typically granted upon entry.

Canadian and Mexican citizens who possess a border pass do not need a visa or a passport.

CUSTOMS

Liquor allowance is one bottle per person, free of tax. Cigarette allowance is one carton per person, free of tax.

All gifts received must be declared. There is a $400 exemption for visitors including US residents (not citizens). From $400–1,000 worth of gifts, there is a 10 percent charge. Gifts worth upwards of $1,000 are charged a "duty right" tax which varies by item.

MONEY MATTERS

American dollar traveler's checks are the safest form of currency. If lost or stolen, most can be replaced. In addition, they are as acceptable as cash in most stores, restaurants and hotels. Banks will generally cash large amounts of traveler's checks.

Foreign currency exchange is available at Sea-Tac (*see At the Airport*), major Seattle banks and at some major downtown hotels. Daily newspapers print exchange rates for major currencies. Tel: 243-1231 for updates.

GETTING ACQUAINTED

TIME ZONES

Seattle is within the Pacific Time Zone (same as California), which is 2 hours behind Chicago and 3 hours behind New York City. On the first Sunday in April, the clock is moved ahead 1 hour for Daylight Savings Time, and on the last Sunday in October, it is moved back 1 hour to return to Standard Time.

Without Daylight Savings Time adjustment, when it is noon in Seattle, it is:
3pm in New York and Montreal
8pm in London
4am (the next day) in Singapore and Hong Kong
5am (the next day) in Tokyo
6am (the next day) in Sydney

CLIMATE

The temperature in western Washington, which is considered west of the Cascade Mountain range, is usually mild. Daytime temperatures typically range from 75–79°F (23–26°C) during summer and 41–48°F (4.5–9°C) in winter.

From October through April, Seattle gets 80 percent of its rain. Snow tends to stay in the mountains which keeps the skiers and most everyone else happy.

WEIGHTS & MEASURES

The US uses the Imperial system of weights and measures. Metric is rarely used. Below is a conversion chart.

1 inch	=	2.54 centimeters
1 foot	=	.3048 meter
1 mile	=	1.609 kilometers
1 quart	=	.9464 liter
1 ounce	=	28.3 grams
1 pound	=	453.5 grams
1 yard	=	.9144 meter

ELECTRICITY

The electricity used by residents is called standard, 110 volts. European appliances brought here require a voltage adaptor since European countries use 220–240 volts. Some hotel bathrooms have electrical outlets suitable for use with European appliances.

TIPPING

Tips are intended to show appreciation for good service and should reflect the quality of service rendered. The accepted rate is 15–20 percent of the bill in restaurants, 15 percent for taxis, hairstylists, hotel bellhops and porters.

BUSINESS HOURS & HOLIDAYS

Businesses are generally open from 9am–5pm Monday–Friday and closed on Saturdays, Sundays and public holidays. Banks are usually open from 9am–3pm Monday–Friday, with many staying open on Saturday mornings. Government agencies, such as the post office, most banks and some businesses close on the following holidays:
New Year's Day, January 1
Martin Luther King's Birthday, January 15
Lincoln's Birthday, February 12
President's Day, third Monday in February
Memorial Day, last Monday in May
Independence Day, July 4
Labor Day, first Monday in September
Election Day, first Tuesday after first Monday in November
Veteran's Day, November 11
Thanksgiving, fourth Thursday in November
Christmas, December 25

RELIGIOUS SERVICES

The Church Council of Greater Seattle, 4759 15th Avenue NE. Tel: 525-1213. Provides referrals by denomination.

FESTIVALS

The events listed below are free except where indicated otherwise.

JANUARY

New Year's Eve, celebrations at restaurants, hotels, nightclubs and homes all over town.
Chinese New Year, based on the lunar calendar, is held sometime in January or February in the International District. Festivities include a parade with dragons, dancers, foods, fireworks.

FEBRUARY

Festival Sandiata, at Seattle Center during Black History month.
Artstorm, over 200 art events held throughout Seattle during the last two weeks of the month including films, seminars and architectural tours.
Chilly Hilly Bike Ride, Bainbridge Island, the third Sunday in February. Hop aboard the ferry to Winslow for this 30-mile ride sponsored by the Cascade Bicycle Club.

Fat Tuesday, Pioneer Square district's own Mardi Gras celebration. This week-long event, held the week before Lent, includes a parade, and music, music, music: cajun, R&B and jazz in the clubs and in the streets. Nightclubs in the area charge one cover price that lets people travel from club to club for the evening.
Northwest Flower and Garden Show, at the Washington State Convention and Trade Center, during President's Day weekend. On almost 5 acres of the convention center floor, landscape architects, nurseries and gardeners try their best to outdo each other at over 300 booths. Admission.
Washington State Games, winter competitive sports held in February at various locations.
Tel: 682-4263.

MARCH

Irish Week Festival, includes events such as the St Patrick's Day Dash, an easy 4-mile run along the waterfront from Jake O'Shaughnessey's on 100 Mercer Street to the Kingdome. Tel: 763-3333.
St Patrick's Day Parade, March 17. Parade travels from City Hall to Westlake Center featuring bagpipes, Irish dancers, marching bands and the ritual laying of the green stripe down Fourth Avenue.
Whirligig, Seattle Center House at Seattle Center hosts this indoor carnival for kids from about mid-February to early-April. Free entertainment; small fee for rides.
All Fools' Day Parade and **Bassett Bash**, downtown Woodinville. Parade, great food, Bassett Hound shenanigans.

APRIL

Daffodil Festival and **Grand Floral Parade**, in Tacoma, one of the country's largest floral parades. Tel: 627-6176.
Skagit Valley Tulip Festival, held on 1,500 acres of colorful tulip fields. Bicycle and bus tours are popular. Tel: 1-42-TULIP.
Artsplash, at Redmond.

MAY

Northwest Folklife Festival, Memorial Day weekend at Seattle Center. Music, dancing, ethnic food and crafts from more than 100 countries. Many people take this opportunity to pack their instruments and join jam sessions which spring up all around the Center's lawns. Tel: 684-7300.
Opening day of yachting season, held first Saturday in May. Yachting Clubs bring out a parade of boats from Lake Union to Lake Washington. Also features a regatta of rowing teams. Seattle Yacht Club, tel: 325-1000.
International Children's Festival, at Seattle Center. Children's performers and theatrical groups from around the world come to entertain at this week-

long festival. Some events are free, but most charge admission.

Pike Place Market Festival, on Memorial Day weekend. Clowns, jazz musicians, and a "kids alley" full of craft activities round out the usual entertainment at the Market.

Seattle International Film Festival, all month long, at various theaters (concentrated in the University district and Capitol Hill). Tel: 324-9996.

University Street Fair, University Way. Held the third weekend in May, the fair features hundreds of artists' booths in a 10-block area. Mimes, clowns and street entertainment. Tel: 523-4272.

JUNE

Fremont Arts and Crafts Fair, on 34th Street. Tel: 632-1285. A well-known neighborhood fair, featuring live music, local crafts, jugglers, mimes and colorful people in general.

Mainly Mozart Festival, Meany Theater, University of Washington. Tel: 443-4740. Mid-June. Seattle Symphony's three-week tribute to the master and other 18th-century composers in acoustically pleasing Meany Hall. Tickets are pricey but worthwhile.

Snoqualmie Railroad Days, Snoqualmie. Tel: 746-4025. Steam trains from the late-19th century. A 10-mile ride from the Snoqualmie depot takes visitors up to the historic depot and quaint town of North Bend.

Mercer Island Summer Arts Festival, 8236 SE 24th Avenue, Mercer Island. Usually held the last weekend in June. The downtown area overflows with display booths of local artists. Sponsored by the Mercer Island Visual Arts League.

Microbrewery Festival at the Herbfarm, 32804 Issaquah Fall City Road, Fall City. Tel: 784-2222. Breweries from the Northwest, Canada and Utah offer samples of their brews, along with barbequed chicken, knockwurst and Bavarian-style beer music. Admission for taste testing.

Special Olympics, at various locations depending on event. Tel: 362-4949. Olympic-style events for the mentally disabled.

In June, July, August and September the Downtown Seattle Association sponsors **lunchtime concerts** in various parks and plazas. For a schedule, call the Daily Events Line: tel: 684-8582.

JULY

Fourth of July Parades: Downtown Bothell, Issaquah, Winslow (on Bainbridge Island) and other neighborhoods; check newspaper for listings.

Fourth of July-Ivar Festival and Fireworks, Mrytle Edwards Park. Tel: 587-6500. A fishing derby, concerts and food at this waterfront park during the day. A fireworks display over Elliott Bay at dusk.

Seafair, late July–early August. Seattle's most spectacular summer festival is really a bunch of events, parades and celebrations that take place over a 2½-week period (usually the third weekend in July to first week in August) in different parts of the city. Highlights include: the milk carton derby races at Green Lake, the Blue Angels Air Show (acrobatic flights), Hydroplane Races on Lake Washington, Bon Odori, festival of dances and food sponsored by the Seattle Buddhist church, Chinatown International District Summer Festival, Hing Hay Park, Soul Festival, including parade, and the Torchlight Parade, a grand, nighttime parade through downtown.

Bellevue Jazz Festival, City Park, 10201 NE 4th Street. Tel: 451-4106. Northwest jazz artists entertain outdoors for three days beginning the third weekend in July. Tickets are needed; one concert in series is free.

Bite of Seattle, mid-July on the grounds at Seattle Center. A taste-testers delight with over 60 restaurants participating. Pay according to your tastes.

Emerald City Flight Festival on Boeing Field, near the Museum of Flight. Includes: air shows, parachuters and food.

Pacific Northwest Arts and Crafts Fair, 301 Bellevue Square, Bellevue. Tel: 454-4900. Sponsored by the Bellevue Art Museum features exhibits and booths throughout the mall including artists at work demonstration booths, musical concerts at the fountain outside The Bon and entertainment for children.

King County Fair, at the fairgrounds in Enumclaw. Tel: 825-7777. Begins third Wednesday in July and continues for five days of music, rodeos, logger competitions, crafts and food. The oldest county fair in the state.

Lake Union Wooden Boat Festival,1010 Valley Street, at the south end of Lake Union. Tel: 382-2628. Features rowing, sailing and boat building competitions, workshops, food, crafts, and water taxis from the Center for Wooden Boats.

McChord Air Show, at the air force base in Tacoma. Tel: 984-5637.

San Juan Island Dixieland Jazz Festival, at Friday Harbor. Tel: 378-5509.

AUGUST

Evergreen State Fair, Monroe. Tel: 794-7832. Held third week in August–Labor Day weekend. A country fair with big-name country stars, plus rodeos, logging competitions, carnival rides, and a chili cook-off.

Seattle Tennis Club Open Tennis Tournament and Challenger Series, during first week in August (order tickets well in advance). Tel: 324-3200.

Santa Fe Chamber Music Festival, Meany Hall, University of Washington. Tel: 622-1392.

Camlann Medieval Faire, Carnation.

Evergreen Classic Benefit Horseshow, Redmond.

Roots Picnic, at Gas Works Park, usually held in September. Gathering of descendants of pioneer families of the black community.

Bumbershoot, music and arts festival at Seattle Center, Labor Day weekend. Big names and local acts perform at this music event. A moderate entry fee is charged which entitles guests to attend hundreds of concerts in all styles of music with soloists and bands performing on stages (and on the grass) throughout the Center complex.

Fiesta de la Sixth de Septiembre, celebrating Mexico's independence from Spain.

Leavenworth Autumn Leaf Festival, last weekend in September, with fall colors, parade, music and free events. Held in the Bavarian-style mountain village of Leavenworth, about 120 miles east of Seattle. Tel: 509-548-5807.

The Puyallup Fair, Western Washington's State Fair, in Puyallup, about 35 miles south of Seattle. A 17-day long country fair extravaganza starting in early September.

OCTOBER

Festa Italia, Seattle Center, held near Columbus Day. Italian dancing, food. Tel: 684-8582.

Greek Festival, St Demetrios Church, 2100 Boyer Avenue E. Tel:325-4347. Held in early October at this Byzantine church with folk dancing, arts and crafts and Greek cuisine.

Issaquah Salmon Days, Main Street. The street is closed to traffic and open to arts and crafts booths with artists from all over the Northwest. Street entertainment, mime, clowns, and musicians are here as well as the salmon jumping up to the hatchery. Big salmon cookout. Tel: 392-7024.

Mushroom Show at the University of Washington, Center for Urban Horticulture. Features 150–300 species of mushrooms. Tel: 522-6031.

Halloween, parades, festivities and pranks at night-clubs and bars. Many shopping centers offer free candy treats for children roaming the mall in costumes.

NOVEMBER

Harvest Festival, late in the month.

Model Railroad Show, Pacific Science Center. Tel: 443-2001. Held during Thanksgiving weekend.

DECEMBER

Christmas Ships, mid-December. Lighted and decorated boats parade around Lake Union and Lake Washington, making stops at public parks while choral groups entertain. Check newspaper for updated schedule.

A Christmas Carol at the ACT Theater, 100 W. Roy Street, Seattle Center. Tel: 285-5110. An annual production of the ever-popular, classic Dickens tale.

Christmas Tree-lighting and caroling in the Barvarian-style village of Leavenworth in the Cascade Mountains. Tel: 509-548-5807.

Community Hanukah Celebration, Stroum Jewish Center, Mercer Island. Tel: 232-7115. Arts and crafts, children's games and candle-lighting ceremony.

The Nutcracker presented by the Pacific Northwest Ballet, Opera House, Seattle Center. Runs from early December through New Year's. Tel: 547-5900.

COMMUNICATIONS

MEDIA

PRINT

The major daily newspapers in Seattle are the *Seattle Post-Intelligencer* in the morning and the *Seattle Times* in the afternoon. On Sunday, the two combine into one large edition. Friday tabloid sections in both papers are useful guides to weekend events. The *Weekly*, a tabloid news-magazine, prints a guide to the week's recreation and entertainment opportunites, including visual arts, theater, music and film. Also included is dining and shopping information. *Puget Sound Business Journal*, is a weekly that covers business activities in the Puget Sound area.

Foreign language newspapers include the *North American Post*, a Japanese daily, the *Seattle Chinese Post,* and *Hispanic News* (a weekly).

Newsstands that sell foreign newspapers and periodicals include:

Bulldog News, 401 Broadway E and 4208 University Way NE. Tel: 328-2881.

Steve's Broadway News, 204 Broadway E. Tel: 324-READ.

Read All About It International Newsstand, 98 Pike Street (in Pike Street Market). Tel: 624-0140.

Public libraries offer reading rooms stacked with periodicals and, at the main branch, a good selection of foreign newspapers and periodicals (ask at the Humanities desk). The main library is located at: 100 Fourth Avenue (Fourth and Madison) and is an excellent place to browse. Hours: 9am–9pm Monday–Thursday, 9am–6pm Friday–Saturday; 1–5pm Sunday from September to end-June. Tel: 386-4636.

TELEVISION

Excluding cable television, seven major stations serve the Seattle area. The public broadcast station is KCTS. It does not air commercials, but supports itself through public donations and grants.

Channel		
4	KOMO	ABC affiliate
5	KING	NBC affiliate
7	KIRO	CBS affiliate
9	KCTS	PBS
11	KSTW	independent station
13	KCPQ	independent
22	KTZZ	independent

RADIO

AM Stations:

570	KVI	popular music, sports
630	KCIS	religious music, interviews
710	KIRO	news, sports
820	KGNW	religious
880	KIXI	hits from '40s, '50s, '60s
950	KJR	classic hits
1000	KOMO	news, adult contemporary
1050	KBLE	religious
1090	KING	news, talk shows
1150	KEZK	business, talk shows, news
1210	KBS	goldies from '50s, '60s, '70s
1250	KKFX	rhythm and blues
1300	KMPS	country
1420	KRIZ	urban contemporary music, blues, jazz, gospel
1590	KZOK	oldies

FM Stations:

88.5	KPLU	jazz and news. Public Radio affiliate.
89.5	KNH	contemporary hits, run by Seattle School District
90.3	KCMU	new wave alternative music
93.3	KUBE	contemporary hits
94.1	KMPS	country
94.5	KUOW	classical, ethnic, swing, public radio, talk shows
95.7	KLTX	soft rock
96.5	KXR	adult rock
97.3	KBSG	rock from '50s, '60s and '70s
98.1	KING	classical
98.9	KEZX	jazz, soft rock, folk, reggae
100	KISW	rock
100.7	KSEA	easy listening
101.5	KPLZ	oldies, sports, traffic
102.5	KZOK	classic rock
103.7	KBRD	easy listening
105.3	KCMS	contemporary Christian music
106.9	KKNW	progressive, jazz, new age
107.7	KNDD	cutting edge, alternative rock

POSTAL SERVICES

The main post office in Seattle is located at 415 First Avenue N. Tel: 285-1690. Hours: 8.30am–5pm Monday–Friday. Travelers who are uncertain of their address in a particular town, may receive mail by having mail addressed in their name, in care of General Delivery at the main post office of that town. Mail will be held there for pick up.

Be sure to include a five-digit zip code for all addresses within the US. Information about zip-codes may be obtained from any post office. Overnight delivery service, Express Mail, is also provided by the post office and some private companies. Check in the *Yellow Pages* under "Delivery Service."

As well as at post offices, stamps may also be purchased from vending machines, which can often be found in hotels, stores, airports, bus and train stations.

TELEPHONES, TELEX & FAX

For long distance calls within the 206 area code, the usual seven-digit phone number must be preceded by a "1". For long distance calls outside the local 206 area code, first dial a "1", the area code and then the phone number. For assistance in long distance dialing, first dial zero and an operator will assist you. Phone numbers that are preceded by "1-800" are free of charge.

To dial other countries (**Canada** follows the US system), first dial the international access code "011", then the country code: **Australia** (61); **France** (33); **Germany** (49); **Italy** (39); **Japan** (81); **Mexico** (52); **Spain** (34); **United Kingdom** (44). If using a US phone credit card, dial the company's access number below, then "01", then the country code. Sprint, Tel: 10333; AT & T, Tel: 10288.

Telegraph services are available through Western Union. Tel: 1-800-325-600.

Fax machines can be found at most hotels and at the airport. Public fax companies are located throughout the city, check the *Yellow Pages* under "facsimile" for the service nearest you.

EMERGENCIES

SECURITY & CRIME

For police, fire or medical emergencies, dial **911**.

The streets of Seattle and most adjoining neighborhoods are safe during the day. However, at night caution is advised. It is best not to walk alone at night on deserted city streets. Lock your car and never leave luggage, cameras or other valuables in view – lock them in the glove compartment or in the trunk. Never leave money or jewelry in your hotel room, even for a short time. Use the hotel's safety deposit service. Carry only the cash you need, using traveler's checks whenever possible.

LOSS OF BELONGINGS

If valuables are lost or suspected stolen, report it to the local police department. A description of the items will be filed and if the items turn up, the police will return them as soon as possible.

Lost Luggage: Most airlines and other transportation companies have insurance for lost customer luggage, but it doesn't hurt to ask the company what its policy is. Be sure to mark all luggage with identification tags. If luggage left at the airport is turned in to Sea-Tac's lost and found (*see At the Airport*), someone from that department will usually bring the luggage to the hotel if getting back to the airport is a problem.

MEDICAL SERVICES

Hospitals and Doctors: Medical care in Seattle is excellent, but prohibitively expensive if a long hospital stay is required. If an illness strikes or medical attention is needed, it pays to have temporary health insurance. Check with your current provider for additional travel coverage.

For **medical emergencies**, tel: 911 or the front desk of your hotel. Most hospitals have a 24-hour emergency room service.

Here are some major hospitals

IN SEATTLE

Children's Hospital and Medical Center, 4800 Sand Point Way, NE. Tel: 526-2000.
Harborview Medical Center, 325 Ninth Avenue (corner of Jefferson Street). Tel: 223-3000.
Providence Medical Center, 500 17th Avenue. Tel: 326-5555.

Swedish Hospital, 747 Summit Avenue. Tel: 386-6000.
University of Washington Medical Center, 1959 NE Pacific Street. Tel: 548-3300.
Valley Medical Center, 400 S. 43rd, Renton. Tel: 251-5185.
Virginia Mason Hospital, 925 Seneca Street. Tel: 624-1144.

IN BELLEVUE

Overlake Hospital Medical Center, 1035 116th NE, Bellevue. Tel: 454-4011.

IN KIRKLAND

Evergreen Hospital Medical Center, 12040 NE 128th, Kirkland. Tel: 821-1111.

Hospital interpretation services offers a 24-hour translation service for hospital patients.Tel: 324-7705 from 8.30am–5pm or 324-7835 after 5pm.

Certain drugs can only be prescribed by a doctor and purchased at a pharmacy. Check the *Yellow Pages* under "Pharmacies" for listings.

GETTING AROUND

MAPS

The King County Convention and Visitor's Bureau in the Washington State Convention Center offers free maps. If these maps are insufficient for a particular destination, the American Automobile Association, better known as "Triple A," can offer advice for planning trips, the best routes to take and detailed maps for a fee. AAA, 330 Sixth Avenue N. Tel: 448-5353.

The Thomas Guides contain detailed street maps in a book format. They are available in most bookstores.

AIRPORT/CITY

Shuttle buses and taxis can be found outside the terminal on the baggage claim level. The exact location of shuttle buses vary depending on destination and carrier. Check with the information booth at the north end of the main terminal on the baggage level. Taxis can be picked up at the north end of the terminal also. STITA (Seattle-Tacoma International Taxi Association) provides services to and from the airport. Tel: 246-9999.

Bus or van companies that link the airport with metropolitan Seattle or Bellevue include:

The Grayline Airport Express, tel: 624-5813. Or for a detailed recording of schedules and stops, tel: 626-6088. Operates buses every 20-30 minutes between the airport and major downtown hotels.

Greyhound, tel: 624-3456. Has several runs to and from the airport and to its downtown station at Eighth Avenue and Stewart Street.

Shuttle Express, tel: 622-1424 or 1-800-487-RIDE. Provides door-to-door van service to and from the airport 24 hours daily throughout the metropolitan Seattle area.

Suburban Airporter, tel: 455-2353. Provides door-to-door service between the airport, Bellevue, Redmond and other eastside suburbs.

Metro Transit, tel: 553-3000. Buses link the airport with various points throughout the city and provide the least expensive method of transportation. The 194 Bus is the most direct, bringing passengers downtown to bus tunnel stops in about 30 minutes. The 174 Bus makes local stops on its way downtown.

Quick Shuttle (in Vancouver, tel: [604] 526-2836; the US, tel: [1-800] 665-2122) operates speedy bus connections between Sea-Tac airport, downtown Seattle (Travelodge, 8th & Blanchard) and downtown Vancouver (Sandman Inn, 180 W. Georgia) eight times daily. Trip between the two cities takes four hours.

Limousines. Washington Limousine Service, a well-established and reliable service, by reservation only. Tel: 523-8000.

LOCAL TRANSPORTATION

Metro Transit bus has both peak and non-peak hour fares. Monthly passes are available. Metro also provides a "Ride Free Area" in the downtown core bordered by the I-5 freeway to the east, the waterfront to the west, Jackson Street to the south and Battery Street to the north. Metro, tel: 553-3000. METRO, 821 Second Avenue, Seattle, WA 98104, Tel: 447-4800 or 684-1739 for TTY/TDD users. **Metro lost and found**: tel: 684-1585. Community Transit: tel: 778-2185.

Metro also operates a **waterfront streetcar**, a 1927 vintage trolley which runs 1½ miles along the waterfront every 20-30 minutes from Myrtle Edwards Park to the Pioneer Square district. Requires exact change. You can also purchase a Metro Visitor Pass which allows one day's unlimited travel on buses and streetcars as well as the monorail. Available at various Metro Customer Assistance offices. Tel: 624-PASS for locations.

The Monorail, which was built for the 1962 World's Fair, runs every 15 minutes between Seattle Center and Fourth and Pine Street to Westlake Shopping Center. The ride is a little under a mile and takes only 90 seconds. It's clean and spacious with big windows.

There are **taxi stands** at major hotels, bus depots, train stations and the airport. Taxi cab fares are regulated. There is an initial hire charge, with each additional mile then costing a flat rate. **Taxi Companies**: Farwest Cab, tel: 622-1717; Graytop Cab, tel: 782-TAXI; Yellow Cab, tel: 622-6500.

RENTAL CARS

A wide selection of rental cars are available. Rental offices are located at the airport and downtown. Generally, a major credit card is required to rent a car and the driver must be 25 and posses a valid driver's license. Local rental companies sometimes offer less expensive rates. Be sure to check insurance provisions before signing anything.

Rental Companies: Avis, tel: 1-800-331-1212; Budget, tel: 1-800-527-0700; Hertz, tel: 1-800-654-3131; National, tel: 1-800-328-4567.

ROAD TIPS

The national speed limit is 55 mph (88 kpm), but outside of populated areas, many states opt for 65 mph (104 kpm). City speed limits usually range between 25–35 mph (40–56 kpm).

Driving around Seattle can be tricky. There are many one way streets and steep hills, but also beautiful views. In the downtown area, which is generally considered to lie between Denny Way and Yesler, the avenues run north and south. The streets run east and west. Streets and avenues can be designated with numbers or names. When locating an address, be sure to note whether the address includes directionals (north, south, east or west). For example, E. Madison Street or Queen Anne Avenue N. will indicate the east or north part of town, respectively.

Avoid driving during the rush hours of 7am–9am and 4pm–6pm. Although extra express lanes open on parts of I-5 and I-90 to help allieviate the backup, it is a time-consuming and sometimes frustrating experience.

A right turn is permitted, after stopping, at a red light unless street signs indicate otherwise.

Parking in Seattle requires that when facing downhill, the front wheels are turned into the curb and when facing uphill, front wheels are turned outward. Doing so will decrease the likelihood of the car rolling downhill. Also be sure to set the emergency brake.

Street signs, usually located on corners, will indicate what type of parking is permitted for that side of the street. However, red-painted curbs mean no parking is allowed and yellow curbs indicate a loading area, for trucks or buses.

There are plenty of traffic police around (except when you need them) who earn their living by passing out fines and having cars towed away. Picking up a towed car is not only inconvenient, but costly (from $40–100 depending on where the car was parked).

Pedestrians always have the right of way.

Although legal, except on freeways, picking up hitchhikers, or hitchhiking, is potentially dangerous.

THINGS TO DO

ATTRACTIONS

Aquarium, 1483 Alaskan Way, (Pier 59 at Waterfront Park). Tel: 386-4320. Seattle's Aquarium, a $5.4 million complex, features an underwater dome with a 360-degree view of Puget Sound sea creatures. The Aquarium houses 14,541 sea mammals and sea shore creatures from around the world on its 200 acres. Open: 10am–7pm during summer and 8am–sunset for the rest of the year. Admission, children age 6 and under free.

Also at Pier 59 is **Omnidome**. Tel: 622-1868. This 70-millimeter, 180-degree screen surrounds viewers with the natural history films shown here, like the eruption of Mount St Helens. Hours: 10am–10pm, April–October; 11am–5pm, November–March. Admission.

The **Hiram M. Chittenden Locks**. Tel: 783-7059. Located in the Washington Ship Canal, the locks raise and lower large fishing vessels, pleasure boats and canoes alike to make the transition from Puget Sound to Lake Union and vice versa. This can be a 6- to 26-ft difference, depending on tides. A **"fish ladder"** with an underwater viewing room allows visitors to watch salmon jumping their way up the ladder and upstream to hatch. A 7-acre **park** and **rose garden** around the locks provide an ideal spot for picnicking and watching the passing boats. Open to the public: 7am–9pm daily. Free.

International District, home for many of Seattle's Asian communities, is located at the southern end of downtown Seattle. Highlights of the area are **Uwajimaya**, a large Japanese supermarket and department store, the **Wing Luke Asian Museum, Kobe Park** and gardens, and the **Chinese Pavilion** in Hing Hay Park. Tours of the district are available, see *Tours*.

Fisherman's Terminal, 1735 West Thurman Street. Presents an opportunity to observe first-hand the workings of one of Seattle's major industries. The piers are open for visitors to stroll and observe hundreds of commercial fishing boats and their crews at work. A newly-built public plaza features signs that detail the development of the local fishing industry. Free. Several excellent seafood restaurants are nearby.

Pike Place Market, at Pike Street and First Avenue, is a bustling marketplace of fresh produce, seafood, artisans, crafts people, gourmet food, street musicians, boutiques, restaurants and much local color. Many describe this as the heart of the city. The **Pike Street Hillclimb**, with its labyrinth of staircases and elevators, connect the market area with waterfront shopping and sightseeing. Free.

Seattle Center, tel: 684-8582. Built for the 1962 World's Fair and home of Seattle's most recognizable landmark, the **Space Needle**. The center's 74 acres form a cultural hub for the city's performing arts groups, housing the **Opera House**, home of the Seattle Opera Company, the Seattle Symphony Orchestra and the Pacific Northwest Ballet; the **Bagley Wright Theater**, the **Seattle Repertory Theater's new house**, and the **Playhouse**, home of the Intiman Theater. Also at the Center are the **Fun Forest amusement park** with a variety of children's rides and arcade games; the **Pacific Science Center**, the **Center House**, with 50 shops and restaurants, the **Coliseum**, which hosts trade shows, concerts and is home of the Seattle Sonics (basketball team); the **Northwest Craft Center**; and more. You can reach the center in 90 seconds via the monorail from Fourth Avenue and Pine Street, in the center of downtown's shopping district.

Pacific Science Center, 200 Second Avenue N. Tel: 443-2870. A hands-on museum with six buildings of science adventure for the whole family. Open: 10am–6pm Monday-Friday, till 7pm on Thursday. Admission, children under 2 free. Features the IMAX theater, laser shows, a planetarium, plus changing and permanent exhibits.

The **Space Needle**, tel: 443-2111. Offers panoramic views of Puget Sound, the Olympic Mountains, the Cascades, and Mount Rainier from its observation deck, 520 feet above ground. Two revolving restaurants at the top turn 360 degrees each hour. Hours: 9am–midnight daily. Admission, children under 4 free. There is no elevator charge for restaurant patrons.

Smith Tower, Yesler Way and Second Avenue. Tel: 622-4004. This 42-story building was the tallest building outside New York City in 1905 when it was completed. The Chinese Room on the 35th floor tells the story of Washington, Alaska and Seattle through intricately carved Chinese characters. An observation deck encloses the room and offers views of Seattle, the Olympics and (sometimes) Mount Rainier. Hours: 10am–10pm daily. Admission.

University of Washington, tel: 543-2000. Its elaborate turn-of-the-century architecture, sculptures, well-designed grounds, a fountain plaza, the Henry Art Gallery, the Medicinal Herb Garden – all reasons to stop by and visit this lovely campus. Gatekeepers hand out free maps of the University grounds. Free.

Washington Park Arboretum, tel: 543-8800. A 200-acre wooded park with plant families from around the world. Guided tours are available by appointment. An authentic Japanese Garden and traditional tea house is located at the south end of the grounds. The arboretum is free and open year-round, but the Japanese Garden is open March through November only. Admission to the Japanese Garden, children age 6 and under free. The visitor center of the arboretum is open: 10am–4pm Monday–Friday, noon–4pm Saturday and Sunday.

Downtown Waterfront, Piers 52–59. The Washington State ferries, Ye Old Curiosity Shop, fresh seafood restaurants, souvenir shops, and a park with elevated walkways that offer wonderful views of Puget Sound and the Olympic Mountains. Free. For the ambitious, stroll along the waterfront past the Edgewater Inn, the *Victoria Clipper* (catamaran to Victoria, Canada) to Pier 70 and visit the shops and restaurants here.

Woodland Park Zoo, 50th Avenue N and Fremont Avenue. Tel: 684-4800. Winner of many awards for its design which simulates the natural habitats of animals, including the African savannah for lions, hippos, giraffes, and zebra; the Nocturnal House, featuring bats, owls, and other creatures of the night; a gorilla habitat, swamps, marshes, a primate house, a petting-farm, pony-rides; excellent gift shop and more. Offers stroller and umbrella rentals. Open: 9.30am–dusk daily all year round. Admission, children under 6 free.

EASTSIDE

Here are telephone numbers of some attractions located in the Eastside:
Bellevue: Champagne Fleet, tel: 286-6232; The Islander, tel: 455-5769.
Bothell: Country Village Shopping Center, tel: 483-2250.
Carnation: Remlinger U-Pick Farms, tel: 451-8740.
Fall City: Herbfarm, tel: 784-2222.
Issaquah: Boehm's Candy Kitchen, tel: 392-6652; Cougar Mountain Zoo, 391-5508.
Redmond: The Balloon Depot, tel: 881-9699.
Woodinville: Molbak's Greenhouse, tel: 483-5000.

GUIDED TOURS

Boeing Plant/Paine Air Field, Highway 526, Everett. Tel: 342-4804. Paine Air Field is located about 15 miles north of Seattle, exit 189 off of Interstate 5. Tours of this commercial aviation plant take place in the world's largest building. Visitors can observe the manufacture of 747s, 767s and future plans for 777s. Tours last 90 minutes, beginning with a 25-minute video presentation of Boeing's history. The tour is free, but space is limited. Tickets are available on a first-come, first-served basis and must be picked up in person at the Boeing Plant. Tickets for the day are handed out at 8am and, in summer, often run out by 9 or 10am. A call in advance is recommended. Children under 10 years are not permitted.

Brewery tours are offered on weekdays by the Rainier Brewing Co., 3100 Airport Way S, tel: 622-2600; and the Redhook Ale Brewery, 3400 Phinney Avenue N, tel: 548-8000. Free.

Chinatown/International District Tours. Tours are run by Chinatown Discovery, tel: 236-0657. Three-hour personally guided tour with a seven-course "dim sum" lunch at a local restaurant included. Mini-tours are scheduled daily in the summer. Admission. **Gray Line of Seattle** (720 S Forest, tel: 624-5077 or 1-800-544-0739; and in the Sheraton Hotel lobby) offers numerous tours including San Juan Islands, Mount Rainier and to North Bend and Snoqualmie Falls of *Twin Peaks* fame.

Kingdome, King Street and Second Avenue S. Tel: 296-3126. Tours of this multi-million dollar indoor stadium are available from mid-April to mid-September when the facililty is not in use by the Mariners (baseball team) or the Seahawks (football team). Telephone ahead to verify times. Admission, children 6 and under free.

Seattle Harbor Tours, Pier 55, Suite 201, at the foot of Seneca Street. Tel: 623-1445. One-hour guided trips along Seattle's waterfront and shipyards.

Skagit Tour operated by the city's utility company, Seattle City Light: a 4-hour excursion to the Diablo hydro-electric project in the North Cascades includes explanatory slide show, train trip, bus to Ross Dam followed by all-you-can-eat chicken dinner. Three departures daily, Thurs–Monday. Reservations required, tel: 684-3030. Admission.

Spirit of Puget Sound, 2819 Elliott Avenue (Pier 70). Tel: 443-1439. Two to 3-hour dining and dancing cruises on the Sound aboard a 600-passenger luxury liner.

Tillicum Tours, depart from Pier 56. Tel: 443-1244. A 4-hour tour combines harbor sightseeing with a trip to Blake Island Marine State Park for Indian-style salmon dinner and traditional tribal dances.

Underground Tours, 610 First Avenue. Tel: 682-4646. A five-block, 1½-hour walking tour of Pioneer Square that includes subterranean sidewalks and storefronts remaining from the 1889 fire.

Whale Watching in the San Juan Islands: Tours from Bellingham by Island Mariner Cruises, tel: 734-8866; from Anacortes by Orca Search affiliated with the Seattle Museum, require advance reservations, tel: 386-4329. You can also go from Friday Harbor by Star of Semiahmoo (2 hours), tel: 1-800-443-4552, or San Juan Boat Rentals (3 hours), tel: 378-3499; or Western Prince (4 hours), tel: 378-5315.

BUS TOURS

Charter bus companies with tours in the area (e.g. Mount Ranier, Mount St Helens, wineries, Whidbey Island) include:
Cascade Trailways, 2209 Pacific Avenue, Tacoma, 98402. Tel: 838-3465.
Gray Line of Seattle, 720 S. Forest Street. Tel: 624-5077.
Greyhound Travel Servies, 811 Stewart Street. Tel: 624-3456.
Puget Sound Coach Lines, 15419 First Avenue S. Tel: 246-3603.

BOAT TOURS

Anchor Excursions, 2500 Westlake Avenue N. Tel 282-8368. Four-hour marine science cruises on Puget Sound.

Gray Line Water Sightseeing, Pier 57. Tel: 441-1887. Two-hour cruises by downtown waterfront, Elliot Bay, the ship canal and Lake Union via the Chittenden Locks.

Major Marine Tours, Pier 54. Tel: 783-8873. One-hour cruises.

Seattle Harbor Tours, Pier 55. Tel: 623-1445. One-hour narrated trips past the shipyards and along the waterfront.

From rowboats and kayaks to fully crewed yachts, charters are available to suit all needs. Here are a few:

Northwest Outdoor Center, Inc., 2100 Westlake Avenue N, Lake Union. Tel: 281-9694. Offers sightseeing tours of Lake Union houseboats, sunset tours, and San Juan Island cruises. Kayak and canoe rentals available on Lake Union. Open: all year.

TOURING BY CAR

What may be Washington State's most spectacular natural site is the 286-ft **Snoqualmie Falls** (100 feet higher than Niagara) which cascade dramatically into the Snoqualmie River, 25 miles east of Seattle. Take Interstate 90 to the Snoqualmie Falls exit (#27) and follow the signs. Power from the falls provides enough energy to serve 16,000 homes. Overlooking the falls is the elegant **Salish Lodge** (rooms with wood-burning fireplaces, whirlpool tubs and refrigerators begin at around $150, single or double) with a good restaurant famous for its hearty breakfasts. Tel: 1-800-826-6124 for reservations. In the park beside the falls is a café and souvenir shop. Not far away and considerably less expensive is The Old Honey Farm Country Inn (tel: 888-9399) which bans telephones, TV sets, smokers and children under 14.

A visit to **Mount St Helens** or to **Mount Rainier National Forest** by car would logically loop right around the region, beginning south on Interstate 5, then southeast on Highway 7 to the old lumber town of Elbe, 60 miles from Seattle. Here you might take a ride on the **Mount Rainier Scenic Railroad** before stopping for dinner at Alexander's (tel: 569-2300), a rebuilt Victorian home in tiny Ashford on Highway 706. There are comfortable rooms here or at the equally old Mountain Meadows Inn (tel: 569-2788) run by Chad, a former lumberman who's a mine of information about the region.

Highway 7 continues down towards **Mount St Helen's National Volcanic Monument** (information from 274-6644) whose visitor center on Highway 504, east of Castle Rock, is open daily. Continuing on Highway 7 brings you into **Mount Rainier National Park** with comfortable inns at Paradise

and Longmire. Advance room reservations are strongly recommended, tel: 569-2275.

Heading across the Sound by ferry to Bremerton on the Kitsap Peninsula offers a chance to head north to the delightful "Norwegian" town of **Poulsbo** (Chamber of Commerce: tel: 779-4848). Taking the ferry to **Winslow on Bainbridge Island** is another easy excursion that doesn't necessarily require a car. **Bremerton**, an old naval town, has a maritime museum and offers tours of the moored *USS Turner Joy*. Buses operate from the ferry dock as far as Poulsbo (tel: 373-BUSS for schedules). Just outside Winslow the **Bainbridge Island Winery** (tel: 842-9463) can be visited on afternoons from Wednesday through Sunday. The local convention and visitors' bureau (tel: 479-3588) offers a free booklet to the Kitsap Peninsula.

Washington State is renowned for its excellent wines and between April and December there are dozens of special celebrations at different wineries. Write to the Yakima Valley Wine Growers Association, PO Box 39, Grandview, WA 98930; or call the Tri-Cities Visitors & Convention Bureau tel: 509-735-8468; in WA 1-800-835-0248) for free schedules and maps.

Tape Tours International offers two self-guiding auto tape tours of the Seattle area. It covers the beaches, parks and scenic drives, the Pike Market, International District and downtown shopping. Tapes can be purchased at the AAA office, 330 Sixth Avenue N. Tel: 448-5353.

TOURING BY FERRY

The **Washington State Ferry** system, the largest in the country, covers the Puget Sound area, linking Seattle (at Pier 52) with the Olympic Peninsula via Bremerton and Bainbridge Island. State ferries also depart from West Seattle to Vashon Island and Southworth and from Edmonds (7 miles north of Seattle) to Kingston on Kitsap Peninsula. It also provides service from Anacortes, 90 miles northwest of Seattle, through the San Juan Islands to Victoria, on Canada's Vancouver Island. For information: tel: 464-6400 or 1-800-843-3779. Passengers to Canada must bring a passport.

Clipper Navigation operates passenger-only ferries, the *Victoria Clippers I, II* and *III*, between Seattle and Victoria with three departures daily from Pier 69. The ride is 2½ hours with food and shopping available on board. Reservations are necessary. Tel: 448-5000.

The **Black Ball Ferry** departs from Port Angeles on the Olympic Peninsula to Victoria, British Columbia in Canada four times a day during summer and twice daily the rest of the year. Ferries carry automobiles. Tel: 622-2222 (Bellevue office) or 457-4491 (Port Angeles office).

Viking Star Charters, 2442 NW Market Street #239, Seattle. Tel: 622-2393. Offers a three-day package cruise through the San Juan Islands, including overnight accommodation at the Rosario Resort.

TOURING BY PLANE

Boeing Field/King County International Airport. Tel: 296-7380. for information on companies that operate at this airport.

Chrysler Air, 1325 Fairview Avenue E, Seattle. Tel:329-9638. Located on Lake Union, operates flights to Vancouver and Victoria in Cananda, the San Juan Islands, Mount St Helens and more. Also offers scenic tours of Seattle.

Elliott Bay Aviation, 8535 Perimeter Road S, Seattle.Tel: 767-3290. Runs helicopter sightseeing tours and charters throughout the Puget Sound region.

Galvin Flying Service Inc., 7205 Perimeter Road, Boeing Field. Tel: 1-800-341-4102 or 763-9706. An on-call, round-the-clock charter service with flights throughout the US and Canada. Also offers sight-seeing tours.

Kenmore Air, 6321 NE 175th Street, Seattle. Tel: 486-8400 or 364-6990. Offers daily flights to British Columbia, Kitsap Peninsula, San Juan and Whidbey Islands and the resort inn at Semiahmoo. Also offers day excursions and overnight packages.

Lake Union Air, 950 Westlake Avenue N, Seattle. Tel: 284-0300. Offers daily flights to San Juan Islands, Victoria, Vancouver, Campbell River and Tofino, British Columbia. Also operates a van service from select hotels and area "Flightseeing" tours.

ESPECIALLY FOR CHILDREN

More than most urban areas in America, Seattle is a place where children can be easily accommodated. Signs around town say, "Seattle is a kids' place," and it's surely one of the reasons why Seattle is consistently rated a livable city in the national press. There are a variety of things for children to enjoy right in town and just a short trip away. Here are a few suggestions.

Take the kids for a **ride on the ferry** on any one of the five routes in and around Seattle. (*See boatrips for details*). It's inexpensive and, through children's eyes, may be one of the highlights of a trip to Seattle. On board, there are wide decks to run around on (ferries are quite informal), get exercise and enjoy the views and fresh sea air. The whole process of loading and unloading cars is fascinating for most (except tired commuters). The indoor areas are also wide and airy feeling with comfortable benches and tables and large windows overlooking the Sound. Cafeterias on board serve sandwiches, burgers and drinks.

Hiking is another great pastime. Some excellent parks for this are the Arboretum, Foster Island Trail (from the Arboretum it leads to Montlake Cut and the Museum of History and Industry in McCurdy Park), Discovery Park, Volunteer Park, Marymoor Park (in Redmond) and beachcombing on any Puget Sound Beach. For a mountainous hike that's not too far away, Tiger Mountain in Issaquah offers well-marked trails. Some trails there allow mountain biking, which active older children would enjoy. A stop by Gilman Village and Boehm's Chocolate factory in town make the adventure a real treat.

Swimming is an option on Lake Washington beaches during the summer. (See *Sports* section for listing). Paddleboating, bicycling, hiking, picnicking, and swimming are some of the activities available at **Greenlake Park**. Just up the hill from Greenlake is the **Woodland Park Zoo and Garden**. Another place to watch animals is the **Seattle Aquarium** at Pier 59, downtown. (See *Attractions*).

Bicycling is ideal for children on the bicycle trails. There are smooth paved roads and no cars to worry about (just the occasional serious bicyclist trying to break a speed record). Try the Burke Gilman Trail, which can be picked up anywhere from Gas Works Park on the north end of Lake Union or the University of Washington area to Log Boom Park in Kenmore. The Sammamish River Trail at Bothell Landing is a quiet and scenic trail which extends for 9 miles to Marymoor Park. Greenlake's trail can get busy, so it's best to try for a weekday ride around the lake. (See *Sports* section for details and bike rental information).

The **Seattle Center** is a wonderland for children. A day or two here is well-spent. The Pacific Science Center, a hands-on museum with displays that children can manipulate to learn scientific principles, offers planetarium shows, laser-light shows and nature/adventure films in the dramatic IMAX theater. At the Center House with its numerous fast food cafés and tourist shops, is the Children's Museum and Piccoli Junior Theater on the lower level. Outside, the Fun Forest offers amusement park rides, arcade games and miniature golf. The elevator up to the Space Needle is a treat as is the view if it's not cloudy. From the Center House, take a ride on the Monorail to the heart of downtown's retail stores.

Chandler's Cove at the south end of Lake Union is home to the Center for Wooden Boats which offers hourly rentals of classic wooden boats. Hop aboard the dry-docked *Wawona* next door, and see what an 1800s fishing vessel looked like. Chandler's Cove also contains several eateries, both fast food and quality restaurants, in addition to interesting shops (especially Pennsylvania Woodworks which features Amish furniture) and a **lakeside playground**.

Pike Place Market is fascinating for children as well as adults. But hold hands, it's easy to get lost in the crowd. While in the **Pioneer Square** district, try a stop at the Iron Horse Restaurant (311 Third Avenue S, tel: 223-9506) where **electric trains** on tracks surrounding the restaurant bring food and drinks right to your table. Not a place for a high-class luncheon, but decent burgers, sandwiches and fries can be had.

The **Chittenden Locks** is another favorite attraction. Children love to watch how they work, see the boats line up, watch the salmon jumping up the fish ladder, and walk through the park and garden that surrounds the locks. (See *Attractions*).

The **Museum of Flight**, located in Boeing airfield, approximately 10 miles south of Seattle, is one the kids won't want to miss. The central room, called the Gallery, contains 20 airplanes including an early 1900 Wright Brothers' model, fighter jets and ultralight gliders hanging from the glass ceiling. (See *Museums*).

The **Puget Sound and Snoqualmie Valley Railroad** provides a living history adventure. The late 1800-vintage steam trains travel between North Bend and Snoqualmie for a half-hour trip through forests, farmlands and over streams. Trains run on Sunday from April–October; on Saturday from May–September; on Friday and Saturday from July–the first weekend in September. While in Snoqualmie, 30 miles east of Seattle, a trip to the **falls** is recommended. Children can explore the trails that surround the 268-foot falls and visit the gift shops and restaurants of the visitor center. The **Salish Lodge** next to the top of the falls has a restaurant with a deck overlooking the falls and splendid accommodation for those who wish to stay overnight. Tel: 888-4230.

Let the kids climb on back of a pony at **Lake Serene Pony Farm** in Lynnwood. The farm conducts 20-minute trail walks for children ages 3–13 on Saturday by reservation. Address: 3915 Serene Way, Lynnwood. Tel: 743-2112.. (See *Sports*).

Try a stroll through **downtown Kirkland** and rest for a while at **Marina Park**, watching the boats and enjoying the view of Lake Washington and Seattle beyond. Follow the signs along Lake Washington Boulevard for a pleasant stroll past restaurants, antique shops and condominiums to still more lakeside parks. Two blocks west of downtown on Central Avenue is Park Place Shopping Center, with **Pinocchio's Toys** and **Park Place Books** of special interest to children. Next to the center is **Peter Kirk Park** with grassy fields, a playground, an outdoor pool and a library.

Edmonds is another town that's fun to stroll through, whether browsing the quaint shops that line Main Street, learning about the history of Edmunds in Old Mill Town, watching the ferries load and unload, or simply enjoying the color of the hanging baskets of flowers that line downtown streets. A long fishing pier extends out into the sound next to Olympic Beach. Curious children love to see what kind of fish people catch. It's also possible to walk along the waterfront from Olympic Beach to Marina Beach, passing Anthony's Homeport, a fine seafood restaurant (tel: 771-4400) and the Edmonds Yacht Club along the way. From the beaches (Marina Park has playground equipment), enjoy the sea breezes and views of Puget Sound and the Olympic Mountains.

Designed for the children in all of us is **Wild Waves and Enchanted Village Amusement Park** in Federal Way, approximately 17 miles south of Seattle. The Wild Waves part of the park contains heated pools, plus one that makes waves, and many water slides and smaller pools for little children. The Enchanted Village part has a farm, numerous cafés, a merry-go-round, ferris wheel, boat rides, train rides, and more rides. The store inside Wild Waves sells bathing suits and any other equipment (rafts, towels, T-shirts) needed. Wild Waves/Enchanted Village, 36201 Enchanted Parkway South, Federal Way, WA 98003. Tel: 838-8676 (when calling from Seattle) or 927-9335 (when calling from Tacoma). Hours: 11am–8pm from last week in June–first weekend in September; 10am–6pm from last weekend in May to third week in June and on weekends only during April, first three weeks in May and September after Labor Day weekend. Exit 142B off Interstate 5.

A little further distance, but worth the trip, is **Point Defiance Park** in Tacoma. The 700-acre park contains a zoo, an excellent aquarium (especially the shark and beluga whale exhibits), **Nisqually Fort Museum** (a restored fur trading post and village *circa* 1830s), **Camp Six** (a lumber museum with a steam train that rides around the camp) and **Never Never Land** with 31 displays from Mother Goose stories. There are also formal gardens, beaches to explore numerous hiking trails with vistas of Puget Sound, Vashon Island and the Olympics. The **zoo** and **aquarium** are open: 10am–7pm.daily. Admission, children age two and under free. Tel: 591-5337.

Farms: There are numerous farms not far from town that offer tours. Here is a sample:

Carnation Research Farm, near the town of Carnation, is approximately 25 miles northeast of Seattle. 28901 NE Carnation Farm Road. Tel: 788-1511. This 1,200-acre dairy farm, is where the Carnation company conducts research for its pet foods, milling and genetics divisions. The maternity and calf barns, milking stalls and Friskies nutrition kennels are open for self-guided tours, as are the formal flower gardens and informal picnic areas. Hours: 10am–3pm Monday–Saturday, March 1–October 31. Free.

The Herbfarm, just outside of Fall City, is approximately 25 miles east of Seattle. 32804 Issaquah-Fall City Road. Tel: 784-2222. An extensive herb garden with over 630 varieties and a lovely gift shop with herbs, gardening books, supplies and dried flowers for sale, are the steady attractions here. Children will enjoy the farm animals and grounds for picnics. The restaurant, for which reservations are hard to come by, is rated among the best in Puget Sound. The farm conducts hay rides, pumpkin picking, stories and games (like a maze made from hay) during its annual Halloween Festival. Open: 9am–6pm daily.

Gold Creek Trout Farm, 15844 148th NE, Woodinville. Tel: 483-1415. Here's a place where anyone can catch a fish. The farm provides poles and bait and also cleans and wraps the fish for guests to take home and cook. Price depends on size of the catch Hours: 10am–5pm daily.

WHERE TO STAY

Rooms for $100 or less are defined as inexpensive; between $100 and $200 as reasonable; above $200 upscale.

NEAR THE AIRPORT

There are few really inexpensive hotels in downtown Seattle, but there are many along the road (Pacific South Highway) to the SeaTac airport. There is one group about halfway between the airport and Seattle, located around 141st Street. The best of these (it has a pool) is the **Ben Carol Motel**, 14110 Pacific Highway South, tel: 244-6464. All the motels in this area are around half the price of even modest downtown eqivalents and are clustered around a comfortable, family-type restaurant and close to an enormous 24-hour supermarket. Also note:

Best Western Airport Executel, 20717 Pacific Highway S, Tukwila, WA 98188. Tel: 878-1814. Amenities: heated indoor pool, sauna, jacuzzi, exercise room, airport transportation, restaurant, lounge, morning newspaper, valet and laundry service. Reasonable.

Comfort Inn, at Sea-Tac, 19333 Pacific Highway S, Tukwila, WA 98188. Tel: 878-1100. Amenities: cable television, exercise room, jacuzzi, airport transportation, valet and laundry service, continental breakfast. Inexpensive.

Red Lion Inn, at Sea-Tac, 18740 Pacific Hwy S. Tukwila, WA 98188. Tel: 246-8600 or 1-800-547-8010 Amenities: concierge, heated pool, balconies, airport transportation, cable television, two restaurants, lounge with entertainment, plus a gift shop. Reasonable.

Seattle Mariott, Sea-Tac Airport, 3201 S 176th Street Tukwila, WA 98188. Tel: 241-2000. Amenities: heated indoor pool, sauna, hot tub, exercise room, airport transportation, cable television, restaurant and lounge, facilities for handicapped. Reasonable.

DOWNTOWN SEATTLE

The Alexis, 1007 First Avenue, Seattle, WA 98104. Tel: 624-4844. Located in a turn-of-the-century building near the waterfront. The Alexis is an elegant hotel of 54 rooms that prides itself on attention to detail and personalized service. Amenities include: 15 rooms with whirlpools, wood-burning fireplaces, complimentary sherry, continental breakfast and morning newspaper of your choice, shoeshines and a reduced-price, guest membership at the nearby upscale Seattle Club or to Northwest Nautilus. There are four restaurants: Cajun Corner, 92 Madison, the Bookstore Bar and its signature restaurant, Café Alexis. Upscale.

The Edgewater Inn, 2411 Alaskan Way, Seattle, WA 98121. Tel: 728-7000 or 1-800-624-0670. Built at the time of the World's Fair in 1962 and completely remodeled in 1989. This is Seattle's only downtown waterfront hotel, which is literally over the water; it stands on Pier 67. Rooms have lovely water views. Amenities include: a dramatic atrium lobby, five large, stone fireplaces and mountain lodge decor. Complimentary downtown shuttle, complete banquet and meeting facilities. 238 rooms. Restaurant features Northwest cuisine. Rates: vary depending on water or city view (water view being the more expensive). Reasonable.

The Four Seasons Olympic Hotel, 411 University Street, Seattle, WA 98101. Tel: 621-1700 or 1-800-332-3442 (in US) or 1-800-821-8106 (in Washington State). A grand hotel in the Italian Renaissance style. Built in 1924 and renovated in 1982. It features 450 spacious guest rooms furnished in period reproductions. Enjoy high tea in the atrium-style Garden Court and shopping off the lobby in stores such as Abercrombie and Fitch, Laura Ashley, Coach Leather or Bally of Switzerland. The hotel currently receives the AAA five-diamond award for service. Amenities include: A health club, heated indoor pool, saunas, jacuzzis, two restaurants, 24-hour room service, complimentary newspaper and shoeshine, a stocked bar, terry cloth robes, and many supplies for parents with small children. Fee for valet parking and massage. There are 12 meeting and banquet rooms. Upscale.

Seattle Hilton-Downtown, Sixth and University Street, Seattle, WA 98101. Tel: 624-0500 or 1-800-445-8667. Amenities: bay windows in each room; Top of the Hilton Lounge (a disco), 24-hour room service, valet/laundry service, concierge, restaurant and gift shop. Reasonable.

Holiday Inn Crowne Plaza, Sixth and Seneca Street, Seattle, WA 98101. Adjacent to Freeway Park. Tel: 464-1980 or 1-800-465-4329. Amenities include: health club with whirlpool, sauna, weight room on the fifth floor; a gift shop; two restaurants: Parkside for formal dining and Parkside Café for breakfast and lunch or dinner. 415 rooms. Reasonable.

Inn At The Market, 86 Pine Street, Seattle, WA 98101. Tel: 443-3600. Located right in the Pike Place Market, most of the rooms have splendid views of Elliott Bay. The 65 rooms are large and the inn surrounds a landscaped courtyard that boasts trendy shops, a spa and the Campagne restaurant serving French country cuisine. A fifth floor deck – fake turf and potted plants – offers one of the best views in town. Amenities: complimentary downtown shuttle bus to shops; complimentary news and coffee; dinner room service from the Campagne restaurant; outdoor deck with chairs overlooking bay from the fifth floor. Reasonable.

Mayflower Park Hotel, 405 Olive Way, Seattle, WA 98112. Tel: 1-800-426-5100 or 623-8700. European-style moderately-sized hotel of 187 rooms. Adjacent to Westlake Center. Amenities: cable television, restaurant, lounge, valet and laundry service. Reasonable.

Pacific Coast Guest Suites, 915 118 Avenue SE, Bellevue, WA 98005. Tel: 1-800-962-6620 or 454-7888. These are one, two or three-bedroom condominium suites located in Seattle, Redmond or Bellevue. Rooms are equipped with full kitchens, washer, dryer, fireplace, cable television, concierge and housekeeping services. Inexpensive.

Residence Inn by Marriott, 800 Fairview Avenue., Seattle, WA 98109. Tel: 624-6000. The Inn offers only suites, 234 in all. Suites are equipped with a full kitchen including microwave oven, coffee maker, full-size refrigerator, range-top stove and dishwasher (but the inn takes care of the dishes). Seventy percent of the rooms overlook Lake Union. Amenities include continental breakfast in the seven-story atrium (complete with waterfall), fitness center on third floor equipped with heated indoor pool, sauna, jacuzzi, exercise room; free covered garage. Upscale.

Sheraton Seattle Hotel and Towers, 1400 Sixth Avenue, Seattle, WA 98101. Tel: 1-800-325-3535 or 621-9000. Top floor (35th) has fitness center equipped with jacuzzi, sauna, swimming pool, bicycles and aerobics area and lounge with panoramic view of the city. Two restaurants: Banner's and Fuller's for formal dining at one of Seattle's finest restaurants. There is also a popular disco. Reasonable.

Sorrento Hotel, 900 Madison Street, Seattle, WA 98104. Tel: 1-800-622-6400. This 1909 hotel was structurally remodeled in 1981 after a castle in Sorrento, Italy and rooms were refurbished with an Italian flavor. The 76 guest rooms on seven floors are sophisticated and stylish, yet due to the moderate size, the hotel prides itself on attentive service. The Hunt Club restaurant continues the theme of European styling. During summer months guests can enjoy dining outdoors in the hotel's courtyard. Afternoon tea with sandwiches and pastries is served daily in the fireside room accompanied by a pianist or guitarist. Amenities: free limousine service downtown, mobile cellular phones, newspapers, shoeshines and valet parking. In-house florist, robes, valet and Shiatzu massage available. Reasonable

Stouffer Madison Hotel, 515 Madison Street, Seattle, WA 98104. Tel: 583-0300. Top two floors are the executive level rooms, with concierge service, complimentary breakfast and appetizers. Amenities include: outstanding views, rooftop fitness center with heated indoor pool, complimentary morning coffee and newspaper delivered to your room, 24-hour room service, one-day laundry, gift shop and hair salon. Valet service. Two restaurants. Upscale.

Westin Hotel, 1900 Fifth Avenue. Tel: 728-1000 or 1-800-228-3000. This is the Westin chain's flagship hotel. It is adjacent to Westlake Shopping Center. Amenities include three restaurants: the stylish Palm Court (overlooking Fifth Avenue shoppers), the Market Café and Fitzgerald's on Fifth (a lounge and disco), and a newer restaurant. The rooms are spacious with views of Puget Sound or the city. There is a heated indoor pool, jacuzzis, saunas and fitness center. Grayline Airport Express stops here. Upscale.

WestCoast Roosevelt Hotel, 1531 Seventh Avenue, Seattle, WA 98101. Tel: 621-1200. A moderately-priced hotel for downtown, it was built in Art Deco style in 1930, renovated in 1987. Rooms are not large, but hotel is convenient to shopping and downtown sightseeing. Inexpensive.

Bush Hotel, 621 South Jackson. Tel: 623-8079. One of the few budget-priced downtown hotels in the somewhat dilapidated area close to the Amtrak station is this 144-room hotel. Coffee shop and restaurants, rooms with TV and all around is Chinatown with some Asian community organizations located in the hotel's basement. Inexpensive.

For inexpensive rooms, consider also the **Claremont Hotel**, Virginia and Fourth, tel: 448-8600; the **Commodore Motor Hotel**, 2013 Second Avenue, tel: 448-8868; the **Cosmopolitan Motor Inn**, 2106 Fifth Avenue, tel: 441-8833; **Days Inn Town Center**, 2205 Seventh Avenue, tel: 448-3434; **EconoLodge**, 325 Aurora Avenue, tel: 441-0400; **Moore Hotel**, 1926 Second Avenue, tel: 448-4851; and the **Pacific Hotel**, 317 Marion Street, tel: 622-3985.

Where the Quick Shuttle bus from Vancouver stops in Seattle is the **Downtown Travelodge Motel**, 2213 Eighth Avenue at Blanchard, tel: 624-6300, which makes it a convenient overnight place if you are traveling between the two cities or planning to go to the airport. Reasonable rates.

NORTHEND

University Plaza Hotel, 400 NE 45th Street, Seattle, WA 98105. Tel: 634-0100. Located in the heart of the University district, with 135 rooms. Amenities include: outdoor pool, cable television, free parking, fitness center, beauty salon, laundry service, restaurant, lounge with entertainment. Inexpensive.

Ramada Inn, Seattle at Northgate, 2140 Northgate Way, Seattle, WA 98133. Tel: 365-0700. Located approximately 7 miles north of Seattle and adjacent to Northgate Mall. Amenities include: heated pool, restaurant, laundry service, room service, facilities for handicapped. Inexpensive.

SOUTHEND

Nendel's Motor Inn, Seattle/Southcenter, 15901 W Valley Road, Tukwila, WA 98188. Tel: 226-1812. Next to the Southcenter Mall with many rooms overlooking Green River. Amenities include: fitness center with heated pool, wading pool, sauna, jacuzzi, airport transportation, restaurant and lounge. Inexpensive.

KIRKLAND

Woodmark Hotel, 1200 Carillon Point, Kirkland, WA 98033. Tel: 822-3700. Features 100 rooms, some with views on Lake Washington, in a ritzy 31-acre shopping/office complex. Carillon Point also features a marina and the popular Ristorante Stresa and Yarrow Bay Restaurant and Beach Café. Amenities include: fully stocked minibars, VCRs with complimentary movies, terry cloth robes, a full complimentary breakfast with a newspaper, and the Carillon Room restaurant. Reasonable.

BELLEVUE

Bellevue Hilton, 100 112th Avenue NE, Bellevue, WA 98004. Tel: 455-3330. Built in 1980 in heart of downtown Bellevue. Amenities include: heated indoor pool, saunas, jacuzzi, airport transportation, cable television. There are three restaurants and a lounge with entertainment. Reasonable. On the weekend all standard rooms are inexpensive.
Best Western Greenwood Hotel, 625 116th Avenue NE, Bellevue, WA 98004. Tel: 455-9444. Amenities: landscaped interior courtyard, heated pool, health club privileges, airport transportation, restaurant, townhouse suites with fireplace. Inexpensive.
Hyatt Hotel and Resort, 900 Bellevue Way, Bellevue, WA 98005. Tel: 462-1234. Luxury Hotel in Bellevue Place, a shopping center that features some of Bellevue's most exclusive clothing stores. This 382-room hotel is the tallest in Bellevue, with 24 floors. On the top two floors the hotel offers its Regency Club rooms featuring special concierge service, continental breakfast and appetizers in the evening. Amenities include: access to adjacent health club for a small fee, and Eques, a highly rated restaurant. Reasonable.
Red Lion, 300 112th SE, Bellevue, WA 98004. Tel: 455-1300 or 1-800-547-8010. Red Lion offers 303 large rooms, some with balconies. Amenities include: heated pool, sauna and jacuzzi; health club privileges, restaurant and night club. Reasonable. Offers lower weekend rates.
Residence Inn, by Mariott Seattle East, 14455 NE 29th Place, Bellevue, WA 98007. Tel: 882-1222. Offers one and two bedroom suites in a village-type setting amid landscaped grounds. Suites are equipped with kitchens, fireplaces and balconies or decks (depending on level). Amenities: heated pool, jacuzzis, laundry, airport transportation. Reasonable.

ISSAQUAH

Holiday Inn, 1801 12th Avenue, Issaquah, WA 98027. Tel: 392-6421
Located opposite Lake Sammamish State Park on the south end of the lake. Amenities include: a seasonal pool, wading pool, sauna, jacuzzi, restaurant and laundry facilities. Inexpensive.

REDMOND

Redmond Motor Inn, 17601 Redmond Way, Redmond, WA 98052. Tel: 883-4900. Amenities: cable television, heated pool, jacuzzi, a restaurant, airport transportation, laundry facility. Inexpensive.

POULSBO

Cypress Inn, Highway 305, Poulsbo, WA 98370. Tel: 679-2119 or 1-800-752-9991 outside WA. Restaurant and coffee shop, outdoor pool. 65 rooms. Inexpensive.

PORT TOWNSEND

The Tides Inn, 1807 Water Street, Port Townsend, WA 98368. Tel: 385-0595 or 1-800-822-8696. On the waterfront; 21 rooms, some with kitchenettes, jacuzzis Inexpensive.
The Port Townsend Motel, 2020 Washington Street, Port Townsend, WA 98368. Tel: 385-2211 or 1-800-822-8696. Similar to above, 26 rooms. Inexpensive.

LEAVENWORTH

Bavarian Leavenworth, c/o Obental Investments, Box 970, Leavenworth, WA 98826. Tel: 1-800-537-9382. There are 78 units altogether, divided between four locations but all reasonably accessible to Cascades National Park. Inexpensive.

LACONNER

LaConner Country Inn, 107 South Second, La Conner, WA 98257. Restaurant and 28 rooms. Inexpensive.

BED & BREAKFASTS

Several bed and breakfast agencies assist in selecting suitable accommodations:
Pacific Bed and Breakfast Registry, 701 NW 60th Street, Seattle, WA 98107. Tel: 784-0539.
Traveler's Bed and Breakfast, PO Box 492, Mercer Island, WA 98040. Tel: 232-2345.
Seattle Bed and Breakfast Inn Association, PO Box 95853, Seattle, WA. Tel: 547-1020.

Bed and Breakfast inns tend to be inexpensive-to-reasonably priced. Some rooms have a private bath; some a shared bath. Here is a small sampling of older, mostly Victorian places in the Seattle area:
Capitol Hill Inn, 1713 Belmont Avenue, Seattle, WA 98122. Tel: 323-1955. Beautifully decorated with antiques, 1903 mansion on Capitol Hill is close to Broadway shops and restaurants.

Gaslight Inn, 1727 15th Avenue. Tel: 325-3654. Nine guest rooms, six private baths, three outdoor decks, a large heated pool. No children or pets.

Salisbury House, 750 16th Avenue E. Tel: 328-8682. On historic Capitol Hill.

Prince of Wales, 133 13th Avenue E. Tel: 325-9692. Good views of city, Sound and mountains.

Williams House, 1505 Fourth Avenue N. Tel: 285-0810. Atop Queen Anne hill; excellent views.

YOUTH HOSTELS

Most hostelries offer clean, no-frills, low-budget accommodation.

YMCA Accommodations, 909 Fourth Avenue, Seattle, WA 98104. Tel: 382-5000. A 178-room hostelry. Amenities include: use of YMCA facilities including lounge, hot tub, indoor pool, sauna, fitness center and laundry service. Membership fee per person plus 14.2 percent sales tax. Weekly rates are available. Bunks can be four to a room. Hostel members also receive discounts on rooms.

Commodore Hotel Youth Hostel, 2013 Second Avenue, Seattle, WA 98121. Tel: 448-8868. Well-kept older hotel of 100 rooms with inexpensive rates. Amenities include: cable television in each room, lobby area and free parking.

Seattle International AYH Hostel, 84 Union Street, Seattle, WA 98101. Tel: 682-0462. A 125-bed hostel. Amenities include: lounge, library and self-service kitchen and laundry available. Membership is free for non-profit groups.

CAMPGROUND/RV PARKS

WEST

Fay Bainbridge State Park, 15446 Sunrise Drive NE, Bainbridge Island, WA 98110. Tel: 842-3931. There are 26 sites available for RVs or tents and an additional 10 sites available for tents only. Amenities include: wide sandy beach on Puget Sound, walking trails through the 17-acre park, boat launch, two mooring buoys, facilities for handicapped, playground equipment, disposal station, picnic shelter and water hookup.

Kitsap Memorial State Park, Poulsbo, WA 98370. Tel: 779-3205 Located approximately 4 miles north of the charming Scandinavian town of Poulsbo. The park has 43 sites for tents or RVs with a 30 foot limit. Amenities include: flush and pit toilets; playground equipment, wooded trails, swimming, boat launch, fishing, disposal station.

SOUTH

Saltwater State Park, 25205 Eighth Place S. Tel: 764-4128. On Puget Sound about 2 miles south of Des Moines (18 miles south of Seattle) off Highway 509, the campground is located inside the state park which has 88 acres and nearly 1,500 feet of Puget Sound beaches. There are 52 sites available for tents or RVs, but no hookups. Amenities include: free use of the park with swimming, boating, a dock, scuba diving, nature trails and a playground. There is also a grocery store, flush and pit toilets. Open: all year.

NORTH

Canyon Mobile Park & RV, 3333 228 Street SE, Bothell, WA 98021. Tel: 481-3005. Primarily a mobile home park, but has 13 RV spaces available. Amenities include: recreation hall. Open: all year.

Twin Cedars RV Park, 17826 Highway 99 N, Lynnwood, WA 98037. Tel: 742-5540. There are 70 sites for RVs on this relatively quiet 3-acre campground. The level gravel sites are set off highway 99. Amenities include: television in recreation room, coin laundry, showers, propane, disposal station, pets are allowed. Open: all year.

EAST

Trailer Inns Inc., 15531 SE 37 Street, Bellevue, WA 98006. Tel: 747-9181 or 1-800-323-8899 (Holiday Travel Park network). There are 100 RV sites on this 4-acre campground. The maximum footage for RVs is 35 feet, with two sites allowing approximately one foot longer. Amenities include: token-operated laundry and propane, a television/game room, a playground, hot tub and heated indoor pool. Pets allowed. A/C or heaters cost a little extra. Weekly and monthly rates are available. Open: all year.

Vasa Park, 3560 W. Lake Sammamish Road SE, Bellevue, WA 98008. Tel: 746-3260. There are 16 tent sites and six RV/or tent sites at this 18-acre campground on Lake Sammamish. Check out time is 10am. Amenities include: a disposal station, beach for swimming, fishing and a playground. Pets allowed. Electrical hookups cost extra; water hookups are free. There are four sewer hookups, no extra charge. Open: May 15–October 1.

FŌOD DĪGEST

Deluxe restaurants are classified as $70 or more; reasonable as $30-70; and inexpensive as under $30. The price includes a meal for two without wine.

RESTAURANTS

Café Alexis, Alexis Hotel, 1007 First Avenue. Tel: 624-3646. Excellent, Northwest cuisine in plush atmosphere of the hotel. Deluxe.

Café Lago, 2305 24 Avenue E. Tel: 329-8005. Quality, rustic Italian fare featuring crusty breads, sumptuous antipasti, and pastas. Serves dinner. Closed: Monday. Reasonable.

Elliott's, Alaskan Way, Pier 56. Tel: 623-4340. Seafood with a view of the bay. Lunch and dinner. Reasonable.

Fuller's, 1400 Sixth Avenue. Tel: 447-5544. In the Sheraton Hotel. Consistently rated one of Seattle's best overall restaurants. Northwest and Continental-style cuisine. Reasonable.

The Georgian Room, 411 University Street. Tel: 621-7889. At the Four Seasons Hotel, a first-class restaurant serving excellent Contitnental-style cuisine in elegant surroundings. Deluxe.

Le Gourmand, 425 NW Market Street. Tel: 784-3463. Classic French cuisine incorporating Northwest ingredients. Reasonable.

The Gravity Bar, Broadway Market entrance, Capitol Hill. Offering imaginative vegetarian dishes, wheatgrass juice and espresso. A great place to people-watch. Inexpensive.

Hiram's At the Locks, 5300 34 Avenue NW. Tel: 784-1733. Quality seafood restaurant overlooking the Chittenden Locks. Outdoor deck for dining enhances boat-watching. Reasonable.

The Hunt Club, 900 Madison Avenue. Tel: 622-6400. In the Sorrento Hotel, Top-notch Northwest cuisine served in plush, clubby atmosphere. Deluxe.

Il Bistro, 93A Pike, Pike Place Market. Tel: 682-3049. Dark, Italian bistro in the Market serves dinner only. Reasonable.

Jake O'Shaughnessey's, 100 Mercer Street. Tel: 285-1897. Pub fare, some seafood, but most come for the local micro-brews. Dinner only. Inexpensive.

Kokeb Ethiopian Restaurant, 926 12 Avenue. Tel: 322-0485. Exotic and spicy cuisine from Ethiopia. Has a loyal following in the University crowd. Food is eaten with fingers. Inexpensive.

Labuznik, 1924 First Avenue. Tel: 441-8899.

Hearty, ethnic Czechoslovakian fare. Reasonable.

Leschi Lakecafé, 102 Lakeside Avenue. Tel: 328-2233. Indoor or outdoor dining, facing Lake Washington. Café fare is the best (fish 'n' chips and hamburgers), good beer and wine list. Open: for lunch and dinner. Reasonable.

Mikado Japanese Restaurant, 514 S Jackson Street. Tel: 622-5206. Excellent sushi and robata bar. Open: for dinner. Reasonable.

The Palm Court, 1900 Fifth Avenue. Tel: 728-1000. Elegant formal dining among the palm trees at the Westin Hotel. Features Continental-Northwest cuisine. Deluxe.

Ray's Boathouse, 6049 Seaview Avenue NW. Tel: 789-3770. One of Seattle's most popular seafood restaurants with a stunning view of Puget Sound and Olympic Mountains. Reasonable.

Rover's, 2808 E Madison Street. Tel: 325-7442. Fresh, contemporary French cuisine expertly prepared. Served in rooms of a frame house filled with flowers and artwork. Open: for dinner. Reasonable

Saleh al Lago, 6804 E Greenlake Way N. Tel: 524-4044. Classic Italian menu, expertly prepared. Reasonable.

Shucker's, 411 University Street. Tel: 621-1984. Seafood restaurant, best known for its fresh oysters, clams and mussels. At the Four Seasons Hotel. Reasonable.

Among the places in a long list of inexpensive restaurants reviewed favorably by *Seattle Times* food critics recently were the following: **Catfish Corner**, 2726 E Cherry, tel: 323-4330; **5 Spot**, 1502 Queen Anne Avenue N, tel: 285-SPOT; **Grady's Pub & Eatery**, 2307 24th Avenue E, tel: 726-5968; **Hokui's Teriyaki Hut**, 3624 Leary Wat NW, tel: 634-1128; **L'Emir**, 1400 80th Street, tel: 523-4196; **Queen Mary**, 2912 NE 55th Street, tel: 527-2770; **Shultzy's Sausage**, 4124 University Way, tel: 548-9461; and **Still Life** in Fremont, 709 E 35th Street, tel: 547-9850.

As *Greater Seattle* magazine points out, visitors to the city don't just want to see the sights, they also want to sample the Northwest's salmon and oysters, which are among the best in the country. For this event, the magazine recommends the previously mentioned Ray's Boathouse, Hiram's At the Locks, and Saleh al Lago, the latter for delicious smoked salmon and pasta. But there's also **Kaspar's by the Bay**, 2701 First Avenue, tel: 441-4805, for grilled king salmon with *pinot noir* cream sauce; **Noggins Brewery Bar & Restaurant**, Westlake Mall, 400 Pine street, tel: 682-BREW, for red pepper ravioli stuffed with smoked salmon; **Takara**, 1501 Western Avenue, tel: 682-8609, salmon teriyaki; **Salty's on Alki**, 1936 Harbor Avenue SW, tel: 937-1600, alder-smoked salmon stuffed with Dungeness crab; and **Satsuma**, 14301 Ambaum Boulevard SW, tel: 242-1747, the place for salmon koganeyaki.

BELLEVUE

Andres Gourmet Cuisine, 14125 NE 20 Street, Bellevue. Tel: 747-6551. French and Vietnamese cuisine. Open: lunch and dinner. Reasonable.
Domani, 604 Bellevue Way, NE, Bellevue. Tel: 454-4405. Italian cuisine conveniently located across from Bellevue Square for lunch, weekdays or dinner daily. Reasonable.
Landau's, 500 108 Avenue NE, Bellevue. Tel: 646-6644. Classic continental cuisine, beautifully presented in a plush and elegant atmosphere. Deluxe.

OUT OF TOWN

The Herbfarm, 32804 Issaquah-Fall City Road, Fall City. Tel: 784-2222. A unique and unforgettable culinary experience if you can manage to get a table. Reservations are taken months in advance, but some tables are set aside for those calling at the last minute. Items on the multi-course meals are based around the herbs grown at the farm. Dining is in a charming farmhouse and meals begin with a tour of the garden. Reasonable.

COFFEE HOUSES

B&O Espresso, 204 Belmont Avenue E. Tel: 322-5028.
Café Septieme, 2321 Second Avenue. Tel:448-1506.
Espresso Roma, two locations: 202 Broadway E. Tel: 324-1866. In the University district, 4201 University Way NE. Tel: 632-6001.
Harvard Espresso Gallery, 810 East Roy Street. Tel: 323-7598.
The Last Exit On Brooklyn, 3930 Brooklyn Avenue NE. Tel: 545-9873.

CULTURE PLUS

MUSEUMS

The Burke Museum, University of Washington campus, NE entrance at 45th Street and 17th Avenue. Tel: 543-5590. A natural history museum of the Northwest with artifacts from Northwest Coast Indians, fossils, dinosaur skeletons and geological information. Hours: 10am–5pm daily, open Thursday, until 8pm. Closed: July 4, Thanksgiving and December 25. Free, except during special exhibits.
Center For Wooden Boats, 1010 Valley Street. Tel:

382-2628. Located on the south shore of Lake Union, with its own marina. This maritime museum maintains a fleet of 75 vintage wooden boats, about half of which are available for rental on Lake Union. The center also runs workshops on wooden boat building, sailing and nautical skills. Also on show is the steam-powered Walowa, featured along with star Marie Dressler in the *Tugboat Annie* films of the 1930s based on Norman Reilly Raine's short stories. Raine's real-life model was Thea Foss, founder of the Foss Launch and Tug Co. (now Foss Maritime).
Coast Guard Museum Northwest, Pier 36, on Alaskan Way S. Tel: 286-9608. Nautical artifacts, ship models, Coast Guard memorabilia and photographs. A 15-minute slide show is also presented. Hours: 10am–4pm Monday, Wednesday and Friday; 1pm–5pm Saturday and Sunday. Free.
Frye Art Museum, 704 Terry Avenue (corner Cherry Street). Tel: 622-9250. Features paintings by 19th- and early 20th-century artists along with changing exhibits by contemporary artists. Open: 10am–5pm Monday–Friday, noon–5pm Sunday.
Henry Art Gallery, University of Washington, 15th Avenue NE and NE 41st Street. Tel: 543-2280. Features historic and contemporary works by American artists. Conducts lectures, events and children's programs in conjunction with changing exhibits. Open: 10am–5pm Tuesday–Sunday; until 7pm on Thursday. Closed: Monday.
Klondike Gold Rush National Historical Park, 117 S Main Street (in Pioneer Square). Tel: 442-7220. This was the site for outfitting the 1897–98 Alaska Gold Rush. Artifacts, gold panning demonstrations and tours. Open: 9am–5pm daily. Closed: January 1, Thanksgiving and December 25. Free.
Museum of Flight, 9404 E. Marginal Way, S. Tel: 764-5720. Located on the site where Boeing began. Museum features The Great Gallery room where vintage planes, experimental planes, fighting planes and cruising planes are suspended from the glass-domed ceiling all around the room. Short films depict Boeing's history and the history of flight. Hours: 10am–5pm daily; to 9pm Thursday and Friday. Admission; children under 6 free.
Museum of History and Industry, 2700 24th Avenue. Tel: 324-1125. Located in McCurdy Park on Lake Washington, it features exhibits on the history of Seattle, and the Pacific Northwest in addition to changing theme exhibits. It also features live radio broadcasts with jazz and progressive-style musicians. Hours: 10am–5pm daily. Closed: January 1, Thanksgiving and December 25. Admission.
Nordic Heritage Museum, 3014 NW 67th Street. Tel: 789-5707. Traces the history and contributions of Scandinavian settlers to the Northwest. Exhibits include: textiles, crafts, costumes, furniture, history of fishing and lumber industries. Phone ahead for guided tours. Hours: 10am–4pm Tuesday–Saturday. Closed: January 1, Thanksgiving and December 24–25. Admission.
Pacific Science Center, Seattle Center. A hands-on

science museum for adults and children, with changing exhibits, IMAX theater, planetarium and unusual science gifts in its gift shop. (*See Things To Do.*)

Seattle Children's Museum, Lower Level, Center House, Seattle Center. Tel: 441-1767. A hands-on educational museum with exhibits that include: a child-size neighborhood, toddler play center, bubble area , a theater, gift shop with unusual toys and three rooms with changing activities, workshops and displays. Hours: 10am–5pm Tuesday–Thursday and Saturday, 10am–8pm Friday, noon–5pm Sunday. Closed: January 1, Thanksgiving, and December 25. Admission; infants age 1 and under, free.

Seattle Art Museum, First Avenue and University Street. Tel: 625-8900. Home to an internationally renowned collection of Asian art, and paintings by the Northwest Mystics group. There are also examples of early European, pre-Columbian, Islamic, African and Persian arts.

The former art museum at **Volunteer Park** , E Galer and 15th Avenue E and E Prospect and 14th Avenue E, houses the Asian collection. Hours: 10–5pm Tuesday–Saturday, noon–5pm Sunday and holidays. Additional hours on Thursday 5–9pm. Tours are given daily at 2pm. Closed: Thanksgiving and December 25. Admission, but free on Thursdays.

Wing Luke Asian Museum, 407 7th Avenue S. Tel: 623-5124. Traces the history of Asian immigrants and their contributions to life and culture in the Northwest. Also on display are paintings and crafts from Asian and Asian-American artists. Hours: 11–4.30pm Tuesday–Friday, noon–4pm Saturday and Sunday. Additional hours are: 11–8pm the first Thursday of each month. Closed: on holidays. Admission; under 5 years free. Free to everyone on Thursday.

BELLEVUE

Bellevue Art Museum, 301 Bellevue Square. Tel: 454-3322. Located on the third floor of the upscale Bellevue Square shopping mall. Specializes in paintings and crafts of Northwest artists. Hours: 9.30am–9.30pm Monday, 9.30am–6pm Tuesday–Sunday. Admission, but children free. Free admission to all on Tuesday.

ART GALLERIES

On the first Thursday of every month, Pioneer Square art galleries host "First Thursday." Visitors may gallery hop, view the new works, sip wine, nibble cheese. Maps are available at most of the Pioneer Square galleries.

Many downtown galleries are closed Monday.

Arthead Art Gallery, 5411 Meridian Avenue N. Tel: 633-5544. Features artists early in their careers. Includes sculpture, photography and paintings.

Center On Contemporary Art (COCA), 1309 First Avenue. Tel: 682-4568. Innovative and avant-garde works on display. Stages large exhibits off-site and some performance art (on-site).

Davidson Galleries, 313 Occidental Avenue S. Tel: 624-7684. Collection of American paintings from mid-1800s and early-1900s; also, local and Chinese painters and many antique prints.

Foster/White Gallery, 311½ Occidental Avenue S. Tel: 622-2833. Exhibits established Northwest artists and work in glass by artists of the Pilchuck School.

Frye Art Museum, 704 Terry Avenue. Tel: 622-9250. Features works by Northwest and Alaskan artists and a permanent collection of turn-of-the-century works.

Greg Kucera Gallery, 608 Second Avenue. Tel: 624-0770. Carries established Northwest artists and known to host controversial shows.

Henry Art Gallery, 15th Avenue NE and 41 Street. Tel: 543-2280. Features historic and contemporary American works.

Linda Farris Gallery, 320 Second Avenue S. Tel: 623-1110. Local, national and Soviet artists displayed.

Mia Gallery, 314 Occidental Avenue S. Tel: 467-8283. Painting, sculpture, furniture and jewelry by Northwest and nationally known artists.

Photographic Center Northwest, 2617 Fifth Avenue. Tel: 441-7030. A school and gallery featuring photographers of local and national reknown and works by students and faculty.

Silver Image Gallery, 318 Occidental Avenue S. Tel: 623-8116. Photographic gallery.

Traver Sutton Gallery, 2219 Fourth Avenue. Tel: 448-4234.

EASTSIDE GALLERIES

Elements Gallery, 10500 NE Eighth Street, Bellevue. Tel: 454-8242. Glassworks, jewelry, textiles, sculpture.

Kirkland Artists' Group Gallery, 145 Park Lane, Kirkland. Tel: 827-7264.

Lakeshore Gallery, 15 Lake Street, Kirkland. Tel: 827-0606. Features local artwork in painting, ceramics, jewelry, glass and sculpture.

Medallion Gallery and School of Art, 1175 NW Gilman Boulevard, Issaquah. Tel: 392-5934.

Nordstrom Fine Arts, 40 Lake Bellevue, Suite 100, Bellevue. Tel: 453-2752. Open by appointment for individual collectors of paintings by Northwest-based artist Loren Salazar and other contemporary artists.

Northwest Gallery of Fine Woodworking, The Gilman Village Barn, Issaquah. Tel: 391-4221. In a two-level barn, exquisite woodworking: tables, cabinets, desks, mirrors, boxes and more.

White/Reese Gallery, 1250 Carillon Point, Kirkland. Tel: 889-9815. Fine art from French Impressionism to contemporary graphics.

OTHER PLACES TO VIEW ART

Seattle and Bellevue art museums, Wing Luke Asian Museum (*see Museums*); Daybreak Star Arts Center (*see Things To Do, Discovery Park*); Safeco Insurance Company, 45 Street and Brooklyn. Exhibitions by Northwest artists on display in the lobby and mezzanine.

Prescott Collection of Pilchuck Glass at Pacific First Center, 1420 Fifth Avenue. Tel: 623-7385. Features internationally renowned artists who are or have been associated with the Stanwood, Washington Glass School.

Sheraton Hotel and Towers, 1400 Sixth Avenue. Tel: 621-9000. Exhibitions on display in the lobby and throughout hotel.

MUSIC & BALLET

Seattle Opera Association, 305 Harrison Street, Seattle. Tel: 443-4711.

The Opera House at Seattle Center, is headquarters of the Seattle Opera Association, which presents six full-scale operatic productions during its September–May season.

Seattle Symphony Orchestra, 305 Harrison Street, Seattle. Tel: 443-4747. The Seattle Symphony Orchestra schedules concerts regularly on Monday, Tuesday and Wednesday evening, September–April with matinees on Sunday and family concerts on Saturday morning for the "Discover Music!" series. Gerard Schwarz is the conductor.

Pacific Northwest Ballet, 4649 Sunnyside Avenue N, Seattle. Tel: 547-5900.

When not in use for operas, you can enjoy performances by the Pacific Northwest Ballet, at the Seattle Center Opera House. Presents six productions from October–May and an annual production of *The Nutcracker*.

THEATERS

Seattle has a thriving theater scene, both classical and fringe. The small fringe groups have formed LOFT (the League of Fringe Theaters) and run a 24-hour hotline for information on performances. Tickets are very reasonably priced. Tel: 637-7373.

Tickets: You can purchase tickets at half price on the day of the show, but you run the risk of a sell-out and take whatever seats you can get (if you're lucky they may be first row at half-price!) This also applies to dance performances and music concerts. Ticket/Ticket sells these last minute tickets and charge a surcharge per seat. Broadway Market, Second Level, 401 Broadway E, tel:324-2744. Open: 10am–7pm Tuesday–Sunday. Cash only. Half-price tickets are also available at Pike Place Market Information Kiosk at the corner of First and Pike Street. **Note**: Ticket/Ticket will not give out ticket availability over the phone.

Another source for tickets besides the box office of the theater or concert hall is Ticketmaster. Tickets can be purchased in person at The Bon (Third Avenue and Pine or Northgate Mall) and Tower Records/Video at 4321 University Way NE or 500 Mercer Street. Tickets may also be purchased by telephone and usually carry a service charge. For tickets or info on performances, tel: 628-0888.

A Contemporary Theater (ACT), 100 W. Roy, Seattle, WA 98119. Tel: 285-5110. Close to Seattle Center. Seattle's leading repertory theater.

Alice B. Theatre, 1535 11th Street, Seattle, WA 98122. Tel: 322-5423.

Bagley Wright Theater, 155 Mercer Street, Seattle, WA 98109. Tel: 443-2222. Northwest end of Seattle Center complex.

Boathouse Theatre, 7312 W Greenlake Drive N, Seattle, WA 98103. Tel: 524-9108.

Broadway Performance Hall, 1625 Broadway, Seattle, WA 98122. Tel: 323-2623.

The Coliseum, First Avenue N and Thomas Street, Seattle Center. Tel: 684-7200.

Empty Space Theater, 107 Occidental Avenue S, Seattle, WA 98104. Tel: 467-6000; 95 S Jackson Street. Tel: 467-6000.

The Ethnic Theatre, 3940 Brooklyn Avenue NE, Seattle, WA 98105. Tel: 543-4327.

Fifth Avenue Theater, 1308 Fifth Avenue, Seattle, WA 98101. Tel: 625-1900. Hosts touring Broadway shows, musicals and plays in an ornate and historic building.

Indian Dinner Theater, at Daybreak Star Indian Cultural Center in Discovery Park.

Intiman Theater, 201 Mercer Street., Seattle, WA 98109. Seattle Center Playhouse. Tel: 626-0782.

Jane Addams Auditorium/Civic Light Opera Company, 11051 34th Avenue NE, Seattle, WA 98125. Tel: 363-2809.

Kane Hall, University of Washington, DG-10, Seattle, WA 98195. Tel: 543-2985.

Meany Theater, University of Washington, George Washington Lane and NE 40th Street, Seattle, WA 98195. Tel: 543-4880.

The Moore Theater, 1932 Second Avenue, Seattle, WA 98101. Tel: 443-1744.

New City Theatre, 1634 11th Avenue, Seattle WA 98122. Tel: 323-6800.

Nippon Kan Theater, 628 S Washington Street, Seattle, WA 98104. Tel: 224-0181. On the National Register of Historic Places.

Paramount Theatre, 901 Pine Street, Seattle, WA 98101. Tel: 682-1414. Presents well-known entertainers.

The Penthouse Theatre, University of Washington, Stevens Way, Seattle, WA 98195. Tel: 543-4880.

Pioneer Square Theater, 512 Second Avenue. Tel: 467-8121.

Seattle Repertory Theater, 155 Mercer Street. Tel: 443-2210. Located in the Bagley Wright Theater in Seattle Center, this is Seattle's flagship professional theater with productions of classic and contemporary works.

Seattle Group Theater, 3940 Brooklyn Avenue NE. Tel: 543-4327. Multicultural theater which has been going for more than a decade.

Washington Hall Performance Gallery, 153 14th Avenue, Seattle, WA 98122. Tel: 325-7901.

MOVIE THEATERS

Most cinemas feature first-run movies only. However, a handful of theaters will run, and sometimes specialize in, old "classics" and foreign films. In Seattle these theaters are: The Guild 45th at 2115 N 45th, tel: 633-3353; The Harvard Exit and its companion, Top of the Exit at 807 E. Roy Street, tel: 323-8986; The Metro Cinemas at NE 45th Street and Roosevelt Avenue, tel: 633-0055; and the Neptune at 1333 NE 45th Street, tel: 633-5545. College and university campuses are another place to check for off-beat films.

Check the newspaper for theater listings and show times.

Jewel Box Theater, Rendezvous Tavern, 2320 Second Avenue. Tel: 682-7064. Host of the Belltown Film Festival and an eclectic selection of films for film buffs.

NIGHTLIFE

Several areas are hubs for evening entertainment where restaurants, clubs and shops open late. They are located around Lake Union or in the Pioneer Square district along the downtown waterfront, or around the University (especially along University Way), and along Broadway on Capitol Hill.

Downtown hotels offer some of the most **elegant lounges** such as: the Garden Court of the Four Seasons Olympic Hotel, the Lobby Bar of the Westin, the Camlin Hotel's Cloud Room (on the top floor, naturally), Stouffer Madison's Visions Lounge or Mirabeau on the 48th floor of the Seafirst building.

In Pioneer Square the **trendiest** and most pleasant bars have a historical flavor such as: Dimitriou's Jazz Alley, the Merchant's Café, the J & M Café and the Old Timers' Café.

Below are some favored nightspots:
The Backstage, 2208 NW Market Street. Tel: 781-2805. Features nationally known rock, jazz, blues, reggae and folk acts in addition to the best of the Northwest.
Central Tavern, 207 First Avenue S. Tel: 622-0209. This large Pionner Square club features well-known and local alternative rock musicians.
Dimitriou's Jazz Alley, 2033 Sixth Avenue. Tel: 441-9729. Presents the top names in jazz in a comfortable and sophisticated atmosphere.
Doc Maynard's, 610 First Avenue. Tel: 682-4649.

Rock 'n' roll and rhythm and blues reign supreme at this Pioneer Square bar.
J&M Café, 201 1st Avenue S. Tel: 624-1670. Burgers and beers and lively downtown crowd.
Kell's, 1916 Post Alley. Tel: 728-1916. Irish restaurant and pub with inspiring Irish sing-a-longs.
Larry's Greenfront, 209 First Avenue. Tel: 624-7665. Blues music.
Murphy's Pub, 2110 N. 45th Street. Tel: 634-2110. Irish pub with tremendous selection of brews and folk music.
New Orleans Creole Restaurant, 114 First Avenue S. Tel: 622-2563. Features creole, ragtime and jazz along with spicy foods in Pioneer Square.
Owl Café, 5140 Ballard Avenue, NW. Tel: 784-3640. A blues joint with a loyal following.
Parker's, 17001 Aurora Avenue, N. Tel: 542-9491. Presents big name acts, usually from the past, with a good sound system and large dance floor.
Scarlett Tree, 6521 Roosevelt Way NE. Tel: 523-7153. Hopping bar north of the University district with a rhythm and blues orientation.
Spinnaker's, 6413 Seaview Avenue NW. Tel: 789-8777. A video-disco overlooking Shilshole Marina. Features a young, single crowd, lip-sync contests and men strutting in tight-fitting Levi jeans.
Top of the Hilton, Sixth Avenue and University Street. Tel: 624-0500. A more sophisticated verison of Spinnaker's Disco features top 40 hits and city-light views.
The Vogue, 2018 First Avenue. Tel: 443-0673. Alternative dance music and new wave fashion showcase. Slam-dancing is popular.

COMEDY CLUBS

Comedy Underground, 222 S. Main. Tel: 628-0303. Presents nationally-known comedians and the best of local talent.
Bailey's Eatery & Bar, 821 NE Bellevue Way. Tel: 455-4494. Offers jazz during weeknights and comedians on weekends.
Also worth checking out are **Giggles Comedy Night Club**, Roosevelt & 53rd Street, tel: 526-JOKE; **Last Laugh Comedy Club**, 75 Marion Street, tel: 622-5653.

SHOPPING

Seattle's climate and outdoor recreational activities have brought about the success of the city's best-known stores like Eddie Bauer (now a national chain), REI (the cooperative, with more stores opening across the country), the North Face and Patagonia. Many of the traditionalists in Seattle look like they just stepped out of one of these stores. Birkenstock sandals are favored by this group during the drier months.

Several areas are well known for shopping, Among them is the Pike Place Market, the downtown retail district, along Broadway on Capitol Hill; and the University District. The latter features ethnic gift shops, specialty food markets and restaurants, bakeries and bookstores. The University Book Store is one of the largest in town with a comprehensive selection of books, maps, and gifts.

Washington has a 8.1 percent sales tax that is added to the price of retail goods and food that is served in restaurants.

DEPARTMENT STORES & SHOPPING CENTERS

Alderwood Mall, Lynnwood (near the north intersection of Interstate 5 and Interstate 405). Features, The Bon, Nordstrom, J. C. Penny and Sears. Many furniture stores and smaller shopping centers are in the vicinity.

Bellevue Square, NE Eighth Street and Bellevue Way, Bellevue. Tel: 454-8096. A 198-store mall featuring Nordstrom, The Bon, Frederick & Nelson, J. C. Penny.

The Bon, Third Avenue and Pine Street. Tel: 344-2121. The flagship of one of Seattle's oldest and finest department stores. Good-quality, moderately-priced clothing, jewelry, toys and sundry items on nine floors. There's also a post office, beauty salon, bakery and restaurants. A garage and a skywalk mean shoppers won't have to step outside on rainy days.

Country Village, 23730 Bothell-Everett Highway, Bothell. Tel: 483-2250. A collection of country farmhouses, remodeled for shopping with meandering brick pathways, landscaped grounds with waterfalls, ponds, gazebos and flowers everywhere in spring and summer. Most stores have a country theme with goods such as quilts, antiques, cookware, yarns, furnishings, and clothing. There are also several cafés.

Edmonds Antique Mall in the restored and historically flavored Old Mill Town. Craft, tourist shops and restaurants.

Frederick and Nelson, Fifth Avenue and Pine Street. Tel: 682-5500. Ten floors featuring a Steuben Glass Shop, Frango chocolates (made in the store) and the Wide World Shop of Antiques.

Gilman Village, Gilman Boulevard, Issaquah. Tel: 462-0594. Country farmhouses and barns that have been remodeled and made into a charming shopping village. Many stores have country-style gifts, clothing, artwork. Features the Gallery of Fine Woodworking, several cafés and restaurants.

I. Magnin, 601 Pine. Tel: 682-6111. High-priced, high-fashion featuring clothes by Adolfo and Hanai Mori, furs, Louis Vuitton leather goods, jewelry and a beauty salon.

Nordstrom, 1501 Fifth Avenue. Tel: 628-2111. Classical piano players at the baby grands are a trademark along with customer service. Quality clothing and accessories for all ages.

Northgate, 555 NE Northgate Way. Tel: 362-4777. This 116-store mall features The Bon, Nordstrom, Gene Juarez Salon, restaurants and bars.

Pike Place Market, First Avenue and Pike Street. Tel: 682-7453. (*See Things To Do.*)

Rainier Square, 1301 Fifth Avenue. Tel: 628-505. Top-of-the-line fashion shops are here such as The Littler and Totally Michael's. Rainier Square adjoins the Hilton Hotel.

Southcenter Mall, Interstate 5 and Interstate 405, Tukwila. Tel: 246-7400. The largest shopping center in the metropolitan Seattle area. Features Nordstrom, The Bon. Many smaller shopping centers featuring furniture, electronics, clothing and food are in the vicinity of the mall.

Westlake Center and Plaza, Pine Street between Fourth and Fifth avenues. Houses 80 specialty shops. Adjacent to Nordstrom, The Bon Marché and Frederick & Nelson. Top floor features 15 fast-food stands from pizza and burgers, to seafood and vegetarian cuisines. Specialty shops include the Disney Store, Brentano's Book Store, Williams-Sonoma (kitchen wares) and the Museum of Flight branch store.

CLOTHING

Baby & Co., 1936 First Avenue. Tel: 448-4077. The ultimate in high-fashion baby wear.

Brooks Brothers, 1401 Fourth Avenue. Tel: 624-4400. High quality men's clothing.

The Coach Store, 417 University Street. Tel: 382-1772. At the Four Seasons Olympic Hotel, the Coach Store is the maker of quality classic leather handbags, belts and accessories.

Michael's Bespoke Tailors, 407 Union. Tel: 623-4785. High quality men's fashions.

Teresa of Hong Kong, 1512 Sixth Avenue. Tel: 622-0455. Traditional Asian fashions such as kimonos, Happi coats, jade carvings.

Osborn and Ulland, 1926 Third Avenue. Tel: 728-8999. One of the best for skiing and tennis apparel.
Yankee Peddler, 4218 E Madison. Tel: 324-4218; and 4737 University Plaza NE. Tel: 526-9656. Quality men's wear.

CAMERAS

Cameras West, 1908 Fourth Avenue. Tel: 622-0066. One of the best places in town to shop for cameras and accessories.

FOOD

A & J Meats, 2401 Queen Anne N. Tel: 284-3885. High-quality meats including specialty cuts and preparation.
Café Dilettante, 416 Broadway E. Tel: 323-6463. Makes exquisitely-rich truffles, irresistible butter-cream filled chocolates, tortes and cakes.
Pike Place Market. See *Things To Do*.
Sivertsen's Bakery, 100 Mercer. Tel: 283-3797. Scandinavian bakery with reputation for heavenly pastries.
Starbuck's Coffee and Tea, 1912 Pike Place, University Village, also Bellevue, and small shops around town. Some of the finest coffees you'll ever find and roasted in Seattle.
Truffles, 3701 NE 45th. Tel: 522-3016. Specialty foods, wine, meats, cheeses.
Uwajimaya, 519 Sixth Avenue S. Tel: 624-6248. Gourmet foods, records and books from Japan.

JEWELRY

Fast Forward, 701 Broadway E. Tel: 352-1313. One-of-a-kind jewelry, fashioned mostly by local artists.
Friedlander Jewelers, 1400 Fifth Avenue. Tel: 223-7474. Established in Seattle in 1886. Offers one of the most extensive offerings of watches, rings and crystal. Custom designs and repair.

MAGAZINES, BOOKS

Bulldog News and Fast Espresso, 4208 University Way NE. Tel: 632-6397. Enormous selection of periodicals, foreign magazines and newspapers.
Elliott Bay Book Company, 101 S Main Street. Tel: 624-6600. Four large rooms and two lofts with over 100,000 titles. The second-largest independent bookstore in the state. Features readings by major authors, two cafés and a graphics store.
Wide World Books and Maps, 1911 N 45th Street. Tel: 634-3453.

MUSIC

Johnson-West Music Service, 500 Denny Way. Tel: 441-7741. Comprehensive selection of sheet music.
Peaches, 811 NE 45th Street. Tel: 633-2990 (in the University district) or 2232 NW Market Street. Tel: 784-9517 (in Ballard). One of the best-stocked record stores around. All types of music are well-represented with special attention to local rock bands.

OUTDOOR SPECIALISTS

Eddie Bauer, Rainier Square. Tel: 622-2766. Also has branch stores in Alderwood and Bellevue Square malls.
The North Face, 1023 First Avenue. Tel: 622-4111. Backpacking clothing and gear.
REI (Recreational Equipment Inc.), 1525 11th Avenue. Tel:323-8333. Branch stores in Lynnwood and Bellevue.

SPECIALTY STORES & GIFTS

Apogee, 4224 E Madison Street. Tel: 325-2848. Located in the charming downtown of Madison Park, this stylish store features unusual gifts, antiques and clothes.
Designer's Fabrics, 1800 Fourth Avenue. Tel: 467-6100. Huge selection of high-quality fabrics.
Keeg's, 310 Broadway E. Tel: 325-1771. Danish furniture and imports such as kitchenware and toys.
Exclusively Northwest, 415 Stewart Street. Tel: 622-9144. Features works by Northwest artisans; sculpture, jewelry, clothing, pottery and Native American art.
Made In Washington, Pike Place Market. Tel: 467-0788. Everything in the store from crafts, local cookbooks, and wines is made in the Evergreen State.
Museum of Flight Store, 9404 E Marginal Way S. Tel: 764-5720. An assortment of aviation gifts: model airplanes, extensive selection of books, T-shirts, pins, photos. Main store at the museum, branch store in Westlake Center.
Molbak's Nursery, 13625 NE 175th Street, Woodinville. Tel: 483-5000. Almost a destination in itself, this is Washington's largest indoor nursery. Offers huge selection of indoor and outdoor plants, trees and shrubs. Also features a café, conservatory, well-appointed gift shop, florist and patio furniture departments.
The Nature Company, 2001 Western Avenue. Tel: 443-1608. Wonderful gifts for the nature and animal lover.
Sur La Table, 84 Pine Street (across from Pike Market). Gourmet cookware. Tel: 448-2244.

CLOTHING CHART

Women's Dresses/Suits

American	Continental	British
6	38/34N	8/30
8	40/36N	10/32
10	42/38N	12/34
12	44/40N	14/36
14	46/42N	16/38
16	48/44N	18/40

Women's Shoes

American	Continental	British
4½	36	3
5½	37	4
6½	38	5
7½	39	6
8½	40	7
9½	41	8
10½	42	9

Men's Suits

American	Continental	British
34	44	34
—	46	36
38	48	38
—	50	40
42	52	42
—	54	44
46	56	46

Men's Shirts

American	Continental	British
14	36	14
14½	37	14½
15	38	15
15½	39	15½
16	40	16
16½	41	16½
17	42	17

Men's Shoes

American	Continental	British
6½	—	6
7½	40	7
8½	41	8
9½	42	9
10½	43	10
11½	44	11

SPORTS

BICYCLING

Seattle was rated by *Bicycling* magazine as the number one city in the US for biking. The Burke-Gilman Trail, a paved road on an abandoned railroad bed, leads from Gas Works Park on Lake Union to Logboom Park on Lake Washington. The 12½ mile trail follows Lake Washington, goes down by the University and is popular with people of all ages, whether biking, jogging or walking. The Sammamish River Trail follows the Sammamish River from Bothell, through Woodinville farmland and ends at Marymoor Park at the north tip of Sammamish Lake. This trail runs for 9½ miles and will soon connect with the Burke Gilman trail. A 2½-mile stretch between the two trails is under construction. Another popular bicycle route is the nearly 3-mile paved trail around Green Lake. It can be quite busy on sunny days, especially if that sunny day is on a weekend, with strollers, joggers, people on rollerblades (lace-up boots with wheels attached), cross-country training roller skis and various homemade concoctions on wheels. From Green Lake bicyclists may choose to take the Ravenna Park Trail to the University of Washington.

Every third Sunday and the first Saturday of the month from May–September, a 6-mile stretch on Lake Washington Boulevard is closed to cars (from the Arboretum to Seward Park). Beautiful lakefront parks and scenery can be enjoyed on this wide paved road for family biking and hiking. Tel: 684-7092.

Marymoor Park in Redmond has a velodrome for racing and was the site of the 1990 Goodwill Games bicycle races. Friday night at 7.30pm races are held from April–November. Tel: 882-0706.

Numerous bicycle rides and races are held in and around Seattle throughout the year. For information on current weekday and weekend events telephone the Cascade Bicycle Club, tel: 522-BIKE.

For **bicycle rentals** here are a few near the above-mentioned trails:
Gregg's Greenlake Cycle Inc., 7007 Woodlawn NE. Tel: 523-1822.
The Bicycle Center, 4529 Sand Point Way NE. Tel: 523-8300.
Alki Bicycle Co., 2722 Alki SW. Tel: 938-3322.

Sammamish Valley Cycle, 8451 164th Avenue NE, Redmond. Tel: 881-8442.

Also check the *Yellow Pages* directory under the heading "Bicycle-rentals."

BIRDWATCHING

Audubon Society, 8028 35th Avenue NE. Tel: 523-4483. The society offers a checklist of birds in the Northwest area and a list of where to purchase birdseed that is especially mixed for native species. The society also conducts birding field trips in Seattle parks.

BOATING

Canoeing, kayaking, rowing, sail boarding and sailing are all available around Lakes Union and Washington. In addition, Green Lake offers paddleboating.

Rentals: University of Washington Waterfront Activities Center. Tel: 543-9433. Offers canoe rentals.

Green Lake, tel: 362-3151. Offers rowboats and paddleboats.

Ray's Boathouse, 6049 Seaview NW. Tel: 782-8322. Offers rowboats, small motor boats (kickers), and fishing gear.

Sailboat Charters and Rentals Unlimited, 2046 Westlake N. Tel: 283-4664.

GOLFING

A call in advance for reservations to the following public golf courses is recommended:

Ballinger Park, 23000 Lakeview Drive, Mountlake Terrace. Tel: 775-6467. Nine-hole; par: 34-men, 36-women.

Bellevue Municipal, 5450 140th NE. Tel: 451-7250. 18-hole; par: 35-men, 36-women.

Foster, 13500 Interurban S. Tel: 242-4221. 18-hole; par: 69-men, 71-women.

Greenlake, 5701 W. Green Lake Way N. Tel: 632-2280. Nine-hole; par: 27 men and women.

Jackson Park Municipal, 1000 NE 135th Street. Tel: 363-4747. 18-hole; par: 71-men, 73-women. Also, nine-hole, par 3 course.

Jefferson Park Municipal, 4101 Beacon S. Tel: 762-4513. 18-hole; par: 70 men and women.

Maplewood Golf Course, 4000 Maple Valley Highway, Renton. Tel: 255-3194. 18-hole; par: 72-men, 73-women.

Tyee Valley, 2401 S 192nd Street. Tel: 878-3540. 18-hole; par: 71 men, 73-women.

Wayne, 16721 96th Avenue NE, Bothell Tel: 485-6237. 18-hole; par: 65-men, 66-women.

West Seattle, 4470 35th SW. Tel: 935-5187. 18-hole; par: 72-men, 74-women.

Golf Seattle, 12822 27th Drive SE, Everett. Tel:338-2148 or 361-2319. This company offers tour packages with pro-shop merchandise and preferred tee times to accommodate traveler's schedules.

HIKING

A good pair of walking shoes, some snacks and a drink are all that's needed (but binoculars and camera are nice to have along). Explore and get a feel for what the land looked like before housing and highways took over.

Carkeek Park, offers wooded trails leading to Puget Sound beach. Playground, picnic, restrooms and high bluff views of the Sound.

Discovery Park, W Government Way and 36th Avenue W. Tel: 386-4236. A 534-acre park of deep wooded ravines, forest, grassy meadows and two miles of beach at the base of Magnolia Bluff. Nature trails wind their way throughout the park. The US Coast Guard's West Point Light Station is accessible by a 1½ mile trail and open for tours from noon–4pm Saturday–Sunday, and Wednesday–Friday by appointment. Tel: 282-9130. The **Daybreak Star Indian Cultural Center**, which includes the Sacred Circle Indian Art Gallery, features Indian arts and crafts. Hours: 8am–5pm Monday–Friday, 10am–5pm Saturday–Sunday. Admission is free. Tel: 285-4425. The park is open daily from dawn–11pm. Guided tours are offered, and a visitor center is open daily 8.30–5pm.

Foster Island Trail, from McCurdy Park or the Arboretum. An easy, level hike crossing wooden bridges and pontoons over Lake Washington to Foster Island.

Marymoor Park, north end of Lake Sammamish, Redmond. Extensive playing fields, playgrounds, trails, picnicking facilities, a bicycle velodrome, model plane airport and historical museum are some of this park's features.

Meadowdale Park, North Edmonds. Wooded hiking trail leads down to level, grassy picnicking area and sandy Puget Sound beach.

St Edward's Park, Juanita Drive, Bothell. Some open grassy grounds for picnicking, soccer or baseball are available on the site of this former Catholic seminary. Wooded trails lead down to still more trails along east shores of Lake Washington.

Tiger Mountain, Issaquah. Numerous trails leading to alpine lakes and mountain vistas. Many of the trails allow mountain biking.

Volunteer Park, E Galer and 15th Avenue E, and E. Prospect and 14th Avenue E. (on Capitol Hill). Tel: 684-4743. Home of the Seattle Art Museum's Asian collection. A conservatory has collections of cacti, orchids and exotic tropical plants and is surrounded by extensive formal gardens. A 75-ft water tower with a spiral stairway provides a panoramic view of downtown Seattle, the lakes and mountains. Hours: dawn–11pm. Conservatory hours: 10am–7pm May 15–September 15; or 10am–4pm the rest of the year.

Washington Park Arboretum, tel: 543-8800. See *Things To Do*.

For **day trips**, try the parks in the Cascade Mountains, especially Mount Rainier and Olympic National Park.

For excellent **maps** of trails in the Puget Sound region there are several places to turn: REI, 1525 11th Avenue. Tel: 323-8333; REI, Lynnwood; or in Bellevue.

US Forest Service/National Parks Service Outdoor Recreation Information Office: 915 Second Avenue. Tel: 442-0170.

The Mountaineers, 300 Third Avenue W. Tel: 284-6310. An outdoor recreation club that runs hiking trips.

Washington Trails Association, 1305 Fourth Avenue. Tel: 625-1367. Has most any information needed on trails in the state.

Mountain Madness, 7103 California Avenue SW, Seattle.Tel: 937-8389. Offers personalized outdoor adventure tours including biking, fishing, moutain climbing and hiking.

HORSEBACK RIDING

Ranches offer guided tours through parks, like Bridle Trails, or mountains, like Squak and Tiger. Length of tours vary from one hour to all day.

Aqua Barn Ranch, 15277 SE Renton-Maple Valley Highway, Renton. Tel: 255-4618.

Gold Creek Stables, 16528 148th NE, Woodinville. Tel: 483-2878.

High Lonesome Ranch, 233 144th NE, Redmond. Tel: 868-5072.

Kelly's Riding and Boarding Ranch, 7212 Renton-Issaquah Road SE. Tel: 392-6979.

Central Park Stables, Bridle Trails State Park. Tel: 827-2900.

SCUBA DIVING

Discovery Park. The parks department offers underwater tours. Tel: 684-4075.

Brackett's Landing, in Edmonds. A sandy beach, next to the ferry landing, especially designed for scuba diving. Underwater park features sunken 300-foot dock and five floating rests.

SKIING

Alpental, Snoqualmie Summit and Ski Acres. Tel: 434-6161 or 232-8182. These three ski areas atop Snoqualmie Pass have joined together to offer extensive choices of trails. They are linked by a free shuttle bus available Friday–Sunday and offer interchangeable lift tickets and night skiing.

Crystal Mountain Resort, Highway 410, 40 miles east of Enumclaw. The site of the 1972 World Cup Championships. Offers a vertical of 3,100 ft and 32 trails from beginner to advanced.Weekend night skiing. Tel: 663-2265

Mission Ridge, 15 miles from Wenatchee, has a vertical of 2,140 ft with 33 runs and night skiing.

Stevens Pass, tel: 973-2441.70 miles northeast of Seattle, 26 runs and a 1,800-ft drop.

White Pass, tel: 1-509-453-8731. Near Yakima. A vertical of 1,500 ft, plus night skiing.

SWIMMING

Beaches on the Sound include: Golden Gardens and Carkeek Park on the north end of Seattle and Alki and Lincoln Park on the south end.

Lake beaches include: the north east end of Green Lake; or, on the western shores of Lake Washington, (from north to south): Matthews Beach Park, Magnuson Park, Madison Park, Madrona Park, Mount Baker Park, Seward Park, Pritchard Island Beach Park. On the eastside of the lake are: Denny Park, Bothell; Juanita Beach and Waverly Park, Kirkland; Meydenbauer Beach Park and Chism Park, Bellevue; Kennydale Park, north Renton; Lake Washington Beach Park, Renton.

Swimming is also available in public swimming pools. These pools, which are located throughout metropolitan Seattle, the suburbs, Bellevue and Redmond, are maintained by the parks department. Tel: 684-4075 for the most convenient location in Seattle; 296-4232 for King County; 455-6885 for Bellevue; 828-1218 for Kirkland; 236-3545 for Mercer Island; 882-6401 for Redmond.

SPORTS IN PUBLIC PARKS

There are playfields for baseball, soccer, football, tennis and paddleball. There are areas for chess games, bocce (lawn bowling), picnicking, kite flying and exploring. Parks vary in what they offer. For information on parks in a particular area or information on facilities, tel: 296-4232 for King County parks; 684-4075 for Seattle parks; 455-6881 for Bellevue; 828-1217 for Kirkland; 236-3545 for Mercer Island; 392-7131 for Issaquah; or 882-6401 for Redmond.

SPECTATOR SPORTS

FOOTBALL

Seattle Seahawks, 11220 NE 53rd Street, Kirkland. Tel: 827-9777.

Seattle's NFL (National Football League) team. is located at the Kingdome, the Seahawk's home arena. Ticket are some of the hottest in town, always.

Husky Stadium, southeast end of University of Washington. Tel: 543-2000. This 73,000-seat stadium hosts the University's football team, The Huskies. The stadium is also used for men's and women's basketball and other athletic events. Husky Stadium has the added attraction of offering views of Lake Washington and the Cascade Mountains.

BASEBALL

Seattle Mariners Baseball Club, 411 First Avenue S, Suite 480, Seattle. Tel: 628-3555. Seattle's major league baseball team, with over 80 games during its April–September season. The Kingdome is the home arena. **The Everett Giants**, Memorial Stadium, Everett (Exit 192 off Interstate 5) Tel: 258-3673. This class-A minor league plays 38 games on a grass field from mid-June through early September at the outdoor Memorial Stadium in Everett. The stadium is intimate, compared to most baseball stadiums, seating only 3,600. The ballpark food here was rated one of the best in the country.

BASKETBALL

Seattle Supersonics, 190 Queen Anne Avenue N, Seattle. Tel: 281-5800. Seattle's NBA (National Basketball Association) team. Season begins in November. Playoffs begin in May. **Seattle Center Coliseum**, which seats 14,250, is the home arena.

HOCKEY

Seattle Thunderbirds, Seattle Center Arena. Tel: 728-9124. Season runs from late September–March (or May if they make the playoffs).

HORSE RACING

Longacres, Exit 1, Interstate 405, West Valley Highway, Renton. Tel: 226-3131. Longacres Track features thoroughbred racing amid beautiful grounds Races are held Wednesday–Sunday, April–September. Approximately 10 races are held per day. The north end of the grandstand is free, but clubhouse boxes offer the best view. Wednesday-Friday racing begins at 5pm, but gates open at 3.30pm. Saturday, Sunday and holidays races begin at 1pm, with gates opening at 11.30am. Saturday and Sunday morning, the track also holds a tour of the backstretch. For tour reservations: tel: 1-800-7-Doo-dah. There are seven restaurants at the track serving cuisine that ranges from hot dogs to fine dining. Wine, beer and cocktails are also available as is a children's play area.

HYDROPLANE RACING

During **Seafair**, hydroplane races take place north of Seward Park on Lake Washington. Boats reach speeds of over 150 mph on the top of the water and follow a two-mile oval course. Tickets in advance or (more expensive) at the gate to prime viewing spots along the beach. There are very privileged seats available for large sums of money at the Captains Club.

SPECIAL INFORMATION

FOREIGN VISITORS

Most Seattleites are conversant only in English. Yet most locals are outgoing and willing to try their best to help visitors despite a language barrier. There are few multilingual signs with the exception of Japanese, due to economic ties to Japan. At Sea-Tac Airport, for example, recorded verbal instructions on the subway trains are in English and Japanese. There is even a separate information booth staffed by persons fluent in Japanese.

Most large hotels in Seattle offer multilingual concierge or front desk staffs who have information regarding city and airport transportation, currency exchange and other visitor services.

If translation is a necessity, there are several places to turn to:

Traveler's Aid Society, 909 Fourth Avenue, Seattle, WA 98104. Tel: 461-3888. Helps with a variety of problems, for example, accommodation, transportation or lost traveler's checks.

Language Bank-American Red Cross, 1900 25 Avenue S., Seattle, WA 98144. Tel: 323-2345. Manages a 24-hour volunteer emergency service. Offers written and oral interpretation in 70 languages.

Seattle Translation Center, 3123 Eastlake Avenue E., Seattle, WA 98102. Tel: 324-7696. Fees are per word for documents or personal letters.

Washington Academy of Languages, 98 Yesler Way, Seattle, WA. Tel: 682-4463. Offers translation services for visitors. Hours: Monday-Thursday 8.30am-9pm, Friday 8.30am-5pm.

The **Seattle-King County Visitor's Bureau** distributes a Seattle tourist brochure in French, Spanish, German, Japanese and English. Maps of the airport are available in French, German, Spanish Japanese, Chinese, Korean and English.

USEFUL ADDRESSES

TOURIST INFORMATION

A wealth of information on attractions, activities, accommodations and restaurants is available from the **Seattle-King County Convention and Visitors Bureau** in the Washington State Convention Center at 666 Stewart Street (Eighth Avenue and Pike Street). Tel: 461-5840. Hours: 8.30am–5pm Monday–Friday, 10am–4pm on Saturday during summer. The bureau also operates an **information center** at **Sea-Tac Airport**, on the baggage level. Tel: 433-5218. Hours: 9.30am–7.30pm daily.

USEFUL NUMBERS

AAA of Washington, tel: 448-5353
American Youth Hostels, tel: 281-7306
FBI, tel: 622-0460
Coast Guard Emergencies, tel: 286-5400
Crisis Clinic, tel: 461-3222
King County Medical Society, tel: 621-9393
(physician referral)
Mountain Road Conditions, tel: 455-7900 (winter only)
Poison Control, tel: 526-2121
Seattle-King County Convention and Visitors Bureau, tel: 461-5840
Seattle-King County Dental Society, tel: 443-7607
(dentist referral)
Seattle Post-Intelligencer, tel: 448-8000
Seattle Public Library, Main Branch, tel: 386-INFO
(for quick information)
Seattle Times, tel: 464-2111
Time, tel: 1-976-1616
Traveler's Aid, tel: 461-3888 or 433-5288
US Post Office, Main Station, tel: 442-6340
Weather, tel: 526-6087

FOREIGN CONSULATES

Austria, 4131 11th Avenue NE, Seattle, WA 98105. Tel:633-3606.
United Kingdom, First Interstate Center, 999 Third Avenue, Suite 820, Seattle, WA 98104.
Tel: 622-9253.
Canada, Plaza 600, Suite 412, Sixth Avenue and Stewart Street, Seattle, WA 98101-1286.
Tel: 443-1777.
Belgium, 2516 42 Avenue W, Seattle, WA 98199. Tel: 623-5005.

Denmark, 1809 Seventh Avenue, Seattle, WA 98101. Tel: 682-6101.
Finland, PO Box 40598, Bellevue, WA 98004. Tel: 451-3983.
France, 400 E Pine Street, Suite 210, Seattle, WA 98122. Tel: 323-6870.
Iceland, 5610 20th Avenue NW, Seattle, WA 98107. Tel: 783-4100.
Mexico, 2132 Third Avenue Seattle, WA 98121. Tel: 448-3526.
Switzerland, PO Box 81003, Seattle, WA 98108. Tel: 762-1223.
Germany, 1617 IBM Building, 1200 Fifth Avenue, Seattle, WA 98101. Tel: 682-4312.
Japan, 1301 Fifth Avenue, Suite 3110, Seattle, WA 98101. Tel: 682-9107.
Philippines, 2033 Sixth Ave, Suite 1125, Seattle, WA 98121. Tel: 441-1640.
Korea, 2033 Sixth Ave, Suite 1125, Seattle, WA 98121. Tel: 441-1011.
Norway, Joseph Vance Building, 1402 Third Ave, Seattle, WA 98101-2169. Tel: 623-3957.
Sweden, Joseph Vance Building, 1402 Third Avenue, Seattle, WA 98101-2169. Tel: 622-5640.

FURTHER READING

Alt, David D. and Hyndman, Donald W. *Roadside Geology of Washington*. Missoula, Montana: Hyndman Mountain Press Publishing Company, 1990.

Anderson, Bern. *Surveyor of the Sea: Life of Voyages of Captain GeorgeVancouver*. Seattle, Washington, University of Washington Press, 1960.

Bauer, E. E. *Boeing in Peace and War*. Enumclaw, Washington: TABA Publishing, 1990.

Brewster, David and Irving, Stephanie, editors. *Seattle Best Places*. Seattle: Sasquatch Books, 1991 (fifth edition).

Caton, Horace R. *Long Old Road*. University of Washington Press, 1970.

Cantwell, Robert. *The Hidden Northwest*. Lippincott, 1978.

Childerhose, R. J. *Pacific Salmon and Steelhead Trout*. Seattle: University of Washington Press, 1981.

Chittenden, Hiram R. *The American Fur Trade of the Far West*. Press of the Pioneers, 1935.

Clark, Norman H. *Washington: A Bicentennial History*. W. W. Norton, 1976.

Cleveland, Carl M. *Boeing Trivia*. Seattle: CMC Books, 1989.

Cobb, John N. *Pacific Salmon Fishing*. Bureau of Fisheries, 1917.

Darvill, Fred T. *Hiking the North Cascades*. Sierra Club, 1982.

Douglas, William O. *Of Men and Mountains*. Harper, 1950.

Faragher, John Mark. *Women & Men on the Overland Trail*. Yale University Press, 1979.

Friedheim, Robert L. *The Seattle General Strike*. University of Washington Press, 1964.

Glassley, Ray Hoard. *Pacific Northwest Indian Wars*. Binford & Mort, 1953.

Goddard, John W. *Washington, The Evergreen State*. Scribners, 1942.

Harford, Cornelius. *Seattle & Environs*. Pioneer Historical Publications, 1924.

Hidy, Ralph L. *Timer and Men: The Weyerhaeuser Story*. Macmillan, 1975.

Holbrook, Stewart H. *The Columbia*. Rinehart, 1956.

Jacobson, Arthur Lee. *Trees of Seattle: The Complete Tree-finders' Guide to History*. Seattle: Sasquatch Books, 1989.

King, Jonathan. *The Northwest Green Book*. Seattle: Sasquatch Books, 1991.

Kirk, Ruth and Carmela Alexander. *Exploring Washington's Past: A Road Guide to History*. Seattle and London: University of Washington Press, 1990.

LeWarne, Charles P. *Washington State*. University of Washington Press, 1986.

Lyons, Dianne J. Boulerice. *Washington Handbook*. Moon Publications.

Meany, Edmond S. *Origin of Washington Geographic Names*. University of Washington Press, 1923.

Morgan, Murray. *Puget's Sound: A Narrative of Early Tacoma and the Southern Sound*. Seattle and London: Universtiy of Washington Press, 1979.

Morgan, Murray. *Skid Road: An Informal Portrait of Seattle*. Seattle and London: University of Washington Press, 1988 (revised edition).

Newell, Gordon. *Totem Tales of Old Seattle*. Superior Publishing, 1956.

Peters, Ed. *Mountaineering: The Freedom of the Hills*. The Mountaineers, 1982.

Ruby, Robert H. and Brown, John A. *A Guide to the Indian Tribes of the Pacific Northwest*. University of Oklahoma, 1986.

Sale, Roger. *Seattle: Past to Present*. Seattle and London: University of Washington Press, 1989.

Saling, Anne. *Great Northwest Nature Factbook*. Bothell: Alaska Northwest Books, 1991.

Speidel, William C. *Sons of the Profits: Doc Maynard, the Man who Invented Seattle*. Seattle: Nettle Creek Publishing Co., 1990.

Steinbrueck, Victor. *Seattle Cityscape*. University of Washington Press, 1962.

Stephens, Dave. *Ivar: The Life and Times of Ivar Haglund*. Seattle: Dunhill Publishing, 1988.

Steves, Rick. *Kidding Around Seattle: A Young Person's Guide to the City*. Santa Fe, New Mexico: John Muir Publications, 1991.

Tierra, Michael. *The Way of Herbs*. Washington Square Press, 1980.

Underhill, Ruth Murray. *Red Man's America*. University of Chicago Press, 1971.

Watters, Reginald Eyre, editor. *British Columbia: A Centennial Anthology*. McClelland & Stewart, 1958.

Whitney, Stephen R. *Nature Walks in and around Seattle*. Seattle: The Mountaineers, 1987.

Woog, Adam. *Sexless Oysters and Self-tipping Hats: 100 Years of Invention in the Pacific Northwest*. Seattle: Sasquatch Books, 1991.

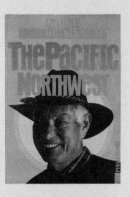

ART/PHOTO CREDITS

INDEX

160 Alaska
155 Alsace
150 Amazon Wildlife
116 America, South
173 American Southwest
158A Amsterdam
260 Argentina
287 Asia, East
207 Asia, South
262 Asia, South East
194 Asian Wildlife,
     Southeast
167A Athens
272 Australia
263 Austria
188 Bahamas
206 Bali Baru
107 Baltic States
246A Bangkok
292 Barbados
219B Barcelona
187 Bay of Naples
234A Beijing
109 Belgium
135A Berlin
217 Bermuda
100A Boston
127 Brazil
178 Brittany
109A Brussels
144A Budapest
260A Buenos Aires
213 Burgundy
268A Cairo
247B Calcutta
275 California
180 California,
     Northern
161 California,
     Southern
237 Canada
162 Caribbean
     The Lesser Antilles
122 Catalonia
     (Costa Brava)
141 Channel Islands
184C Chicago
151 Chile
234 China
135E Cologne
119 Continental Europe
189 Corsica
281 Costa Rica
291 Cote d'Azur
165 Crete
184 Crossing America
226 Cyprus
114 Czechoslovakia
247A Delhi, Jaipur, Agra
238 Denmark
135B Dresden
142B Dublin

135F Düsseldorf
204 East African
     Wildlife,
149 Eastern Europe,
118 Ecuador
148A Edinburgh
268 Egypt
123 Finland
209B Florence
243 Florida
154 France
135C Frankfurt
208 Gambia & Senegal
135 Germany
148B Glasgow
279 Gran Canaria
169 Great Barrier Reef
124 Great Britain
167 Greece
166 Greek Islands
135G Hamburg
240 Hawaii
193 Himalaya, Western
196 Hong Kong
144 Hungary
256 Iceland
247 India
212 India, South
128 Indian Wildlife
143 Indonesia
142 Ireland
252 Israel
236A Istanbul
209 Italy
213 Jamaica
278 Japan
266 Java
252A Jerusalem-Tel Aviv
203A Kathmandu
270 Kenya
300 Korea
202A Lisbon
258 Loire Valley
124A London
275A Los Angeles
201 Madeira
219A Madrid
145 Malaysia
157 Mallorca & Ibiza
117 Malta
272B Melbourne
285 Mexico
285A Mexico City
243A Miami
237B Montreal
235 Morocco
101A Moscow
135D Munich
211 Myanmar (Burma)
259 Namibia
269 Native America
203 Nepal

158 Netherlands
100 New England
184E New Orleans
184F New York City
133 New York State
293 New Zealand
265 Nile, The
120 Norway
124B Oxford
147 Pacific Northwest
205 Pakistan
154A Paris
249 Peru
184B Philadelphia
222 Philippines
115 Poland
202 Portugal
114A Prague
153 Provence
156 Puerto Rico
250 Rajasthan
177 Rhine
127 Rio de Janeiro
172 Rockies
209A Rome
101 Russia
275B San Francisco
130 Sardinia
148 Scotland
184D Seattle
261 Sicily
159 Singapore
257 South Africa
264 South Tyrol
219 Spain
220 Spain, Southern
105 Sri Lanka
101B St Petersburg
170 Sweden
232 Switzerland
272 Sydney
175 Taiwan
112 Tenerife
186 Texas
246 Thailand
278A Tokyo
139 Trinidad & Tobago
113 Tunisia
236 Turkey
171 Turkish Coast
210 Tuscany
174 Umbria
237A Vancouver
198 Venezuela
209C Venice
263A Vienna
255 Vietnam
267 Wales
184C Washington DC
183 Waterways
     of Europe
215 Yemen

You'll find the colorset number on the spine of each Insight Guide.